THE JESSE JAMES NORTHFIELD RAID

CONFESSIONS OF THE NINTH MAN

The Jesse James Northfield Raid

CONFESSIONS OF THE NINTH MAN

John Koblas

NORTH STAR PRESS OF ST. CLOUD, INC.

Koblas, John J., 1942-
    The Jesse James Northfield Raid: confessions of the ninth
man/John Koblas. —1st Ed.
    272 p. 25 cm.
    Includes bibliographical references and index.
    ISBN 0-87839-125-8 (alk. paper). —ISBN 0-87839-124-X
(pbk.: alk. paper)
    1. Bank Robberies—Minnesota—Northfield—History—19th
century.
2. Stiles, Bill, d. 1937. 3. James, Jesse, 1847-1882. I. Title.
HV6661.M62K63   1999
364.15'52'09776555—dc21   99-30770
                                                                        CIP

Copyright © 1999 John Koblas

Second edition: November 1999

ISBN: 0-87839-124-X (paper)
ISBN: 0-87839-125-8 (cloth)

Cover art: John Stevens

Printed in Canada by Friesens.

Published by
        North Star Press of St. Cloud, Inc.
        P.O. Box 451
        St. Cloud, Minnesota 56302

For my mother, Susan, and cousin Gary.
And to the memory of my father, Johnny, brother Bobby,
and of course, Dodo,
who long ago taught a young boy
that the Wild West begins in Northfield.

Contents

The Jesse James Northfield Raid

Confessions of the Ninth Man

Chapter 1

An Old Man's Tale

BILL STILES: MAN OF THE CROSS

i.   Bill Stiles
Man of the Cross,
Did Jesus die for you?

ii.   Man of water, clay and grass . . .
Boulder and granite . . .
Fine layers of mica or schist . . .
A universal man for all mankind,
Yet an emerald sinner
The sole grain of sand in the clam shell

iii.   Was it you, Bill Stiles, who
swept the humble adobe floors
and pathways at the mission?
You, a peaceful man,
Inherited brother to
St. Francis

iv.   Yea . . . Miraculous!
Sweeper of floor, man with
hushed hand, gracing the
mixed seed in the marble garden
for the sparrows and wrens...
a kind sorcerer holding your holy,
hollow palm up to the sun,
The seed becomes a spray of colored stardust
in a sweep of your arm.

v.   You, whose seed borne
of dark humus,
thrust into dusty village streets

vi.   Did you live on after the
business of 1876 . . .
to travel lonely lands . . .

1

vii. Or were your dying breaths
whisked along into
history
From the dusty streets
of Northfield . . .

viii. Your gentle, dying breath
merging with the Tao,
the spring rains,
winter snows
and freezes . . .
glazed branches

ix. Your body and soul
transfigured onto a single
craggy trunk of oak,
somewhere in the lonely Minnesota countryside
—Chip Stroebel, 1983

ON JULY 19, 1913, A DEAD MAN WALKED into Los Angeles, monitoring actions of the Santa Fe and Southern Pacific Railroad.[1] This dead man, desperado Bill Stiles, a former member of the notorious Jesse James gang, had been killed in the dusty streets of Northfield, Minnesota, September 7, 1876, during a robbery attempt. Or had he?

Leaving Los Angeles a few weeks later, Stiles disappeared into the mountains near Pisgah Brande and met with old outlaw friends with whom he had visited earlier in Seattle and Tacoma.[2] For a month the outlaws remained in hiding, laying plans for a daring train robbery. Upon returning to the city the night before the would-be heist, Stiles found cover for his accomplices who were wanted men.

Sauntering down Main Street, Stiles became frightened when he noticed a police officer walking in his direction.[3] Fearing he was being followed, the outlaw ducked into a service at the Union Rescue Mission, then located at 145 North Main Street. Hoping to shake his pursuer, Stiles took a seat near the front, losing himself in the audience.

Stiles later recalled: "I did not hear much of the service, for my mind was upon the work for the next day. I felt a little uneasy, for I had left my suitcase in my room, and in it some of the 'soup' (nitroglycerin), some high explosives, and my guns. I had everything ready and so far my plans had gone smoothly; but as I say, I felt worried, and was just getting up to leave when one of the workers came to me and asked me to give myself up to God."[4]

Stiles told the evangelist, Mel Trotter, he did not believe in God because of the horrible lifestyle he had been forced to live.[5] Stiles stood up to walk away and found he had no control over his legs.

"I do not know what you think," recalled the outlaw, "but I know my legs were fastened to the floor by a power not of this earth. I kept trying to get up, when a woman came and sat down beside me, and urged me to go up to the altar. I listened to her pleadings for a time and then consented to go, thinking it would do me no harm anyway. What seemed so strange to me was that I did not have any power to resist. It was not the woman, for I had been a woman-hater since my early life; it was the power of God. As soon as I gave my consent my legs were released, and I went up and knelt at the altar."[6]

During the prayers, Stiles began weeping, feeling remorse for the outlaw life he had led. Mother Benton, wife of mission superintendent, Fred Benton, played the piano, all the while "coaching" the inspired Stiles through his conversion to Christianity. In spite of seeing the light, Stiles did not stay at the mission that night, but returned to his hotel room.

The following morning, Stiles sought his outlaw cronies and told them he was through with the old life of crime.[7] When he refused to take part in the train robbery, his confederates told him he was crazy and left. (The two men were later killed in separate holdups.)

Stiles showed up at the Union Rescue Mission early the next morning. Finding the door locked at such an early hour, he began tapping at the window until a startled Mother Benton let him in.[8] She was more startled, however, when he carried in a suitcase, and informed her it was full of soup. The frightened evangelist told him she would have to tell the police in fear mission workers could be considered accessories. Stiles gave her his consent to inform the authorities because he had not done anything with the explosives and had turned them in. The police came, removed the suitcase and Stiles was not charged.

Taking Mother Benton into his confidence, Stiles confessed he had been a criminal since the age of fourteen when he commenced life as a pickpocket on the streets of New York.[9]

Bill Stiles (left) and Mel Trotter, evangelist, who converted him. (Photo from the *Los Angeles Examiner*, July 8, 1931)

Stiles grew up in a fashionable home, his father a successful doctor. To curtail his criminal activities, his parents sent him abroad to the *Schoolship St. Mary*. Young Stiles would have none of it. Upon learning of the plan, he ran away to the Midwest.

Continuing his not-always-successful outlaw career, he served three one-year prison terms. Then he joined the James-Younger gang and participated in the robbery of the First National Bank of Northfield, Minnesota. Stiles maintained he escaped from Northfield and eventually made his way to Omaha, Nebraska. Sentenced to life imprisonment in 1900 for a different crime, he was released in 1913. Friends found honest work for him in Washington lumber towns, but his past caught up with him. He was fired after only two months. Deciding to return to crime, he journeyed to Los Angeles to rob a train.

"For a number of days I sat in the mission," recalled Stiles. "I was happy—happy for the first time in my life. Finally I began to come to myself and to think about the law, knowing that I was liable to be arrested, for I had revealed my past life. I thought about going away. . . ."[10]

But Stiles did not go away after his conversion. He stayed on at the mission helping with odd jobs, sweeping floors and cutting wood, shunning offers from old outlaw chums to return to a life of crime. Some of his old friends even tempted him with money, but Stiles remained true to his conversion and became the mission's night watchman.

Said a mission staff member, shortly before Stiles' demise: "A wonderful change had been worked in the heart of Bill Stiles and he has lived a Christian life ever since. We have learned to love him for his kind and genteel manner. Although he is eighty-two years old he is still our faithful night watchman, alert and watching while his fellows sleep, much as he used to, only for a different purpose."[11]

Stiles remained the mission's night watchman until his death in 1937. He had spent the final twenty-four years of his life as a devout Christian and was respected by all who had known him. But during a July 8, 1931, interview the man called Stiles made a full confession as to his true background. Still, respect for him never wavered.[12]

During the interview conducted by writer Ed Earl Repp and staff members of the Union Rescue Mission, Stiles maintained he had ridden with Frank and Jesse James during the holdup of the First National Bank of Northfield, Minnesota. Eight robbers were known to be involved in the holdup but Stiles professed there were nine; himself being the ninth highwayman.[13] Cole, Jim, and Bob Younger were captured near Madelia,

4

Minnesota, while two unidentified men believed to be Frank and Jesse James escaped. Three of the robbers were killed: Clell Miller, Charlie Pitts, and Bill Chadwell alias Bill Chadwick alias Bill Stiles.

During the 1931 interview, the man purported to be Bill Stiles claimed that Bill Chadwell and Bill Stiles were two separate outlaws riding in the same gang and not the same person. In a 1932 letter to a Minnesota resident, Union Rescue Mission Superintendent I.L. Eldridge wrote: "In a former letter you stated there were eight men in this raid. In reality there were nine but only eight of them were seen in the square in front of the bank. Bill Stiles, as I have stated before, was placed as an outer guard on the road leading out of town to keep the way clear for the get-away. This without a doubt will explain to you why there was [sic] apparently only eight."[14]

Eldridge went on to vouch for Stiles' integrity and said no one at the mission had ever doubted the former outlaw's connection with the James gang. He added, "[Stiles] is a straight-forward, clean-cut Christian gentleman, eighty-two years of age and

Bill Stiles (on the right). (Courtesy of the Union Rescue Mission, Los Angeles)

has no reason of trying to identify himself with the group unless he had been connected with them. At the time of his conversion nineteen years ago our Board of Directors and Management went into the matter quite thoroughly and have always been satisfied as to the truthfulness of Mr. Stiles' statement."[15]

Not everyone was convinced the ninth man theory was valid. After a second article appeared, this one in the *Sunday-School Times*, Philadelphia, Pennsylvania, July 23, 1932, by William A. Corey, mail from readers flooded the offices of the Union Rescue Mission, *All-Western Magazine* and *The Sunday School Times*. One of these angry letters came from G.M. Palmer, cofounder of the Hubbard Milling Company in Mankato. He maintained there was no question that Bill Stiles had been killed in the streets of Northfield.

In his closing paragraph, Palmer stated, "I am writing merely to find out whether or not the statement made in our reports to the effect that Bill Stiles was one of the two men killed in Northfield is correct, which I think is the case. If anyone else is posing under the name of Bill Stiles, in accordance with your article, we should certainly be glad to know it. There were eight in the gang at Northfield—two were killed there, six got away, but of the six three were captured, one was killed, and the two James Bros. escaped and were never apprehended."[16]

The Sunday School Times replied to Palmer's letter three weeks later and passed on an answer from William A. Corey, who had written the Stiles piece in their publication. Corey, via *The Sunday School Times*, said he was very familiar with the opinion held by many that Stiles had been killed in Northfield. He added many persons considered his Northfield death an error.

Said Corey, "If Mr. Palmer is not willing to take Stiles' own word for it, or the word of men of spiritual discernment who have known him for about twenty years and have the fullest confidence in him, I suggest he get Mr. Repp's account and read it. I submit to any thinking man that lying and hypocrisy that does not show itself or manifest itself in twenty years is in all probability not lying and hypocrisy at all. Especially as there could be no apparent motive for it."[17]

Corey went on to say the Union Rescue Mission, the oldest gospel mission in Los Angeles, had over the years been invited to hold services at different churches. Each time, a few of the Union's converts were taken along to testify as to their faith. Quite frequently Bill Stiles was one of these.

"[Stiles] always gives his testimony in brief, modest words, never boastful, and always with sorrow for the past, and giving all the glory to God who saved him on the eve of adding another terrible crime to his already long list," wrote Corey. "You may doubt a man's words but you cannot doubt his life; and when life and words agree, the words are pretty apt to be true."[18]

Palmer again wrote *The Sunday School Times* responding to Corey's argument. He contended there were eight men involved in the robbery and did not believe a ninth man was left at the edge of town guarding the escape route.[19] Palmer took objection to Repp's statement in *All-Western* magazine that the men who killed the two robbers in Northfield were on horses because there were no mounted men. He also attacked Repp's statement that Bill Chadwell's face "was blown to a mass utterly unrecognizable," stating the outlaw's face was not disfigured at all.

The Mankatoan also took umbrage at Repp's statement that Jim Younger was shot through the mouth and added the only Younger hit at Northfield was Bob, who suffered a broken arm. Repp's article also implied the fleeing James brothers and Stiles took a route northeast, then north across the border of Wisconsin when the robbers had really taken a southwesterly path.

"[Stiles] says a farmer with whom he was acquainted took the winded horses and gave them fresh ones—another misstatement; two of the robbers stole two horses from a friend of mine and escaped across the country to the Nebraska or South Dakota line," wrote Palmer. "He says they approached the town of Grantsburg in Wisconsin—absolutely wrong, as these robbers did not go anywhere near the Wisconsin line at the time of this raid. He says they went on until they crossed the Illinois line—another misstatement. He says that presently they arrived in Missouri without interference."[20]

Palmer did agree with the Los Angeles Bill Stiles that Frank and Jesse James were involved in the holdup. Beyond that, he said *All-Western* magazine was simply a magazine of wild west stories and the author of the article, Ed Earl Repp, knew nothing about the Northfield raid. "The robbers," added Palmer, "captured a farmer three miles from Mankato and some of them wanted to kill him but the others did not, and as soon as he was liberated he gave the alarm here, and the robbers were seen in this immediate vicinity but were not captured until they had gotten about thirty miles away."[21]

Shortly after receiving the letter from Palmer, William A. Corey stopped by the Union Rescue Mission to see Superintendent I. L. Eldridge and the alleged ninth man, Bill Stiles. Eldridge was not in when Corey called. Eldridge did write the author a few days later and asked him to call on Monday and set up an interview with Stiles.

"There has never been any question in our minds about [Stiles'] identity and his connection with the James boys," wrote Eldridge. "I think where you made a mistake in your article was that you took it from say-so and articles written by men who usually stretch the truth and get things all mixed, which the writer of the article in the *All-Western* magazine did."[22]

The author in question, Ed Earl Repp, may have embellished his article. A noted pulp writer, Repp was a master of science fiction stories and was well-known for pieces like Radium Pool and Stellar Missiles. He was also a western adventure writer with such novels as Hell in the Saddle and Tenderfoot Trail.

Corey interviewed Stiles and quickly wrote a four-page letter to Palmer. In the opening paragraph, he wrote that he would spare no effort to get to the bottom of the ninth-man matter. Then he went on to say, "In the first place I wish to say that I, The *Sunday School Times*, Mr. Stiles, and all concerned appreciate and echo your desire to vindicate truth in this issue. I think we all owe you our thanks for insisting upon a 'show-down' in the controversy."[23]

Corey said he had before him three accounts of the Northfield raid; Palmer's account, the one which appeared in *All-Western* magazine and a copy of *The Rise and Fall of Jesse James* by Robertus Love. The latter had been published by G.P. Putnam's Sons in 1926. Corey also informed Palmer he had had a "conference" with Mr. Stiles and also had a long letter from him with a newspaper clipping. Included with the letter to Palmer were statements of confidence in Mr. Stiles from those who knew him at the mission.

Said Corey: "First as to the three accounts, and beginning with yours, you were not, I take it, an eye-witness of the battle in the street. You compiled your account from others. And while teh [sic] facts as you state them are in the main correct— much more nearly so be it admitted, than the *All-Western* account—you will pardon me I am sure for saying that I think you weaken your main contention by claiming too much. You seem to assume a photoghaphic [sic] accuracy that, in the nature of the case, is open to question."[24]

Referring to the shoot-up in the Northfield streets, Corey reminded Palmer that "where there is dust, and noise, and excitement," anyone could make a mistake since no one could see everything at once. He said the *All-Western* story was unfortunate for everyone and that Palmer had been correct in questioning its validity. Stiles, he said, was not pleased with the story and had repudiated many of the statements, notwithstanding his signed endorsement as printed.

Corey asked Palmer to keep in mind that Stiles was a man nearing his middle eighties, and since the former outlaw was quite deaf, it was very difficult to interview him and even more difficult for Stiles to understand. Corey went on to say Stiles had had little contact with writers and it was difficult for him to express himself on paper. He added Stiles had more than likely signed the statement following the interview without reading it, only seeing the article when it appeared in print.

"On the other hand," continued Corey, "Stiles claims you are mistaken in some details. He says, there were nine men instead of eight—that one was posted on the outskirts of town as a guard. He says Jim Younger was shot in the mouth, and that they were all badly shot up, etc. As to the other three killed, the A.W. [*All Western*] story got him wrong, he says there were but two, Bill Chadwick, and Clell Miller. As to the direction they took out of town, he is not positive, his memory is uncertain. He speaks of a man named Graves, who had a small store near the bank, and of his [Stiles] escaping on a fine black stallion."[25]

Corey continued by stating the crux of the controversy was in identifying Bill Chadwick a.k.a. Chadwell, the slain bandit. Stiles had never known if Chadwick was his real name or only an alias. He did know Chadwick was the son of a prominent Minnesota family but the young man had turned to outlawry to feed a craze for adventure. Corey reiterated that Palmer's mistake and that of other Northfield accounts, were in not taking into consideration the possibility Stiles and Chadwick were two separate men.

"In this connection," wrote Corey, "Mr. Stiles showed me an old newspaper clipping bearing on this Stiles-Chadwick mix-up. Some years ago *The Lake Crystal* [Minnesota] *Tribune*, made a window display of copies of old newspapers. A lady, Mrs. Retta Clark a former resident of your state, later of Los Angles sent to *The Tribune* a copy of *The New York Times* of September 26, 1876. This copy of *The New York Times* carries a St. Louis dispatch, which says: 'The Chief of Police of St. Louis, a member of the police force in that city, and Mr. C.B. Hunn, Superintendent of the United States Express Company, arrived in this city Sunday morning for the purpose of establishing the identity of the dear [sic] and wounded Northfield bank robbers. After examining the body of the man killed at Madelia, they without hesitation pronounced it that of Charley Pitts, and from photographs [sic] they are satisfied that those killed at Northfield were Bill Chadwick and—[Clell] Miller.'"[26]

The most convincing argument in Stiles' behalf was probably unknown to Corey. Following the Northfield raid, Stiles' own father made the trip from his home near Grand Forks, North Dakota to Northfield to identify his son's body. He left Northfield with peace of mind. The body was not that of his son's as evidenced in one of several newspaper accounts:

"Confirmatory of the fact that Chadwell was not Bill Stiles is a letter in the same paper from Elisha A. Stiles, of Grand Forks, D.T. [Dakota Territory], in which he denies the published statement that he recognized the portrait of the man killed at Northfield as that of his son; also that he was a horsethief. He also claims to have received letters from Peterman, of Cannon Falls, denying that he made the affidavit that has been published; and claiming that in the letter he received from Texas, Stiles asked him for money instead of offering him some.

"Although it looks as though Bill Stiles is likely to establish an alibi; and there exists considerable doubt whether the two men who escaped of the Northfield gang were really the James brothers."[27]

In light of the fact Elisha A. Stiles found the dead man someone other than his son, Bill Stiles' credibility has to be seriously considered. The writer of the article also implies Stiles survived the Northfield shoot-out but was involved in the melee when he said "Stiles was likely to establish an alibi." One also must consider Elisha A. Stiles' home near Grand Forks, North Dakota. Following the raid on Northfield, the two [or three] fleeing bandits chose a westerly path which led them into eastern South Dakota. From here, it is believed they headed southeast toward their home in Missouri.

Jesse and Frank would have been aware of the dangers ahead as they swung toward Missouri. Every law official in the Midwest would anticipate the move. Could the James boys have ridden north instead of south and taken temporary refuge in the home of Elisha Stiles? Since Elisha's son was believed to have been killed in Northfield, why would anyone suspect the senior Stiles of harboring fugitives? And, of course, no one would suspect a northerly diversion where the fugitives could lay over for a few days, obtain fresh horses and confuse their pursuers.

Did the real Bill Stiles die in Northfield? Perhaps so; perhaps not. The identities of the three slain robbers created quite a controversy, and even a century later, no one can be absolutely certain who the fleeing bandits were. We do know Bill Chadwell, Clell Miller and Charlie Pitts were killed, but once Chadwell's corpse was put in the ground, there could be no positive identification of Bill Stiles.

Not only was Chadwell confused with Chadwick and with Stiles, but there was even a minor disagreement that Clell Miller's body was really that of Chadwell's. Shortly after the unpleasantness in Northfield, a lady in Cato, Crawford County, Kansas, wrote a letter to the St. Paul *Pioneer Press* stating the man pictured in the newspaper as Clell Miller was really William Chadwell. She said Chadwell had worked for her husband five years earlier and stayed with her family for several months.

Chadwell, she claimed, was only eighteen years old at the time, a harmless, inoffensive young man, although not particularly brilliant. Because he was easily swayed, he was influenced by another boarder in the household who was corrupt.

Chadwell's mother, a member of the local Baptist church, lived in the community and had grown increasingly uneasy over her son's wild and reckless habits. Yet Mrs. Chadwell, as well as the entire community, were startled when they learned Bill had become a member of the Younger gang and helped rob the Baxter Springs bank in Kansas.

"As I look at his likeness in your paper which lies before me, the exact resemblance of him as I last saw him, now nearly a year since, as he raised his hat on addressing me and brushed back the curls that clustered around his forehead, my heart prompts me to drop a tear of regret over his terrible fate," read the letter from the Kansas woman. "I have thus set these facts before you; and you can make such use of them as you may see fit; the identity of the man shown as Clel [sic] Miller can be established as Wm. Chadwell without a doubt in the community where he has been so long known."[28]

Chadwell. Chadwick. Stiles. Even Miller. A confusing issue that may never be laid to rest. It has been established Clell Miller was not Bill Chadwell, but what about Stiles? If anyone believed in the Los Angeles Bill Stiles, it was William A. Corey:

"Let me say a word about the testimonials, which I am sending you," wrote Corey in his letter to Palmer. "I have underscored the words in Mr. Eldridge's letter, which carries his endorsement of Bill Stiles. I have replied to it, stating that I never saw the *All-Western* story until I had sent my story to *The Sunday School Times,* and that I had already seen Mr. Stiles. The officials of the Union Rescue Mission have known Stiles for twenty years. He has long served here as night watchman, and literally hundreds of friends would vouch for him."[29]

Corey sent copies of affidavits for Palmer's perusal. Among these was one from evangelist Tom Mackey who was well-respected throughout the country. Mackey had preached in some of the largest churches in Minneapolis and St. Paul and was very familiar with the Minnesota countryside Stiles had spoken of Mackey's endorsement of Stiles read as followed:

"I can only say I have always believed in Bill Stiles. All I ever knew is his testimony at the mission."[30] Mackey's affidavit went on to give Mother Benton's address in the state of Washington.

An affidavit from Samuel Ware Packard was also included with Corey's letter. Packard had been a director at the Union Rescue Mission for several years and had practiced law for over fifty years. At the age of twenty-six, he had won a case before the United States Supreme Court and received a fee of $20,000. Corey told Palmer that Packard was one of the brightest legal minds in the country.

11

Packard's affidavitt read: "I have known Bill Stiles since his conversion at the Union Rescue Mission. He has lived a conservative Christian life since then and I think the Minnesota man (Palmer) is mistaken."[31] (Packard's writing at this point becomes illegible.)

Corey, in concluding his letter to Palmer, rested his case. "Now Mr. Palmer I cannot prove that our Los Angles Bill Stiles was not killed at Northfield more than fifty years ago, you cannot prove that he was. I think the fair presumption is with us. Anyway we have both had our say and I think we should shake hands call it a day and quit."[32]

Corey added a final paragraph to his letter disagreeing with Palmer over another issue. Palmer stated Cole Younger had broken his parole by going to Missouri secretly. Corey was certain Cole had been granted a full pardon by the Minnesota Prison Board of Pardons and there was no secrecy involved with his leaving.

Palmer tested Corey on the issue, writing Warden Sullivan about the difference of opinion. He asked if the warden could clear the air by informing him whether Cole Younger was paroled or pardoned and allowed to return to Missouri. He received the following reply from Stillwater: "Robert Younger died in prison on September 16, 1889, Cole and James were paroled on July 14, 1901, James committed suicide on October 19, 1902. Cole was pardoned, while on parole, February 4, 1903, and died at Lee's Summit, Missour [sic] in 1917."[33] Corey had been correct.

The Mankatoan then penned another letter to Corey thanking him for his help. Palmer continued, "I can readily account for many of the discrepancies in the *All Western* magazine, for probably the writer drew upon his own imagination about as much as he did on the story given him by Stiles."[34] He then went on to ask Corey if Stiles could have been one of the two outlaws who escaped, which he felt drew doubt as to whether the James boys were implicated in the raid. He asked Corey if he could interview Stiles again and ask him about their escape.

Palmer insisted the matter was important. He said a personal friend of his had been one of seven men who went into the swamp near Madelia, captured the robbers and killed one of them. According to Palmer, his friend received a slight scratch from a bullet fired by one of the outlaws. He added his friend was saved from being killed because he had a pipe in his pocket which was flattened by the bullet.

Corey did not respond immediately, but instead referred Palmer's letter to mission superintendent I.L. Eldridge. Eldridge responded on November 1: "You are correct as to the escape of both Jesse and Frank James. Stiles was an outer guard stationed on the road leading out of Northfield. He followed the two James boys as a rear guard and probably was not seen by the people who saw Frank and Jesse leave."[35]

Eldridge reported Stiles had named the robbers as Jesse James, Frank James, Bill Chadwell, Clell Miller, Charlie Pitts, Bob Younger, Jim Younger, Cole Younger and Bill Stiles. Stiles via Eldridge said Palmer had been correct in assuming the three robbers slain were Bill Chadwell, Clell Miller, and Charlie Pitts. Eldridge added, "Jesse was shot in the hip. Stiles was wounded with a shot gun in the back but was far enough away so that it was not a serious wound. Frank was also hit I understand."[36]

Eldridge concluded his letter by saying if Palmer needed further information on the matter, he would again be glad to talk with Mr. Stiles and clear the air. He reiterated, "We have never doubted his connection with the James boys."[37]

On November 8, Corey answered Palmer's letter, apologizing for the delay, and stating he had referred the Mankatoan's letter to Eldridge since he was in closer touch with Stiles. Said Corey, "The fact of the matter is Stiles has allowed this discussion regarding his past life to get on his nerves. He feels hurt that Christians should doubt his word. I think he even harbors a suspicion that a trap is being laid for him to his injury. Of course no one else has any such thought but we must remember that he lived for long years as a hunted man, and while for twenty years he has been free from it and in peace the questioning of his word and the scrutiny of all the details has brought back to some extent the old feeling. So it is really impossible to get any further real information out of him. He has written me two long letters but they convey little real information beyond what he has already given us."[38]

Corey then summed up all he had been able to gather about the robbers in the Northfield raiding party: "They approached the town in two squads and from two directions. They left a guard on the outskirts of the place along the main street at each end of the street. Bill Stiles was one of these guards. When the bank had been entered and the fight started Stiles heard the firing and dashed into the town to aid his comrades. He took little or no part in the actual fighting but escaped with the wounded survivors, riding his black stallion."[39]

Corey added the robber was personally convinced Frank and Jesse James had escaped. He said Bob, Jim, and Coleman Younger were all captured, Bob dying in prison, Jim dying by his own hand following parole, and Cole pardoned and returning to Lee's Summit, Missouri where he lived until his death. Corey said Clell Miller and Bill Chadwick were killed at Northfield, and Sam Wells, alias Charlie Pitts, met a similar fate near Madelia.

"Bill Stiles escaped," added Corey. "Whether he escaped in company with the Jameses or not I can't say. There are some details Stiles will not reveal because he fears it might injure individuals still living in Minnesota [who] gave them aid in the getaway. This accounting, you will see, makes nine in the whole party, as Stiles has all along contended. Also it identifies Stiles and Chadwick as two separate men which is where most accounts have got confused."[40]

Corey said he hoped the information he had provided Palmer would present a somewhat clear understanding of the incident, at least as far as his own knowledge of the affair went, adding: "I am satisfied there are some things that Bill Stiles will carry to his grave untold. But we can all readily see how this would very naturally be. Also we can appreciate his sensitiveness and even nervousness about the discussion. I am writing him today to say to him that, for my part, I am sorry that I was the indirect cause of distress to him. I appreciate your historical society's interest in the matter. But you see Bill Stiles hardly looks at it from just that standpoint."[41]

Palmer wrote his final letter to Corey November 12 and thanked him for all his help. He said he in no way wished to cause Mr. Stiles any trouble but had only wanted the facts regarding the incident he called "the most spectacular of anything that had been pulled off in Minnesota." He ended his missive by saying, "I shall pursue the matter no further and have not given it any publicity here in this state. I should dislike at this late date to make this old man any further trouble, and while I do not think publicity would result in that, it would create great interest and perhaps some unpleasant results might accrue to Mr. Stiles."[42]

Whether Palmer was convinced The Los Angeles Stiles was in earnest is uncertain. Palmer did relate to a friend that Stiles was a fraud.[43] However, the correspondence is undated, so it is unclear whether he made this statement prior before or after his association with William A. Corey.

But there were some who were convinced, including U.G. Kniss of Northfield: "Northfield historians who are posted on the story of the Waterloo of the James-Younger gang in their attempted raid on the First National Bank of Northfield September 7, 1876, don't know quite all there is to know about the historic event that put Northfield 'on the map.'"[44] Kniss based his theory on the July 8, 1931, interview with Los Angeles Bill Stiles.

The most convincing argument, of course, to establish Los Angeles Bill Stiles' credibility, remains the fact his own father saw the body of the man killed in the streets of Northfield and walked away a happy man. The elder Stiles was unable to identify the corpse but was certain it was not that of his son. But Stiles was reportedly seen by others years after the robbery.

Frank Dalton, who falsely professed to be the real Jesse James, was one of these "witnesses" to Stiles' continued existence. Although he himself was exposed by author Carl W. Breihan and other scholars in the Circuit Court and Appeals Court and $10,000 supposedly awarded the James family, it is peculiar why he would raise the ghost of Bill Stiles.[45] He certainly had no reason to "back" Stiles' claim. Although Dalton was not Jesse James, he knew many former outlaws. Had Stiles survived the Northfield raid, Dalton would probably have known him.

In a 1943 letter, Dalton wrote: "I saw Bill Stiles—who was under the name of 'Bill Chadwell' and was thot [sic] to be killed during the bank robbery—on one of my frequent boat trips down the Mississippi River in 1911. He was a fisherman just below Vicksburg. (He died in 1922 or I wouldn't be telling of meeting him.) He was under an assumed name of course. He knew me, as I did him, as we had been in the same Company with Quantrill during the war. He didn't know my wife, having never met her. She was with me, as she always was whenever possible. Bill was married and had a fine wife and family. We stayed a week talking over old times. His wife knew who he was, as also did Annie, my wife. Annie and I were writing stories and selling them to the newspapers of the towns along the river, but you can be assured that that's one feature story that we didn't write. This is the first time I've ever told it. You can use this in any way you wish if you think it of interest."[46]

The reference to the year 1911 would certainly give support to Stiles' claim. The mention of 1922 as Stiles' date of death is a mystery. Was it just one more piece of fraudulent information or had Dalton only thought Stiles had left this world? This was still two years before Stiles entered the mission in Los Angeles and told his story. In 1911, he was still living in obscurity under an assumed name, afraid of apprehension for past deeds. Or was Bill Stiles just another fake Jesse figure?

Little else was said regarding the man in Los Angeles believed by some to be veteran westerner Bill Stiles. and The matter was eventually forgotten after his death. But in 1970, a story appeared in *Real Frontier* magazine under the title, "The James Gang and the Bounty Hunters" by Bill Stiles, as told to Ed Earl Repp.[47] An editor's note appeared with the story stating the material in the article was obtained by Repp from personal interviews with Mr. Stiles, eighty-six, before his death in 1939, as well as from written material given to Mr. Repp from Mr. Stiles.

The editor's note also stated Stiles was discovered by Repp who was then a Los Angeles newspaperman. Stiles, it said, was found living in seclusion at a North Main Street Rescue Mission after having spent thirteen years of a life sentence in Sing Sing for involvement in a New York killing. Repp commented on Stiles terrible handwriting in which he used no punctuation or upper case letters.

Repp also referred to a feud between Stiles and Emmett Dalton which assumed Dalton recognized Los Angeles Bill Stiles as the real Stiles. According to Repp, Stiles was still tough at eighty-six, and his deadly enemy was still Dalton. Repp thought Stiles was joking when he said he would put a slug in Emmett if he ever got the chance. When Emmett fired back he'd like nothing better than to slit Stiles' gullet, Repp realized they weren't kidding. Repp knew them both, for they lived only eight miles apart in Los Angeles, and didn't know it.

Emmett Dalton believed in Bill Stiles, his hated enemy. Frank Dalton, whatever his status, believed in Bill Stiles. People in and around a mission in Los Angeles believed in Stiles as did writers like Repp and Corey. Most importantly, so did Stiles' father.

There were eight men who robbed the Northfield bank, but was a ninth waiting on the edge of town guarding the escape route? We may never know. But we can piece together the facts we do know about what happened in the dusty streets of Northfield, September 7, 1876, a year when George Armstrong Custer and his troops were massacred near the Little Bighorn River, Wild Bill Hickok was murdered, and the notorious James-Younger gang was defeated in Minnesota.

Notes

1 Art Palmer, Union Rescue Mission, telephone interview with author, February 3, 1982; Art Palmer letter to author dated February 24, 1982; Thomas R. Ankrom, Union Rescue Mission to letter to author dated April 5, 1982.

2 Helga Bender Henry, Mission on Main Street, W.A. Wilde Co., Los Angeles, 1955, p. 73.

3 41st Annual Report of the Union Rescue Mission, Los Angeles, California, 1931.

4 Helga Bender Henry, Mission on Main Street, p. 73.

5 Los Angeles Examiner, July 8, 1931; Helga Bender Henry, Mission on Main Street, pp. 73-74.

6 Helga Bender Henry, Mission on Main Street, p. 74.

7 41st Annual Report of the Union Rescue Mission.

8 Helga Bender Henry, Mission on Main Street, pp. 75-77.

9 Ibid. pp. 72-73.

10 Ibid. p. 76.

11 41st Annual Report of the Union Rescue Mission.

12 *Los Angeles Examiner,* July 8, 1931.

13 I.L. Eldridge, Superintendent of the Union Rescue Mission letter to G.M. Palmer of Mankato, Minnesota, dated November 1, 1932. The letter is in a collection at the Blue Earth County Historical Society, Mankato; Ed Earl Repp, *All-Western* magazine, January and March 1932, Dell Publishing Co., New York.

14 Eldridge letter to Palmer, November 1, 1932.

15 Ibid.

16 G.M. Palmer of Mankato, Minnesota, letter addressed to *The Sunday School Times,* Philadelphia, Pennsylvania, dated August 3, 1932. Blue Earth County Historical Society collection.

17 The editors of *The Sunday School Times* letter to G.M. Palmer, dated August 24, 1932. Most of the material in the letter was copied from a William A. Corey letter. (Blue Earth County Historical Society).

18 Ibid.

19 G.M. Palmer letter to *The Sunday School Times,* dated September 14, 1932. (Blue Earth County Historical Society).

20 Ibid.

21 Ibid.

22 I.L. Eldridge letter to William A. Corey, dated October 8, 1932. (Blue Earth County Historical Society).

23 William A. Corey letter to G.M. Palmer, dated October 11, 1932. (Blue Earth County Historical Society).

24 Ibid.

25 Ibid.

26 Ibid.

27 *Faribault (Minnesota) Republican,* October 25, 1876, p. 3.

28 Ibid.

29 October 11, 1932 letter from Corey to Palmer.

30 Copy of Tom Mackey affidavit enclosed in Corey's October 11, 1932 letter.

31 Copy of Samuel Ware Packard affidavit.

32 October 11, 1932 letter from Corey to Palmer.

33 Undated letter (written between October 18 and 21, 1932) from Warden Sullivan's office at Stillwater State Prison to G.M. Palmer.

34 G.M. Palmer letter to William A. Corey, dated October 21, 1932. (Blue Earth County Historical Society).

35 I.L. Eldridge letter to G.M. Palmer, dated November 1, 1932. (Blue Earth County Historical Society).

36 Ibid.

37 Ibid.

38 William A. Corey letter to G.M. Palmer, dated November 8, 1932. (Blue Earth County Historical Society).

39 Ibid.

40 Ibid.

41 Ibid.

42 G.M. Palmer letter to William A. Corey, dated November 12, 1932. (Blue Earth County Historical Society).

43 Undated postcard from Maynard S. Tyrrell to Thomas Hughes.

(Blue Earth County Historical Society).

44 Undated 1931 *Northfield News* article.

45 Carl W. Breihan letter to author dated February 12, 1982.

46 Frank Dalton letter to Mr. O.L. Hawk, Puallup, Washington dated February 12, 1943, in possession of Rice County Historical Society, Faribault, Minnesota.

47 Bill Stiles, as told to Ed Earl Repp, "The James Gang and the Bounty Hunters," *Real Frontier*, I, No. 4, August 1970.

Chapter 2

Yankee Gold

TOMORROW'S THE DAY

"Tomorrow's the Day," Jesse said
      To me while we watched the road
From bushes along the river bank.
      "Tomorrow's the day." And his eyes showed
He was seeing' the loot—Yankee loot—
      Waitin' for us to take it away.
'Twas Bill Stiles said 'twould be easy:
      "They're farmers: milking cows, making hay;
We'll walk right in and bust the bank
      (Fat with carpetbaggin' Ames'
And Spoons Butler's stolen goods)
      They'll be no match for our game
And we'll make the thievin' Yanks pay
      For bringin' ol' Jeff Davis down."

And so we came to Minnesota
      A drinkin' and a gamblin' our
Way around Minneapolis,
      Shakopee, and New Ulm to scour
What information we could find
      About banks and streets and highways.
We posed as land speculators
      And cattle buyers; our sly ways
Foolin' the simple small town folk;
      And news came in by twos and threes
Until Jesse said, "Mankato
      Is where we'll find our life of ease."

We rode to town that lazy day
      Of summertime with thoughts of gold
Jest fillin' up our hearts and minds.
      But 'tweren't to be—we had to hold
Those thoughts of gold for another day.
      For millin' round the bank so bold
We saw a crowd of folk so large—

We knew, we jest knew, they'd been told
Someone was plannin' a heist that day.
So's we jest turned our horses round
And galloped right back out o' town
And threw our bedrolls on the ground
While Jesse formed a grand new plan
To strike at Yanks and make them pay,
And fill our pockets deep with gold:
We'd leave Mankato right away
And make our way to Northfield town,
To Northfield town that very day.
For there that evil disgustin' pair
Of Yankee thieves (Butler and Ames)
Had put their stolen goods at int'rest
To maximize their ill-gotten gains.

"Tomorrow's the day," Jesse said
To me while we watched the road
From bushes along the river bank.
"Tomorrow's the day!" And his eyes showed
He was seeing' the loot—Yankee loot—
Waitin' for us to take it away.

—Christopher W. Hawes

ON JULY 7, 1876, A MISSOURI PACIFIC TRAIN was robbed by eight outlaws near Otterville, Missouri.[1] The robbery, also known as Rocky cut, had been committed by the notorious James-Younger gang consisting of Jesse and Frank James, Cole and Bob Younger, Clell Miller, Bill Stiles, Charlie Pitts, and Hobbs Kerry. Kerry, a raw recruit, began boasting of his participation in the hold-up, and when arrested, quickly gave the names of his confederates in exchange for two years in prison.

Jesse and Frank James had been robbing banks and trains throughout Missouri, Arkansas, Texas, Iowa, Kentucky, and as far east as West Virginia.[2] The Younger brothers had been opportunists also in much of the same territory, and like the Jameses, could hide out with relatives and friends "as long as they didn't bring any of the loot with them."[3] Members of the gangs were almost always reliable men, cohorts they could depend on during any crisis. Hobbs Kerry was the exception, but for the next holdup, the James-Younger gang would not have another like him.

The James home in Clay County, near Kearney, Missouri, frequently served as a not-so-secret rendezvous for the gang, and although under the watchful eye of local law authorities, their comings and goings often went unseen. Zerelda James, mother of Frank and Jesse, had married Dr. Reuben Samuel on September 26, 1855,

Jesse James, 1868. (Courtesy of the Armand De Gregoris Collection)

20

The footpath leading into Monagaw Cave. (Photo by Marley Brant)

Monagaw Cave lookout above Osage River. (Photo by Marley Brant)

four years after the death of her first husband, Robert James, and three years following the accidental death of her second, Benjamin Simms.[4]

But it was perhaps in nearby Monagaw Cave that plans for a raid on a Minnesota bank were agreed upon.[5] The cave was a natural fortress overlooking the Osage River—an ideal meeting place, because any intruder could easily be watched coming up the narrow footpath which led to the opening.

The idea to venture so far north may have originated

with Bill Stiles. Stiles had once lived in Monticello, Minnesota as well as in Rice County, and knew too-well the fat banks in the state which were ripe for plucking. Stiles was particularly adept in his knowledge of the southern part of the state and he was familiar with many of the roads leading in and out of many villages.[6] He had once been convicted for horse theft in Minnesota and still had relatives living in the state. Writing frequent letters to his brother-in-law in Minneapolis, Stiles stayed in tune with events in the state.

Stiles reportedly had been seen in various parts of Minnesota only a year before the raid on Northfield.[7] He stayed for awhile in Cannon Falls. For six weeks, he roomed in a boarding house with a flour mill worker. He studied the layout of the roads in the Cannon Falls area and may have been making preparations for a future strike somewhere in the area.

Two years before the raid, Stiles returned to his native Wright County. A warrant had been issued for his arrest for selling liquor to the Indians and law officers were in pursuit of him. His father had owned a farm here, although at the time of Stiles' visit, the spread was owned by a W.P. Barnett. The Stiles family had moved to Brainerd in northern Minnesota where they kept a primitive shack and had since migrated to Grand Forks, North Dakota. Before Bill Stiles left Cannon Falls, he stole a bottle of perfume from the window of Barker's Drug Store.[8]

Jesse was an attentive listener as Stiles told stories of the rich northern banks and easy trains to rob. According to Stiles, the farmers in the rich Minnesota rural communities couldn't identify an outlaw band if it surrounded them, and the northern banks were far more prosperous than those of the hard luck states. Fruitful Minnesota was easy pickings and Stiles said the gang could make a getaway with a large haul.[9] His knowledge of the towns, roads, the rivers and lakes, the bridges, and most importantly, the banks, was tempting; so tempting, Jesse visited Bob Younger in a Kansas City hotel and talked him into the scheme. It never took much to interest Bob in a holdup.

Bob, ready to marry, was anxious to obtain land for a large farm in Missouri. Cole had been trying to talk the family into settling in Texas but Bob was tired of his nomadic lifestyle. In the past six years, he had moved from Missouri to Texas to Virginia to Florida to Louisiana to Texas to Missouri and wanted to rebuild the land his father had left behind. He rode with the gang mostly out of revenge for the killing of his brother John. When Jesse spoke of one more "big" job, Bob saw the means of financing his plans and agreed.

Bob Younger probably had as much to do with planning the Minnesota caper as did Jesse James and Bill Stiles.[10] Bob was very close to Jesse and they maintained a special friendship. Bob resented being told what and what not to do by his older brother Cole, and he found in Jesse, a means of escape from the habitual advice. Jesse continually offered Bob options and encouraged the independent side of him. Still, Bob was usually reasonable and rational and could be talked out of impulsive acts by a wiser Cole.

Cole and Frank were against the holdup but Bob and Jesse told them they were going to do it anyway. When it came to pulling off a bank robbery in Minnesota, Bob stubbornly refused to be guided by his brother or anyone else who opposed it. Cole, who was jealous of Jesse, had no choice but to come along.

Jim Younger was not present at the sessions at the Kansas City hotel, Monagaw Cave, and at the James home.[11] The role of an outlaw had never suited Jim; he was in California working an honest job and seldom missing a day of work. He was in no way eager to ride the outlaw trail again, but after several refusals, he reluctantly set off for Missouri to join his brothers and their companions. Like Cole, Jim was not going to allow his little brother to pull this off without him.

Todd M. George, who befriended Cole Younger, presented a different version of the plan to visit Minnesota: "On a certain date which I do not remember correctly the word had been circulated among the then known bushwhackers of Missouri that wealthy merchant dealers in the northeast on certain dates in the fall season would share an express coach on a train carrying a bountiful lot of cash through the northern states to purchase a large quantity of grain to be shipped back east, always making a deposit in cash for these purchases in each town where they visited." According to George, the gang led by Cole

The Younger house in Jackson County, Missouri. (Photo by Marley Brant)

went to Minnesota to obtain the date they would be passing through Northfield, so they could rob the train. "It was so planned," continued George, "that it would be their last attempt of this kind and they would divide up the money and scatter in far away states and get away from the law. Unfortunately, they arrived in Northfield two days after the train had gone through. Most of them, then being short of cash, decided to remain over night and rob the bank."[12]

There has been speculation as to whether the outlaw band rode their splendid horses into Minnesota or journeyed by rail. One scholar has written through correspondence: "These guys wouldn't go anywhere without the finest horses—especially out of state. Now, if they did obtain new horses and trained them (and I don't think they would have had to put too much time into training them—they knew what they were doing) it would be only natural to do so in St. Paul where their cover would be good and they could obtain information and conduct other business. Don't forget that the Youngers' father was in the horse-selling business as well as Jesse and Frank knowing quite a bit about horses so why would they have to take weeks to train horses. I don't think so."[13]

Rumors of a mysterious Farmer Brown circulated following the robbery attempt in Northfield. Many persons believed Brown owned a farm somewhere in southern Minnesota, where it was alleged the horses belonging to the James-Younger gang were trained for the raid on Northfield. No trace of an illusive farmer named Brown was ever found.

"Maybe Farmer Joe Brown lived right outside of the Minneapolis/St. Paul area," wrote the same scholar. "I only think this story makes any kind of sense if such were the case. Why would they take good horses (again, the only kind they would ride only to leave them 'where' in Council Bluffs, board a train and start all over again. There really wasn't that much time. Especially when you relate it to the Otterville robbery being so close behind them. The time and effort involved in riding up there really wouldn't have been practical and that's one quality each one of those men possessed."[14]

During his incarceration in Minnesota's Stillwater Prison following the Northfield raid, Jim Younger wrote to his sweetheart and told her about the gang's horseback ride to Minnesota.[15] Jim described each of the horses and how each one rode, and related how well-trained each of the horses were. But there was a story recounting the riding of horses only as far as Council Bluffs where the outlaws then boarded a train. Another account insisted they had taken a train all the way to Red Wing, Minnesota, where they procured and trained mounts. But there would have been little time.

Excerpts from a letter written by Jim Younger give substance to the horse riding theory. "The truth of my ride from Kansas City, Missouri to Northfield, Minnesota in August of 1876." "Stopped at Albert Lea (Minnesota) to purchase fresh mounts." "Met with Frank J. party on September 7, 1876." "Appreciate unselfish loyalty of Pitts."[16]

Cole Younger, on the other hand, repeatedly contradicted himself, stating in his memoirs the outlaws had come to Minnesota by train, but through his correspondence and interviews, he hinted of a long ride in the saddle. Cole, however, liked to confuse the media, often fabricating events to protect his confederates.

Although he did not specifically mention the word "horse," it is more than apparent he referred to mounts in a letter he wrote while a Stillwater inmate: "On going to our destinations we went by different routes. Four including Bob went the southern route. Jim, myself, and the other two by the northern route. On the 6th of September (we) stayed at Janesville. Rested on west side of river."[17]

Also apparent was Cole's undying loyalty to his companions. He referred to the two outlaws believed to be Frank and Jesse James merely as "the other two."[18] Although he was never called a liar, at least not to his face, he was the story teller in the Younger family, and from time to time was known to do a little stretching around the edges. Jim, however, did mention both Frank and Jesse by name in some of his correspondence, perhaps the only real proof of their involvement.

Since the men probably traveled to Minnesota in separate bands, it is possible that one group came by horse, the other by rail; or at least part of the way. Cole did allude to this in his autobiography and there is some evidence fresh horses were purchased in Minnesota. Cole, with Bill Stiles, perhaps came by train. The pair would have arrived in Minnesota much earlier

James farm near Kearney, Missouri. (Photo by Diana Pierce)

than the others, and with Stiles already familiar with the country, the pair could put everything in its proper perspective.

Gang members assembled secretly at the James home three miles southeast of Kearney, which lay back from the road a quarter mile on the slope of a hill.[19] It was late July and the house seemed deserted, the doors were closed and locked, and no sound came from within. A few yards away, a black boy sat lazily on a stump, his eyes searching nervously in every direction. He would continually glance at the door of the barn, take his seat back on the stump, and moments later, repeat the ritual.

The boy's name was Perry Samuel and he had been born on the James farm September 15, 1868.[20] His mother was named Charlotte and was a former slave, but Perry never discussed his father. The 1880 Census lists Perry Samuel not as a Negro but as a mulatto, and family legend has it his father may have been Dr. Reuben Samuel.[21] Perry Samuel had been raised on the James farm and remained there until 1890 when he was twenty-two years old. In a deposition completed in the 1930s, Perry Samuel stated, "he had seen Jesse James on each occasion that he came home."

Perry remained outside the barn for a long time, and once the sun had disappeared behind the surrounding hills, a voice from within the barn broke the stillness of evening. "Perry, you may open the door."[22] This was the signal the young man had been waiting for. Making sure the coast was clear, he rushed to the door, unhooked it, and flung the doors open. A covered wagon pulled by a team of horses moved slowly out of the shadows. Only one man, the driver, was seen. He flipped the boy a coin. The young boy saluted the driver as if he were a soldier and the wagon disappeared in the direction of the highway

There is some speculation that the outlaws paused at the home of Myra Belle Shirley, the infamous Belle Starr on the way to the fat banks of Minnesota.[23] Here the men continued preparations and rested up for the next leg of the journey. Leaving Belle's, the outlaws split up only to meet again at Fort Osage Township in Jackson County, Missouri.

Near Parkville, Missouri, the boys were rowed across the Missouri River by Charlie Turner, a brother-in-law of one of the men. One man at a time was rowed across the river to avoid suspicion, with each of the horses swimming alongside the boat.[24] At least some of the band rode across Iowa and into southern Minnesota.

According to an 1876 resident of Woodward, Iowa, who owned a general store, implement store, livery stable, and two farms, the gang members stopped at his home on their journey north. "Jesse James and his band of about eight men stayed at the Fred Miller home in Iowa for a week. They faced the benches in the house toward the windows to see any oncoming attempt at capture. Mrs. Miller refused to cook for them unless they would say 'grace,' which they then did. They paid for the food and feed for the horses and left."[25]

The Miller Family History Records state Jesse James was accompanied by his band of about eight men. If these figures are correct, nine men would have visited the farm on their way to Northfield. Los Angeles Bill Stiles claimed nine men went to Minnesota, not eight as accepted by James historians.

In Southern Minnesota, two of the men went into a town and purchased eight thoroughbred saddle horses.[26] Scholars disagree upon the town in question, but Jim Younger in a letter to his sweetheart identified the town as Albert Lea.[27] Near Worthington, Minnesota, the gang stopped to rest under a walnut tree and was fed by a family named Ackerman.[28]

All the men were well-dressed, well-mounted and well-equipped.[29] Each of the riders carried a carbine strapped to his saddle and a pair of colts under his long linen duster. They rode leisurely in separate scouting parties through the countryside. Two or three would enter a town and strike up friendships with local citizens. They pretended to be horse buyers and sellers, grain dealers, civil engineers, or real estate speculators; whatever they felt would be the most believable in a given situation.[30] This was an old ploy and they had used it many times before.

Whenever possible, the riders avoided towns in favor of visiting local farmers whom they found easy to talk to, and they had no difficulty in giving a plausible account of themselves.[31] Everywhere they went, however, they attracted curiosity and many people were suspicious of them. Nonetheless, they made a favorable impression on most they encountered and were well-respected.

During that August, a Minnesota farmer was driving his team of horses along a rural road on his way home from a small village.[32] He would make the journey into town about once a week, selling his produce and purchasing supplies for his family. At the top of a hill where the road veered sharply to the right, he came upon four men in the midst of a friendly argument in the middle of the road.

Four horses bearing expensive saddles were tied to a fence post near the men, and about a hundred yards further up the road, four more men were standing, their horses also tied to the fence. The startled farmer was suspicious, and when greeted by the men, he stopped and asked what had brought them to the rural country road.

The farmer introduced himself as Joe Brown and each of the strangers shook hands with him. They conveyed to the farmer that they were from Tennessee and were planning to ride further north to look for timber lands.[33] The strange men did have a slight southern accent which lent their story credibility, and as Brown chatted incessantly about northern Minnesota, he never doubted their tale. In fact, he told them he lived only a mile up the road and they were all welcome to spend the night at his farm. The men insisted on paying for their accommodations and thanked him profusely for coming to the aid of weary travelers.[34]

As the horsemen began following Brown up the road, the farmer noticed one of the horses was riderless. Suddenly, a wagon was driven out of the woods and joined the procession. In reaching the Brown farm, the riders dismounted at the barnyard, but the wagon moved behind the barn, just out of sight from the road. The issue becomes a bit clouded here, for if there had been eight men standing in the road, who was driving the wagon? A ninth man? Or did one of the men step into the woods while Brown was filibustering?

Brown asked the men about the wagon and was told it carried the supply camp. He did not notice the guns and ammunition that were hidden inside, and accepted the explanation. The riders then saw to their horses' needs, unsaddling, watering and bedding them down. Two of the men carried wood from a nearby thicket, started a fire and began cooking a meal.

Bob Younger, who prepared the meal, was considered by Brown to be a very serious young man, although the farmer did not know him by name. Brown noticed Bob seemed much younger than the rest, seldom speaking unless spoken to, and whenever he did, he was almost apologetic. Once he asked Frank James, whom he referred to as Buck, to fetch a pail of water from the well so he could boil potatoes for the men.

As Frank walked to draw the water, he overheard Joe Brown trying to explain the men's presence to his wife. He was not having an easy time of it as Mrs. Brown accused him of always bringing strangers home. Frank enjoyed the little family squabble, and with a full bucket of water in his hand, continued his vigil on the combatants. His eyes met the gaze of Mrs. Brown, and as he looked away embarrassed, she ripped, "Well, if you are after water, get it, and don't stand there paralyzed."[35]

Frank James (Courtesy of the Armand DeGregoris Collection)

Frank, assuming the air of a saintly man, answered, "Mrs. Brown, the good book says in St. Matthew, Chapter 25, Verse 41, 'Then shall He say also to them, on the left hand, Depart from me, ye cursed, into everlasting fire, prepared for the devil and his angels; for I was hungered, and ye gave no meat: I was thirsty. and ye gave me no drink: I was a stranger and ye took me not in naked, and ye clothed me not.'"[36]

Then Frank asked her to turn to Chapter 7 and he recited, "Judge not, that ye be not judged. For with what judgment ye judge, ye shall be judged." He slung the strap of the bucket over his shoulder and walked away to join the others. Mrs. Brown was a religious woman, and following Frank's recitation of the scriptures, she suddenly changed her opinion of the men her husband had brought home. "That man is a preacher," she exclaimed to Joe Brown.

This was not the first time Frank assumed a dramatic role.[37] He had always entertained a fondness for Elizabethan drama, and it was Cole Younger who was deeply interested in theology and historical research. The other men were not so polished, and their rougher aspect took on the coarseness of the lowbrow type. They were ruthless individuals and had no conscience when it came to shooting somebody down. But in the company of the polished Frank and Cole, they could be depended upon to act cordially in the presence of law-abiding citizens.

The morning after Frank's theological lesson, the men mounted their horses and told the Browns they were leaving, but would return in the evening.[38] They asked permission to leave their wagon in the barn and consent was given with no questions asked. They left the farm early the next three mornings, and while the Browns wondered about their activities, they did not pursue the matter since their guests were so liberal with their money.

What were the outlaws doing? They were doing what they had been instructed to do during the Civil War. As guerrillas, they had received perfect training which prepared them for banditry. They were highly mobile, utterly ruthless and they seldom committed themselves to battle organized forces. The key word here is mobile. The horses had to respond to neck-reining, and each rider had to learn the peculiarities of his mount before it could be trusted to perform well in a raid. For any of the outlaws who may have arrived in Minnesota, this was especially important.

"The James and Younger brothers were always painstaking in their preparations," at least two news sources printed. "It is a known fact that these men, when in tight places, would take the bridle reins in their teeth, guide their horses by a touch of the knee or a touch of the rein on his neck, while using a gun in each hand as they rode at breakneck speed."[39]

While at the Brown farm, the James-Younger gang had the opportunity to train its horses in secluded areas near or on the farm to jump fences, creeks, and mudholes, and, should the need arise, make certain that the animals did not spook under fire.

According to these newspaper accounts, the training of horses at the Brown farm continued until September 1. On that morning, the men supposedly rode off like other mornings, but this time, did not return. Brown was puzzled why the wagon was left in his barn and it was never claimed. He never heard from any of the men again.

If the outlaws did train horses on or near the Brown farm, they could not have tarried long, and certainly not until September 1. Some members of the gang were seen as far north as Minneapolis and St. Paul in mid-August and others visited the towns of Red Wing, Mankato, St. Peter, Lake Crystal, Madelia, St. James, Garden City, Janesville, Cordova, Waterville, Millersburg, Cannon City, and, possibly, New Ulm.[40]

Was there really a Joe Brown, and, if so, what was his real name? If the Brown rumors are true, he must have lived somewhere in Freeborn County. Jim Younger stated in a letter the men bought horses in Albert Lea, and it was shortly after this they met Brown on the road.

The 1870 Federal Government Census, taken every ten years, lists a Joseph Brown living in Oakland Township, just east of Albert Lea.[41] The geography is right but Brown is not listed in the 1880 census. Furthermore, he is not listed in the 1875 Minnesota State Census which casts a doubt on his being the "right" Joe Brown.[42] This Brown must have moved from the county at least two years before the outlaws arrived.

The 1875 State Census for Freeborn County does list another Joseph Brown, but this one was only five years old that year. The name of the infant's father was B.J. Brown. Although there is a long-shot chance the man's middle initial stood for Joseph, it would be stretching it a bit to consider his being the Brown in question. A survey of the surrounding counties turns up nothing as well, a six-year-old Joseph in Faribault County, a J.E. Brown in Dodge County, and none at all in Waseca and Steele counties.

Gang members did presumably visit the town of Freeborn and stopped at a general store. "My father clerked there and my folks lived where I live," recalled a local woman. "It was during this time that the Northfield bank robbery took place. The Sunday before the robbery, early, a bunch of men on horseback came to the door of our house (across the street from the store) and asked my father to open the store so they could buy some things. He did not know who they were, nor was he in the habit of opening on Sunday, but when he saw that they were armed he did not refuse. They were very polite, and after their purchases rode away and he later learned who they were."[43] That night the men camped in a grove north of town.

While some members of the gang surveyed Freeborn County, others showed up in Minneapolis as early as mid-August. It is believed that the men in Minneapolis were Cole Younger and Bill Stiles who spent a week in the city sightseeing, playing poker, and more importantly looking for horses.[44]

Stiles had already staked out Minneapolis two months earlier. Police officer Patrick Kenny, who had arrested him several years earlier in the state of Iowa, recognized the outlaw immediately. Stiles recognized Kenny as well and informed the peace officer that since his release from custody, he had gone straight and was on his way to the Black Hills.[45]

When Cole and Stiles failed to procure horses in the mill city, they turned their attention to St. Paul, where they lingered for another week. Gambling, not horses, appears to have been their first priority, and they spent some of their time at the Chinn and Morgan gambling house on Robert Street.[46] Lady luck, which had never been theirs during the ill-fated Minnesota trip, eluded them again. The two were stripped of about $200 by St. Paul sharpies.[47]

It was exceedingly warm in the gambling hall, and either because of the stifling heat or hoping to throw a little fear into the competition, the outlaws removed their coats, unstrapped their cartridge belts, and displayed their pistols and knives. The message was received by the gamblers who attempted to make it clear they were playing fairly; the inference was, the visitors would have it no other way.

The frightened owner of the establishment asked the men to cover up their weaponry. He then locked the door and allowed the game to proceed well into the night. The two armed men had arrived at the gambling parlor in a hack and the hackman called for them several times during the course of the evening. He was finally dismissed and the game continued.[48]

The club's proprietor recognized the shorter of the two bandits as Bill Stiles. He remembered Stiles had been in the city seven or eight years earlier, "sporting" and living by his wits. The owner also recalled this same scheming Stiles having been engaged in trickery that necessitated adroitness of manipulation and had succeeded in palming off several counterfeit bills.

Regarding the presence of the two outlaws in St. Paul, the local newspaper later reported, "While on the visit in question, they were asked, in thieves' parlance, if they were 'working the trains,' that is, were they engaged in burglarious or similar attempts? To this they gave a tacit acknowledgment."[49]

Where the outlaws stayed that night is a matter of conjecture, but it is quite evident they remained at the gambling hall until morning. However, two strangers fitting their descriptions were discovered sleeping in a deep cut on Sibley Street at its junction with Fifth by two St. Paul citizens, L. E. Reed and Richard Marvin. The St. Paulites were astonished in finding the two strangers asleep in such a fashion, for they were not attired as tramps but were clean, good-looking, well-dressed men. They became frightened, however, in discovering the sleeping men had cartridge belts strapped around their waists, although no weapons were exposed.[50]

On August 19, Bob Younger and Clell Miller were seen stepping from a train. The following day they visited Hall and McKinney's Livery Stable on Robert Street. One of McKinney's assistants showed the pair the horses that were for sale, but the visitors were not impressed. Disgruntled, they departed, only to return in an hour or two, one of them parading a handsome black mount which he said he had purchased from a farmer on the street for $110. His companion said he had also purchased a mount, a very capable bay, which had not yet been delivered.[51]

The outlaws were deceiving McKinney for they had purchased the horses at the William A. Judd Livery Stable on Fourth Street. They had commenced negotiations with Judd the day before, and it was apparent to the livery man his customers were good judges of horseflesh and would settle for nothing short of his finest mounts. Judd sold them the black and the bay during a second meeting, and in doing so, parted with two of his finest mounts.

Prior to their negotiation sessions with Judd, the pair had called at the Charley Colter Livery as well as at several others in the city. Bob and Clell even had the audacity to seek out the United States Marshall in St. Paul and make inquiries about purchasing a very fast horse.[52] General R.A. McLaren, the marshall, and Charles Reichow, deputy United States Marshall, were both seated in their office when the two intruders entered and made their inquiry.

Both Bob and Clell were wearing dusters and it was obvious to the two lawmen the pair were traveling men. General McLaren did have a horse for sale, temporarily being quartered at Judd's Livery, and he asked his assistant Reichow to accompany the men to the stable.

The colt had never been ridden but it took to the saddle the stable hand put on its back. Bob Younger mounted the colt and dashed down Fourth Street in zigzag fashion. Reaching a hotel, the horse and rider turned for home galloping and jumping rodeo style. Bob admired the horse and told Reichow so, but still, it was not quite the horse he wanted.

Returning to McKinney's, Bob and Clell purchased two McClellan saddles for the pair of horses they had purchased from Judd. The saddles were next to new, one of which was marked with a masonic emblem. A single bridle was also purchased, and since no other bridle suited the pair, McKinney accompanied one of the men to Norton & Ware Wholesale Store on Robert Street. There, a second bridle was purchased.[53]

The bandit who accompanied McKinney to Norton's selected a light-colored bridle and a fine bit comparable to those used on cavalry horses, featuring long curved arms on either side which he and the livery man added to the bridle. A saddle blanket was also sought but none in stock suited the Missourian.

The stranger rejoined his confederate at McKinney's, the horses were equipped, and the man on the black horse treated onlookers with a riding exhibition in the middle of Wabasha Street. Horse and rider galloped back and forth at a lively canter, the rider testing both his steed and his new equipment. The other Missourian remained a spectator, and when the rider dismounted, the pair lauded their purchases.

McKinney wondered about the identities of his two unusual customers and made several inquiries as to the nature of their business. The men told him they were from Missouri and had come to tour Minnesota. Much joking followed and the pair scorned the popular belief that it was necessary to travel about on horseback for the benefit of one's health.

One of the bandits directed his glance at McKinney and boasted, "Do I look like a man who was out of health?"[54] A hearty laugh ensued from all present and the pair rode away intimating they were bound for the sister city of Minneapolis.

Horses had always been a top priority. In September 1874, during a robbery of a stagecoach near Hot Springs, Arkansas, the boys had even gone so far as to "borrow" the mounts from the coach they were holding up, leaving their own Indian ponies as trade.[55]

But horses were not the only purchases Bob and Clell made in St. Paul. One of them visited Burkhardt's Gun Shop on Third Street, scrutinized the artillery, and finally selected a large Bowie knife.[56]

On the east side of Robert Street, midway between Third and Fourth Streets, was a curious stone arch which led to a passageway some forty feet long between McLeod's Ladies' and Gents' Restaurant and Sample Room at 312 Robert, and a hotel and billiard supply store at number 316.[57] The elegant restaurant occupied two floors, featuring "oyster parlors" upstairs, and it employed seven waiters and four bartenders. A small stable was situated in the rear of the restaurant where owner Archie D. McLeod, a successful real estate man, housed his two horses and buggies.

Bob and Clell were not the only gang members to dine at McLeod's. Cole Younger and Bill Stiles were still in the city and dined at the restaurant for two days, attracting little attention. They appeared to be fine, handsome gentlemen who conversed quietly amongst themselves and always minded their own business. Both of the men had enormous appetites which they did not neglect. Neither Cole nor Bill drank or smoked, but they bought rounds of drinks for many of the people they met in the bar.

While the days were spent lolling at McLeod's, their evenings were given to gambling at Chinn's.[58] Cole was a very sharp poker player and had won $3,000 one winter he spent in Florida, but he considered Stiles the best he had ever seen. The gambling house and the restaurant were conveniently located just up the street from the Merchant's Hotel where the pair were staying. The boys became friendly with both casino manager Guy Salisbury and his bartender Charles Hickson.[59]

Still smarting from the fleecing they had suffered by the sharpies previously, Stiles and Cole returned to the gambling den. This time luck was with the boys and they were nearly $300 richer when Bob Younger walked in and insisted on playing. Cole immediately left the table, for he would never gamble in his brother's presence.

The following evening, Jack Chinn, proprietor of Chinn and Morgan's gambling house, called upon McLeod at the restaurant. Chinn asked McLeod if some men of his acquaintance could leave their horses in the stable behind the restaurant for a short while. McLeod gave his permission.[60]

About 9:30 the same evening, McLeod's porter informed him a number of horses had been hitched in the rear stable. McLeod informed his employee he had given his consent. The following morning, the porter reappeared and conveyed to McLeod that the riders had ridden out through the stone arch shortly after midnight.

Other members of the gang filtered into Minneapolis and St. Paul. These men did not join their friends at the Merchant's Hotel in St. Paul, preferring to stay at the fashionable Nicollet House on Washington Avenue between Nicollet and Hennepin Avenues at Bridge Square in Minneapolis.[61] Possibly as many as six of the robbers roomed at the Nicollet at one time or another. One of the men becoming ill during his stay and did not leave his room.[62] The hotel management was suspicious of the strangers and the night watchman took it upon himself to shadow them during their stay.

During their sojourn at the Nicollet, the strangers were seen on the balcony in their linen dusters and white hats, and they amused the curious by dropping fifty cents and one dollar pieces to the gawkers below.[63] To those with whom they spoke, they claimed they were looking for cattle to buy or a location for a railroad. They were courteous to everyone they encountered and were considered fine gentlemen.

One evening in late August, three of the men hired a hack and asked to be driven to a house of ill-repute kept by local madam Mollie Ellsworth.[64] Miss Ellsworth was dressing for the

Jesse James, 1869. (Courtesy of the Armand DeGregoris Collection)

34

night when one of the men entered her room. Stepping from the shadows, he asked her if she had once operated a similar house in St. Louis, and if her real name was Kitty Traverse. The surprised madam replied in the affirmative, and as the stranger came nearer, she recognized him as Jesse James.

Miss Traverse had known Jesse fairly well in St. Louis and she instantly recalled an incident involving his former girlfriend, Hattie Floyd. Jesse had purloined a $1,500 shawl and had given it to Hattie as a gift. Young Hattie had been eager to display her new possession and soon began wearing it on the street. She was arrested. Because she could not reveal the identity of her benefactor, she was sentenced to five years in prison.

The madam then asked Jesse if he knew what had happened to Hattie Floyd following her sentencing. Jesse laughed and replied she had died years ago.

Kitty recalled another incident in St. Louis when Jesse visited another "house." A wealthy banker was a guest at the establishment, and after drinking more than he could handle, he began flashing a stocking full of money. James quickly drew Kitty aside and whispered, "Stand aside while I drop onto that."[65]

Drop into it he did, for he was soon quarreling with the man. Jesse then struck the banker over the head with a club, seized the bag of money and began to flee. Kitty attempted to block his path, even though she realized the banker had probably stolen the money to begin with (he was later dismissed from the bank). Jesse would have killed Kitty had she not let him pass. She did.

Kitty was now surprised to see Jesse James in Minnesota and asked him what he was doing so far from home. Jesse replied he was doing nothing; he would be going into the country for a few days, but would return to take her to the centennial observances. Kitty was certain Jesse was up to something and pleaded with him not to commit any crimes in Minnesota.

"You don't want to drop into any cases around here," she advised, using one of Jesse's favorite terms.[66]

Jesse assured her there was nothing to worry about. Discovering he was carrying three or four large revolvers, she asked him what he planned to do with the firearms. He insisted he was going to use them on a man he knew uptown. Again, she cautioned him about getting into trouble. The confident outlaw, with a flair for dramatics, remarked, "I shall die like a dog or eat the hatchet."[67]

Kitty Traverse had known Jesse for thirteen years and was convinced he had always been a thief and always would be. But she felt he was too smart for any lawmen or bounty hunters and doubted if anyone would ever be able to bring him to justice.

If Jesse James should die like a dog, she hypothesized, it would only be through an act of treachery.

She noticed Jesse was wearing two boots of different sizes and his small feet could wear nearly any shoe. She was also aware he was carrying a great amount of money, and when she inquired about the roll, he told her he had everything he wanted. But he did not stay long that evening. He and his companions were very much cognizant of their vulnerability of being arrested in such a large city.

Following Jesse's leave, Kitty Traverse, alias Mollie Ellsworth, did talk to local law officials about her nocturnal visitor, perhaps only because she did not wish to be implicated should the James gang attempt to pull off a caper in the city. She reported this same group of men, or at least some of them, had been playing cards at a public place in Minneapolis prior to their appearance in St. Paul. The police, however, were not overly concerned, especially because Kitty Traverse never revealed the suspicious men were members of the notorious James gang.

Concluding their business in the Twin Cities, the robbers fanned out into the surrounding countryside. It is quite probable some of the gang members visited Wright County, specifically the town of Rockford, just west of Minneapolis.[68] Little documentation exists as to their activities there; the only newspaper covering the area was published in distant Monticello where Bill Stiles once lived.

Jesse James in Clarinda, Iowa, circa 1873. (Courtesy of Erich Baumann)

Farther west, the town of Chaska was visited by some of the robbers; in particular, the Minneapolis Hotel located uptown on the northwest corner of Fourth and Chestnut Streets.[69] Either because of the congeniality of its host, Herman Brinkhaus, or his patrons, the hotel had become a favorite hangout with its evening poker games.

In late August, F.E. DuToit, the county's young sheriff and a regular at the hotel's poker table, was deadlocked in a tight game when three strangers entered the hotel. After checking in and cleaning up, the three newcomers made their way into the saloon where

DuToit was playing cards. Since the strangers seemed interested in the poker game and appeared to be of an amiable sort, they were asked to sit in. After a pleasant evening playing cards, the party broke up without mayhem, and the strangers returned to their sleeping rooms.[70]

The following morning, the men saddled their horses and rode out of Chaska. Even after the raid on the Northfield bank, the presence of James gang members in Chaska, playing cards with the enterprising young sheriff, was not recorded in the local newspaper, probably because this same F.E. DuToit owned the *Weekly Valley Herald*, the town's only newspaper.

Members of the gang, attired in linen dusters and riding fine-looking mounts also appeared in nearby Shakopee on the Minnesota River. Three of the men paid a visit to John A. Dean's blacksmith shop. Dean, a pioneer farrier, mistook the men for dudes from over Excelsior way, a not-too-distant community on Lake Minnetonka. Englishmen and Easterners were both quite common in the Lake Minnetonka area during the summer months, and since the three strangers had queer notions, at least to 1870's Shakopean standards, their requests were usually honored.[71]

Dean considered the three men to be intelligent, but supposedly, the men requested their horses be shod backwards. Reportedly, the James boys resorted to this unusual shodding because it would often throw off a pursuing posse. The lawmen would gallop furiously down a trail pursuing a quarry, and instead of catching up with outlaws, the posse would end up at the crime scene.[72]

While Dean resorted to the unusual request, the strangers remained silent, listening to the din of clanging anvils and nervous horses. Away from the shower of sparks and roaring forges, an unobtrusive Frank James leaned in a dim corner watching and waiting.

Reportedly a James trademark, the brothers' horses were reputedly shod in this fashion in Kansas City too, and during preparations for the assault on a Minnesota bank, in both Shakopee and Red Wing. Blacksmith Jim Dewar claimed to have had shod horse hooves backwards for the Jameses, Youngers, and Daltons on numerous occasions, calling the strange practice "their trademark." In his shop, eighteen men allegedly shoed 200 horses a day, and when Jesse James entered, the men all knew what to do. Jesse would say a word to owner Aleck McIntyre, and the owner would ask his men if they knew who the horses belonged to. The men would shake their heads and the shoes would be put on backwards.

According to Dewar's account, these backward shoeings led the sheriff's posse to where the men had been, not to where they were. He claimed this method of foolery was the James gang's vaccination for sheriffs and the boys couldn't be caught.

It is quite improbable, however, the horses were ever shod in such a fashion. Had the shoes been affixed backwards, the entire hoof could not be covered and an imprint would reveal a vacant spot on the ground. The only effective procedure for covering the entire hoof would be through making a special shoe and adding a quarter inch, thus eliminating the vacant spot and enabling an imprint to be formed on the ground.[73]

Even with an added quarter-inch of shoe, the shodding in reverse would be a detriment since the outlaws making good their escape would require swift, sure-footed mounts. Although some blacksmiths might argue the point, at least one smitty believes a swift getaway next to impossible.

According to farrier Dean, he considered the unorthodox shoeing just another quirk of these Eastern dudes. The leader of the trio, whom Dean later identified as Jesse James, tipped Dean's helper fifty cents, a pretty fair sum at the time. Then the mysterious trio rode off.[74]

Other members of the gang allegedly visited the blacksmith shop of Frank Juergens, also in Shakopee. Several local citizens including Mayor John McDonald and Sheriff Dennis Flaherty stopped by to see the fine looking horses. Juergens, too, was supposedly ordered to shod horses backwards, although these strangers were not as friendly with their smitty as was the other trio.[75]

The riders did not waste any time in Shakopee once their mounts were shod. It was still daylight when they were seen riding away in the direction of Minneapolis.[76]

At two o'clock the following morning, Shakopee pioneer druggist, A.M. Strunk, was called to furnish spirits of niter for a sick horse belonging to a stranger, who was in reality one of the bandits. Regardless of what has been written, it was probably H.H. Strunk, brother of A.M. Strunk, who had been called out to administer the potion.[77] There has been some doubt cast as to the validity of the Strunk story since the robbers had left Shakopee in the daylight hours. However, the robbers did camp that night near the Bloomington Ferry Bridge so the nervous druggist was probably taken to the Minnesota River site.

As few as four robbers and as many as eight showed up in Red Wing on or about August 26.[78] Four strangers disembarked from the noon train and proceeded directly to the National Hotel where they registered as J.C. Hortor, Nashville; H.L. West, Nashville; Charles Wetherby, Indiana; and Ed Everhard, Indiana. The four men were probably Jesse and Frank James, Jim Younger and Clell Miller.[79]

The foursome stayed at the National over a period of four days.[80] During their stay at the hotel, they offered to bet $1,000 Minnesota would go for Tilden in the presidential election later that year. There were no takers.

It is presumed one of the robbers came to Red Wing a couple days prior to that of his confederates, arriving as early as the twenty-fourth.[81] This man went first to the local express office and sent a package, a box of cigars, to a pal who was an inmate in the Missouri State Penitentiary at Jefferson City. The package was sent in care of the prison warden for a prisoner in cell #8. The stranger informed the express agent, a Mr. Blodgett, that he had a good friend in the penitentiary and he was not ashamed of it.

The prisoner in cell #8 was a second termer named Joyce, serving four years for grand larceny. Sheriff Chandler of Red Wing later learned from a letter he received from the warden in Jefferson City that the man who sent the cigars went by the name of Kelly and was himself an ex-convict discharged the previous May. The name Kelly, of course, was an alias.

Another report states the outlaws rode into Red Wing on horseback, between ten and a dozen men, all wearing linen dusters and wide, black felt hats.[82] The numbers ten or twelve were probably exaggerated although Los Angeles Bill Stiles claimed there were more than eight men involved.

The riders explored the town, mainly the buildings, and most of the townspeople thought they were part of a show troupe since many of the showmen traveled by horse. After procuring dinner at the National Hotel, four of the men purchased two sorrel horses from A. Seebeck, a well-known horse dealer in the Red Wing area.[83] Leaving Seebeck, the men went over to the livery stable of J.A. Anderberg and bought one nine-year-old bay mare with an off-white hind foot, very thick neck and white spot on its forehead. Another horse, a five-year-old bay gelding with both hind legs white from the ankles down and a small white spot on its forehead, was purchased at the same livery.

With their four new horses, the men proceeded to E.P. Watson's Harness Shop and purchased three new saddles. The fourth man must have retained the saddle from his previous mount because there is no record of any fourth saddle purchase.

During all these business transactions, the strangers were reluctant to discuss their business, whether real or bogus, and the stories each told conflicted those of the others. At one of the liveries, they professed to being cattle drovers en route to St. Paul, and to others they claimed to be an exploring party from Kentucky, heading for the Black Hills of South Dakota.

The robbers also called at Whitney's Gunshop and purchased some number 44 pistol cartridges. The gunsmith was puz-

District 113 Hay Creek Schoolhouse in Featherstone Township. (Courtesy of the Goodhue County Historical Society)

39

zled why the men asked for 44s since the cartridges were so unusually large.[84]

Still searching for the right bank to rob, the men were considering one of three different banks in Red Wing: The First National on Plumb (not Plum) and Main; the Goodhue Savings Bank, which was located upstairs of the First National; or the Pierce, Simmons and Company, situated at 93 Main Street.[85] They apparently abandoned their plan to rob a Red Wing bank when they learned only two roads led out of the city. Escape would be difficult.

Red Wing was out but they still planned to rob a Minnesota bank. For the past ten years, the gang had robbed banks and trains in and out of Missouri. These banks and trains had been on the Union side during the Civil War and the banks charged high interest rates on loans to people trying to rebuild their farms and businesses after the war. Furthermore people were forced to pay high taxes to support railroads which in turn charged high freight rates to farmers trying to ship crops and livestock to market.[86]

Yankee money. Fat Minnesota banks. Many Missourians had fought on the side of the Confederacy during the war and these same people never shed a tear when the James gang robbed a train or a bank. But that was in "The Robber State." Now in Minnesota they were faced with Union greenbacks and strike they would.

Before departing from Red Wing, the men visited a blacksmith shop located near the hotel.[87] At the old stone brick building they had the shoes of their horses caulked and weighted in the same manner which cavalry men practiced. Reports the men had the shoes of their horses shod backwards that day were probably false.

On Monday, one of the strangers left Red Wing on the Pine Island Stage.[88] Later that day, the other three men rode off in a northerly direction towards Faribault. But they did not go far that evening, stopping to rest in nearby Featherstone Township, just outside the town of Hay Creek.[89]

Two of the robbers may have stopped for the night at the farm of Robert Beveridge outside Featherstone. A Mrs. Herschler, whose husband was renting the farm from Beveridge at the time, was terrified in receiving visitors after dark although she later said the men acted like perfect gentlemen. The following day the men had dinner at a house near Minneola, exercised their horses there, and traded an English saddle for a larger one.

Other members of the gang stopped at the District 113 Hay Creek Schoolhouse.[90] Farmers in the Featherstone area who had witnessed the men riding into the area grew suspicious of the

strangers. No one in the valley rode a horse quite like that and any strangers, regardless of their actions, were looked upon with suspicion in the tiny communities outside Red Wing.

Left to right: Cole, Jim, and Bob Younger. (Photo by L. Peavey of Faribault) (Coutesy of the Minnesota Historical Society Collection)

The strangers went into the schoolhouse and all was quiet for a couple hours. Then two of the men walked across the creek to the Thomforde farm and requested ham and butter which they were given by the frightened family. They did not pay for the food nor were they asked to. They were also given oats for their horses.

Returning to the schoolhouse, the men came out no more that evening. The light in the school could be seen across the valley, and the neighboring farmers, afraid to venture forth from their homes, stayed up all night and watched the eerie glow of the schoolhouse. No one had any idea who the strange men were, but no one was eager to ask any questions.

The following story was related to Elfriede Struss Meyer by Mrs. Louis Thomforde during a visit: "Grandfather Henry Germann and grandmother together with Aunt Bertha, who was then only six years old, were standing in front of their farm home watching some unusual activities at the schoolhouse across the creek about a quarter of a mile away. Two men came down the hill road to the school. A moment later two other men came from the direction of the Alms farm, and a short time later, two men came from the direction of the John Struss farm. All were on horseback and they tied up their horses in the woods at the back of the schoolhouse. The farm and schoolhouse are about three miles west of the little village of Hay Creek.

"As my grandparents and little Bertha watched, one of the men had ridden over to the farm house, unnoticed until he was beside them. He demanded a ham and two pounds of butter which grandmother gave him without hesitation, because it was evident by this time that the men were up to no good."[91]

The Featherstone School was a perfect hideout—out of the way, small, isolated, and far enough removed from Red Wing where their movements could be unrestricted. Only a few frightened farmers knew of their presence, and, of course, Bill Stiles had boasted these people wouldn't know an outlaw band if they were surrounded by them.

Why the robbers did not buy more food in Red Wing before their departure is a mystery. Yet, fresh farm meat and produce was a delicacy and the men were not bashful when it came to asking for supplies. According to Mrs. Meyer:

"Some members of the family stayed up all night but they didn't think it was wise to ride into Red Wing because their movements could have been easily detected from the schoolhouse. A little after three in the morning they heard the men ride off.

"After daylight several members of the family went to the schoolhouse where they found the top of the stove covered with grease. The men had written their names on the blackboard including those of Jesse James and his brother Frank. Grandfather learned from the Alms family that the men had obtained bread from them."[92]

The outlaws quite certainly spent part of the night in the schoolhouse. This account has been documented by several families in the area, such as the Germanns, Strusses, Thomfordes, and Almses. The signatures of the outlaws scrawled on the blackboard are hardly believable, however, since the robbers would not announce their presence so carelessly.

About the twenty-eighth, two of the outlaws, pretending to be land speculators, stopped at the home of John Mulligan at Brush Prairie near Northfield. The strangers offered to buy Mulligan's land and horses, and when a deal was approved, the men said their money was in a bank in Red Wing. They would go get the money and return for the deed. The strangers pumped Mulligan with questions about the kind of people who lived in the area. Of course, they had no intention of returning for Mulligan's property.[93]

Meanwhile, the remaining gang members in St. Paul left the city separately. Cole Younger and Charlie Pitts arrived in St. Peter; Bill Stiles and Bob Younger to follow shortly thereafter. The latter pair missed their train, however, and were delayed, throwing a wrench into the plan to meet in either St. Peter or Mankato. Cole and Charlie had arrived in St. Peter on the twenty-sixth and the concerned outlaws watched the newspapers nervously for news of any arrests.[94]

Cole and Charlie registered at a local hotel under the names J.C. King (Cole) and J. Ward (Charlie), both of Virginia. There was some jibing on the part of some of the townsfolk who thought Cole bore a resemblance to Congressman William S.

King of Minneapolis. When asked as to the nature of their business, the outlaws professed to be cattle dealers.

Following a dispute with the landlord who refused to serve them meals in their rooms, the outlaws moved to the American House, a nearby hostelry. Staying in their rooms as much as possible, they did venture out to some of the local liveries to procure horses. One mount was purchased from a Mr. Hodge, another from a man named French. Stylish blankets, McClellan saddles, new bridles, and rubber coats were picked up from another dealer, and the fancy gear attracted much attention from the locals.

While training the new horses in St. Peter, Cole made the acquaintance of a little girl who would later become one of the most earnest advocates for his parole. The little girl informed the outlaw that she, too, could ride a horse. Cole lifted the child onto the saddle next to him and rode up and down the street. When asked her name, the girl replied, "Horace Greeley Perry."

Cole was quick to answer: "No wonder you're such a little tot, with such a great name."

"I won't always be little," Miss Perry countered. "I'm going to be a great big girl and be a newspaperman like my pa."

The soft-hearted Cole was quite taken with the little girl. "Will you still be my sweetheart then and be my friend?" he asked. The youngster answered in the affirmative, Cole never dreaming what lay ahead. (Many years later a party visited Stillwater Prison where Cole was incarcerated, and amongst them, Miss Horace Greeley Perry, then about 16.) Cole reminded her of her promise to always be his friend. The girl, at about the age of 18, became the editor of the St. Peter Journal before moving to Idaho.[95]

With Stiles and Bob still delayed, Cole and Charlie left St. Peter temporarily, planning to return later and rendezvous with their tardy confederates. Leaving on Monday, they spent the night in Cleveland, before continuing on to Madelia in southwestern Minnesota and as far as the most eastern part of Cottonwood County. Their plan was to familiarize themselves as much as they could with the surrounding countryside.

The pair arrived in Madelia on the thirtieth and registered at the Flanders Hotel, Madelia's finest at the time.[96] Horsemen did not make any impression on the local citizens, who were used to new faces riding in and out of town, but they considered these two newcomers and their mounts more than ordinary. As before, Cole and Charlie professed to be cattle buyers, and the former struck up a friendship with Col. Thomas L. Vought, the hotel's proprietor, making inquiries about the lay of the land for his imaginary cattle drives.

One of the strangers was described as being about six feet tall; the other rather short and very heavily built. The men stayed all night at the hotel and were shaved by the barber. While each of the strangers was being shaved, the other sat and watched the barber. The men then rode off in the direction of St. Peter.

On the twenty-ninth, two of the strangers rode into Northfield, leaving their horses tied in front of a brick building near the railroad tracks. While the building owner was engaged in selling a plow to a local farmer, one of the strangers interrupted the conversation and asked about the best roads in the area to take. The two men directed questions to other townsfolk pretending to be conducting interviews about land purchases.[97]

Two other gang members met the strangers in the Northfield area and the four men rode back to St. Peter where they discovered Bob Younger and Bill Stiles had finally arrived by train. The two had arrived September 2, registering at the hotel as B.T. Cooper and G.H. King, both of Illinois.

Meanwhile on the second, Jesse, Frank, Jim Younger, and Clell Miller rode into Mankato with every intention of robbing at least one of the city's three banks.[98] According to at least two accounts, five men, nor four, descended on Mankato, which gives Los Angeles Bill Stiles' story some credibility, since four men remained in St. Peter. The men made purchases at some of the stores, attracting attention to their fine horses and horsemanship, and entered the First National Bank to get change for a fifty-dollar bill.

Two of the outlaws registered at The Clifton House and two at the Gates House, while the fifth stayed at the home of George Capps, in Kasota, five miles south of Mankato. On Sunday night, two of the outlaws were seen at a notorious resort kept by Jack O'Neil across the river frequented by known criminals. It is believed the men consulted with other highwaymen about the raid and escape route. On a Mankato street, Jesse was recognized by Charles Robinson, someone who knew him, and the men were shadowed by police until midnight and bankers put on guard.

The following day, the robbers rode to the First National Bank, deciding to strike about noon when the work force would be reduced over lunch and the streets not too busy. Arriving at the bank, they noticed several citizens on the sidewalk in front of the building and one was apparently drawing another's attention to the approaching horsemen.

Fearing their plan may have been discovered, the riders left the scene, but decided, nonetheless, to strike an hour or so later. When they returned, they found the same group of persons in front of the bank, and the strangers quickly left town, convinced their actions had been found out. However, they were not suspected, and the man who pointed at them, was merely admiring their horses. The men on the street were there to attend the weekly meeting of the Board of Trade and were observing some repairs on an adjacent building.

According to one account, seventeen-year-old Adolph Forsberg of St. Peter witnessed some riders cross the Minnesota River and disappear into a hill shortly after the aborted Mankato robbery. The boy was not afraid and followed the men into a cave and groped his way through the darkness. He said a group of men were sitting around a fire with their coats off, each one wearing five guns. When the boy asked them why they were wearing guns, he was told, "Don't ask any questions, kid, but you can eat with us if you want." He did. The boy later identified the men as those who had robbed the bank in Northfield.[99]

Cole's party arrived in LeSueur Center, now LeSueur, county seat of LeSueur County, on Monday, the fourth.[100] Finding no place to spend the night, they found shelter in the courthouse. According to Cole Younger, court was in session, and the bandits had to sleep on the floor with lawyers, jurymen and witnesses. Their sleep was constantly disturbed by the uproarious conduct of the judge but Cole later said they had a high old time that night.

Commissioners' reports, however, indicate Cleveland was the county seat in 1876 for LeSueur County. The bandits did stop at the Adams Hotel in Cleveland with intent to rob the county treasurer's office. A church served as the court house, and while the gang waited to enter the treasurer's office, a poker party inside lasted until 2:00 A.M. The plan had to be abandoned.

Two of the robbers were reportedly in New Ulm at this same time.[101] Registering at the Merchants Hotel, the men walked into the billiard room. Each wore a long linen duster. They stayed a short time and left.

The pair appeared again a few days prior to the robbery, leaving their "spirited chestnut-colored" horses at the McCarthy Livery Barn where they insisted on feeding them themselves. While registering at the Merchants as Charles and King, the men handed proprietor Charles Brust two heavy packages for safekeeping during the dinner hour. After eating and paying their bill, the men asked Brust to bring the packages out to them. Brust toted the heavy packages and jokingly asked if they contained gold. One of the men answered, "yes."

While some of the robbers were in Cleveland, Bob Younger and his group arrived in Janesville. Passing a store, the boys were handed cigars by a friendly clerk before registering at the Johnson House as George Pryor, Dave Smith, John Jones, and James Johnson. In registering, the clerk noticed the four capital

"Js" were in a bold dashing hand. One of the visitors rode a buckskin horse, one a black, another a bay, and one had a sorrel. The men claimed to be railroad engineers and the owner of the hotel found them to be men of good conduct. The men stayed in their room most of the time and no word or sound was heard from them. They remained at the Johnson House until 3 o'clock the following afternoon. After they left, it was discovered one of the men had forgotten a double handful of white pearl buttons on a table.[102]

Tuesday morning two of the bandits called at Jennison and Miner's Store, wanting to purchase a pair of pants of the highest quality for the taller one. The tall stranger grew impatient with Jennison, who was having trouble finding the right pair of pants. Turning on his heel and walking toward the door, the customer bellowed, "You know what I want better than myself."[103] The man went to an adjoining store and made his purchase. Jennison later remembered him as a "pretty fiery customer."

That evening, they were in Waterville and registered for the night at a hotel. Clell Miller engaged in a game of pool with one of the local citizens.[104] Everything was peaceful, the townsfolk finding the strangers quiet and polite, although reticent.

Taking leave of the hotel, a man stopped Jesse, mistaking him for a dishonest acquaintance. The accuser told Jesse to get on his horse and go someplace. Jesse wheeled and exploded, "Go to hell, you sonofabitch."[105]

The accuser informed Jesse he'd wait and ride off with him. Jesse put his hand on his gun and said, "I have a mind to blow your brains out." Some of the outlaw's confederates calmed him down and the outlaws rode peacefully out of Waterville, Jesse still angry.

Meanwhile, four of the men rode into Cordova and spent the night at the Dampier House, registering under the names Cooper, King, Lyon, and Ward, all of Illinois.[106] The men had to share a room with a man named W.W. Barlow of Delevan, Wisconsin, who later recognized Stiles. Barlow was told by the men they were cattle dealers, and when they rode off Wednesday morning with a tip of hats, he had no reason to suspect anything.

The following night, these same four men spent the night at Millersburg in Rice County, nine miles from Faribault. That same day, the others, including Bob Younger, were seen crossing the Cannon River near the Bean Brothers Mill in Faribault. They rode their fine horses down Seventh Street to Main, and turned up Main towards the Fourteenth Street bridge. Here they crossed the Straight River and proceeded to Cannon City, four and a half miles from Faribault and twelve miles southwest of Northfield where they stayed overnight.[107]

The men now knew their destination. Word had reached them that General Benjamin F. Butler, whom they called "Silver Spoons Butler" from his New Orleans experiences during the Civil War, had $75,000 invested in the First National Bank of Northfield.[108] Butler's son-in-law, J.T. Ames, whom the gang dubbed "the carpet-bag governor of Mississippi" also had a bundle invested in the bank. The gang bore a grudge against Butler for his treatment of Southerners during the war.

When Cole Younger and Bill Chadwell visited Northfield just prior to their assault, they found the bank doing big business and carrying a large amount of cash. After asking about town as to whether the town had any gun shops and being told there were none, the pair stopped at the town's two hardware stores. In examining the meager stock of weapons, they came to the conclusion the citizens were incapable of stopping a would-be robbery. The day they were foiled at Mankato, they had decided on Northfield.[109]

On Thursday morning, September 7, the gang was reunited on the west side of the Cannon River, a little outside Northfield. About 11 a.m., three of the boys rode into Northfield to look over the bank. A few minutes later, two more horsemen rode across the bridge over the Cannon River and followed them into the business district. The local citizens eyed them suspiciously. A local citizen, G.E. Bates, told a reporter for the Minneapolis-St. Paul *Pioneer Press* the next day that "nobler looking fellows he never saw but there was a restless, bold swagger about them that seemed to indicate that they would be rough and dangerous fellows to handle."[110]

Hitching their horses behind the train depot, the men walked through the business district. John Archer, a Northfield citizen, examined their horses noting "they were all first-class horses and would attract attention anywhere." At noon, the five men enjoyed ham and eggs at J.G. Jeft's restaurant. Each man requested four eggs. The strangers jokingly argued politics, with one offering to bet the restaurant owner $1,000 the state would vote Democratic in the fall election. Jeft declined the wager.

Following a hearty lunch, the five strangers left Northfield and retired to a site west of the Cannon to finalize tactics. They were ready for the raid. Cole urged on the boys "that whatever happened we should not shoot anyone."[112]

Notes

1 Robertus Love, *The Rise and Fall of Jesse James*, Blue Ribbon Books, New York, 1935, p. 176-188.

2 *Sioux Falls* (South Dakota) *Argus Leader*, March 22-June 4, 1924, Second in a series of articles by J.A. Derome under heading "Northfield Bank Robbery Most Daring Work of James-Younger Gang in Southern Minnesota."

3 Margarette B. Hutchins letter to author dated March 6, 1983.

4 Carl Breihan, *The Day Jesse James Was Killed*, Bonanza Books, New York, No date given, p. 29-31.

5 Marley Brant Letter to author dated March 15, 1983.

6 Robertus Love, *The Rise and Fall of Jesse James*, p. 190-191.

7 *New Ulm Journal*, undated.

8 Ibid.

9 Tom Ryther letter to author dated October 27, 1982; William A. Settle, Jr., *Jesse James Was His Name*, University of Nebraska Press, Lincoln, 1977, p. 95; George Turner, *Secrets of Jesse James*, Baxter Lane Company, Amarillo, Texas, 1975.

10 Marley Brant letter to author dated November 22, 1982.

11 *Sioux Falls Argus Leader*, March 22-June 4, 1924.

12 Todd M. George letter to Owen Dickie dated February 22, 1968, Nicollet County Historical Society, St. Peter.

13 Marley Brant letter to author dated November 22, 1982.

14 Ibid.

15 Tom Ryther letter to author dated October 27, 1982.

16 Jim Younger letter to Cora McNeil dated August 16, 1898 in collection of Wilbur Zink, Appleton City, Missouri.

17 Cole Younger letter to Cora McNeil dated June 1897 in collection of Wilbur Zink.

18 Wilbur Zink letter to author dated November 11, 1982.

19 *Norborne* (Missouri) *Democrat & Leader*, Friday, January 3, 1936, Harry Hoffman, "The Younger Boys Last Stand."

20 Milton F. Perry, James Farm Superintendent letters to author dated August 25, 1982 and November 9, 1982.

21 A photograph of Perry Samuel at the James farm depicts a light-skinned person, as was his daughter, who resided in Liberty, Missouri.

22 *Norborne Democratic Leader*, Friday, January 3, 1936.

23 Dallas Cantrell, *Northfield, Minnesota, Younger's Fatal Blunder*, The Naylor Company, San Antonio: 1973, P. 10-11. James D. Horan, Desperate men. *The Complete Factual Eye Witness Story from the Sealed Vaults of the Pinkerton Detective Agency*, Avon Publishing Company, Inc., New York, 1951, p. 119-120.

24 Carl W. Breihan, *Saga of Jesse James*, The Caxton Printers, Ltd., Caldwell, Idaho, 1991, p.81.

25 Miller Family History in possession of Millie Miller; Millie Miller letter to author dated January 28, 1982.

26 *Madelia* (Minnesota) *Times-Messenger*, March 27, 1936, "The Inside Story of the Northfield Bank Robbery."

27 Jim Younger letter to Cora McNeil dated June 1897. Wilbur Zink

collection.

28 Faribault County Historical Society Historic Sites Project Nomination Form, Blue Earth, Minnesota. The tree was later cut down and furniture was made from the wood. A small stand, made by T. W. Kaiser, was given to Alice Kaiser in commemmoration of the "Jesse James Tree."

29 James D. Horan, *Desperate Men: The Complete Factual Eye Witness Story from the Sealed Vaults of the Pinkerton Detective Agency*, Avon Publishing Company, Inc., New York, 1951, p. 119-120.

30 Robertus Love, *The Rise and Fall of Jesse James*, p. 193; Phillip W. Steele and George Warfel, *The Many Faces of Jesse James*, Pelican Publishing Co., Inc., Gretna, Louisiana, 1995, p. 51.

31 George Huntington, *Robber and Hero, The Story on the Raid of the First National Bank of Northfield, Minnesota*, Ross and Haines, Inc., Minneapolis, Minnesota, 1962, p. 2-3. On page 3, Huntington mentions the possible involvement of the ninth man, Stiles, but gives it little credibility.

32 *Norborne* (Missouri) *Democrat & Leader*, Friday, January 3, 1936.

33 *Kansas City Star*, Sunday, February 16, 1936, "The Inside Story of the Northfield Bank Robbery."

34 *Norborne Democrat & Leader*, Friday, January 3, 1936.

35 Ibid.

36 Ibid.

37 Robertus Love, *The Rise and Fall of Jesse James*, p. 192-193.

38 *Norborne Democart & Leader*, Friday, January 3, 1936.

39 *Kansas City Star*, Sunday, February 16, 1936; *Madelia Times Messenger*, Friday, March 27, 1936.

40 Cole Younger, *The Story of Cole Younger by Himself*, The Henneberry Company, Chicago, 1903, p. 77;   Robertus Love, *The Rise and Fall of Jesse James*, p. 193-194.

41 Federal Government Census for 1870 and 1880, Minnesota Historical Society, St. Paul.

42 *Minnesota State Census for 1875*, Minnesota Historical Society, St. Paul.

43 Letter written by Laura Gilmore, born about 1885, in collection of Freeborn County Historical Society, Wells, Minnesota; Tracy Christensen, Freeborn County Historical Society, Wells, Minnesota, letter to author dated June 2, 1982; Mrs. B.A. Gilmore, Freeborn, Minnesota, letter to author dated November 8, 1982.

44 Cole Younger, *The Story of Cole Younger*, p. 77.

45 *Minneapolis Tribune*, Friday, September 8, 1876; reprinted in Hennepin County History, Winter 1966, p. 23.

46 *St. Paul Pioneer Press*, Saturday, September 9, 1876; Carl Weicht Collection, Northfield.

47 *The St. Paul Dispatch*, Sunday, September 10, 1876, gives the figure as $300.

48 *The St. Paul Dispatch*, Sunday, September 10, 1876.

49 Ibid.

50 *St. Paul Pioneer Press*, Saturday, September 9, 1876.

51 Ibid.

52 Undated *St. Paul Pioneer Press* article in Carl Weicht Collection, Northfield.

53 *St. Paul Pioneer Press,* Saturday, September 9, 1876.

54 Ibid.

55 Larry Rhodes, "The Return of the James Gang," *The Ouachita Mountaineer,* Spring 1996, Murfreesboro, Arkansas, p. 31.

56 *St. Paul Dispatch,* Sunday, September 10, 1876.

57 Undated 1927 *St. Paul Dispatch* article in Carl Weicht Collection, Northfield.

58 Cole Younger, *The Story of Cole Younger,* p. 77-78.

59 Cole stated Guy Salisbury, later to become a minister, was the proprieter of the casino but it appears he was probably the manager. The gambling house was owned by Jack Chinn.

60 Undated 1927 *St. Paul Dispatch* article in Carl Weicht Collection, Northfield.

61 *St. Paul Pioneer Press,* Wednesday, September 20, 1876.

62 Dallas Cantrell, *Northfield, Minnesota, Younger's Fatal Blunder,* p. 16.

63 *Sioux Falls* (South Dakota) *Argus-Leader,* series of articles by J.A. Derome under "Webster Man tells of Capture of Younger Bandit Gang at Madelia," March 22 to June 4, 1924.

64 *St. Paul Pioneer Press,* Wednesday, September 20, 1876.

65 Ibid.

66 Ibid.

67 Ibid.

68 Mouraine Hubler letter to author dated April 11, 1983; Mrs. Malcolm Jamieson, curator Wright County Historical Society, interview with author March 9, 1983.

69 Shirley Brewers, curator Chaska Historical Society, letter to author dated August 26, 1982; Booklet, no author given, *Chaska, A Minnesota River City,* Volume I - The 1800's, p. 163.

70 Tracy DuToit Swanson letter to author dated May 2, 1983.

71 Ter, North Ridge Farms, Wayzata, Minnesota, interview with author April 16, 1983.

72 Ibid.

73 Ibid.

74 *The Southern Minnesotan,* July 1931; Tracy DuToit Swanson, letter to author dated May 2, 1983.

75 Ray Juergens letter to author dated April 21, 1983.

76 *The Southern Minnesotan,* July 1931.

77 Julius A. Collier II letter to author dated April 20, 1983.

78 *St. Paul and Minneapolis Pioneer Press and Tribune,* Saturday, September 9, 1976.

79 Dallas Cantrell, *Northfield, Minnesota: The Youngers Fatal Blunder,* p. 17.

80 *St. Paul Dispatch,* Saturday, September 16, 1876.

81 *Red Wing Argus,* Thursday, September 14, 1876; *St. Paul Dispatch,* Saturday, September 16, 1876.

82 *Red Wing Daily Republican,* February 11, 1976, "Reminiscences Atop the St. James Balcony," by Harry B. Robertson.

83 *St. Paul and Minneapolis Pioneer Press and Tribune,* Saturday, September

9, 1876.

84 *St. Paul Dispatch*, Saturday, September 16, 1876.

85 *Red Wing Daily Republican*, February 11, 1976.

86 Robert L. Dyer, *Jesse James and the Civil War in Missouri*, University of Missouri Press, Columbia, 1994, p. 3.

87 *Red Wing Daily Republican*, February 11, 1976.

88 *Red Wing Argus*, Thursday, September 14, 1876.

89 *St. Paul Dispatch*, Saturday, September 16, 1876.

90 *Red Wing Republican Eagle*, May 16, 1968; October 1, 1969; May 15, 1971.

91 Elfriede Struss Meyer, "The James Brothers at Featherstone Township Schoolhouse 1876," unpublished manuscript at Goodhue County Historical Society, Red Wing.

92 Ibid.

93 Dallas Cantrell, *Northfield, Minnesota: The Youngers Fatal Blunder*, p. 18

94 Cole Younger, *The Story of Cole Younger by Himself*, p. 78-79; *St. Paul and Minneapolis Pioneer Press & Tribune*, Saturday, September 9, 1876; Dallas Cantrell, *Northfield, Minnesota: The Youngers Fatal Blunder*, p. 18-19.

95 Cole Younger, *The Story of Cole Younger by Himself*, p. 78-79.

96 *Sioux Falls Argus Leader*, series of articles by J. A. Derome under "Webster Man Tells of Capture of Younger Bandit Gang at Madelia," March 22-June 4, 1924.

97 Dallas Cantrell, Northfield, Minnesota: *The Youngers Fatal Blunder*, p. 20.

98 George Huntington, *Robber and Hero, The Story on the Raid of the First National Bank of Northfield*, Minnesota, p. 5-7; *The Southern Minnesotan*, July 1931, p. 26; Carl W. Breihan, *Saga of Jesse James*, p.82.

99 *Mankato Free Press*, Monday, July 7, 1969 under "Where Jesse James Legend Lived, Highway Erased St. Peter Caves" by Mike Larson.

100 *The Southern Minnesotan*, July 1931, p. 25.

101 Brown County Historical Society: "Origins" by Charles Brust, July 30, 1926, donated by Hugh Walters, April 1952; Charles Brust Recalls James Gang's Visit Here; *New Ulm Journal*, June 30, 1896 under "Northfield Bank Robbers Stopped at Charles Brust Sr., Hotel Here;" Notes of Lydia Schilling, May 31, 1956 under Younger Brothers: Chas. Pomeroy; Brown County Heritage, December 1964, Vol. 2, No. 7, "The James-Younger Gang Reconnoiter the Brown County Region" by Charles Brust.

102 Donna Fostveit letter to author dated August 27, 1982; *Faribault Republican*, Wednesday, September 20, 1876, "The Outlaws, Incidents Relating to their Movements on the way to Northfield," p. 3; Dallas Cantrell, Northfield, Minnesota: *The Youngers Fatal Blunder*, p. 21.

103 *St. Paul Pioneer Press*, Friday, September 22, 1876; *Faribault Republican*, Wednesday, September 20, 1876.

104 *St. Paul Pioneer Press*, Wednesday, September 20, 1876; *Faribault Republican*, Wednesday, September 20, 1876.

105 *Faribault Republican*, Wednesday, September 20, 1876; Dallas Cantrell, Northfield, Minnesota: *The Youngers Fatal Blunder*, p. 21-22.

106 Ibid p. 22; *Faribault Democrat,* Friday, September 15, 1876.

107 *Faribault Democrat*, Friday, September 15, 1876.

108 Cole Younger, *The Story of Cole Younger by Himself*, p. 77.

109 George Huntington, Robber and Hero, *The Story of the Raid on the First National Bank of Northfield,* pp. 9-10; Don Coulston, "The Youngers 'Rebels with a Cause,'" *The* (Stillwater) *Prison Mirror*, p. 8; Marilynn Cierzan letter to author dated July 13, 1982.

110 Donald L. Gilmore, "Showdown in Northfield," *Wild West Magazine*, August 1996, Leesburg, Virginia, pp. 36-37.

111 Ibid.

112 Cole Younger, *The Story of Cole Younger by Himself*, p. 80.

Chapter 3

"They're Robbing the Bank!"

THE BATTLE OF NORTHFIELD'S BEGUN

Somebody special just rode into Northfield,
     Somebody famous and bold,
Long linen dusters concealing their pistols,
     They've come to steal all our gold.

James boys and Youngers, they're up from Missouri,
     Riding so slow into town,
Mighty warm welcome in South Minnesota,
     We're going to cut that gang down.

Peace-loving farmers, we're New England yankees,
     Swedes and Norwegians here too.
We've got a college and we've got some churches,
     We've got a bank, yes we do.

Up to the windows and ready your rifles,
     The Battle of Northfield's begun!
Blasting those bandits right out of their saddles,
     Dropping them dead in the sun,
The Battle of Northfield's begun,
     The Battle of Northfield's begun!

Mister Gustavson, he couldn't speak English,
     He didn't do what they said.
After they killed him they murdered another:
     Bank-teller shot in the head.

Out in the street, now we're using our shotguns,
     This time we've evened the score.
'Couple of outlaws stretched out on the sidewalk:
     They won't rob banks anymore.
We'll put Cole Younger in Stillwater Prison,
     Twenty-five years in a cell.
Time to think over September the seventh,
     Northfield turned into Hell.

Up to the windows and ready your rifles,
    The Battle of Northfield's begun!
Blasting those bandits right out of their saddles,
    Dropping them dead in the sun.
The Battle of Northfield's begun,
    The Battle of Northfiled's begun![1]

              —by Steve Eng

ON THURSDAY, SEPTEMBER 7, 1876, EDWARD BILL, his wife, and their two daughters, Maude and Luna, rode into Northfield by horse and buggy from their farm in nearby Waterford. Bill, who had spent three years with General William T. Sherman during the Civil War, visited the hardware store operated by A.R. Manning and was about to cross the street at about two o'clock so his daughters could visit their uncle Fred Shatto, who ran a grocery store.[2]

Ten-year-old Maude noticed three horsemen riding across the bridge on the west side of town. As the riders passed the Bills, the youngster was impressed by the big hats and clean linen dusters the men wore over their riding clothes. Maude was also dazzled by the beautiful horses each of the men rode, noticing the bridles decorated with silver. Five more men rode into town from the south and met the others in front of the First National Bank.

"They came riding over the old Cannon River bridge, two by two," she recalled years later. "They were elegantly mounted with gorgeous saddles on sturdy horses. We saw a few of them come into the square first to look things over. We were suspicious."[3]

The family had just reached Maude's uncle's store when shooting broke out less than a half-block away. Fred Shatto was physically handicapped and couldn't respond, but, when the shooting commenced, Edward Bill grabbed a pistol and ran into the street. Just as he emerged from the store, a shot hit the window directly above his head, shattering the glass. Amid the shouting and shooting, terrified Maude and Luna held onto their mother and begged their father to take them home.

"Father told me not to worry," recalled Maude Bill Ordway. "The men were trying to rob the bank and wouldn't hurt me. I wasn't very convinced."[4]

Mr. and Mrs. Charles Gress and their twenty-year-old son, Harry, lived above the shoe store they operated directly across from the First National Bank. They witnessed riders galloping away from the bank up Division Street. When shots rang out, Charles grabbed his musket and rushed to the roof.

"[Harry] ran up the back way to see where [his mother] was, and she was at the front window to see what was all going on," recalled a family member. "He pulled her away and told her they would shoot her, as they were firing at all the men on the roofs. When he returned to check on her a second time, I guess he found her at the window. She couldn't resist all that excitement."[5]

Margaret Ann Sumner was on her way home to Northfield from a visit to Canada that same day when newsboys ran through her train in St. Paul shouting "Big Robbery in Northfield" and "James and the Younger Brothers have shot and killed many Northfield residents." She became sick with worry, believing her husband, Ira, a photographer, might be among the dead residents. Great was her relief when she found him standing on the platform waiting for her.

"A close neighbor of mine in Northfield ran home on that memorable day to grab his rifle, and Mr. Manning was credited with killing one of the two robbers shot that day," said Ira. Margaret's daughter said, "Father never got over regretting that he had gone hunting that day, for the prairie chickens were flying."[6]

The town of Northfield lies about forty miles directly south of St. Paul on either side of the Cannon River. The river was spanned by a bridge at Fourth Street with the east end of the structure opening into a square that extended a block, about twice the width of an ordinary street. Running north and south, Division Street merged with Fourth, which formed part of the square. The bank building faced the south side of the square, located on the west side of Division. On the end facing the square in 1876 were two stores with the bank entrance situated at the rear of the building facing Division.[7]

John W. North had chosen the site of Bridge Square to build a town in early 1855. By the end of the following year, he had constructed a dam, a sawmill, and a gristmill. The two mills provided lumber for construction and a place where farmers could have their grain processed into flour. The Ames Mill, built in 1869, pioneered new milling processes, which gave Northfield flour the highest rating at the 1876 Centennial Exposition in Philadelphia.[8]

The first major downtown commercial building was constructed for $15,000 by Hiram Scriver, Northfield's leading merchant and first mayor. The Scriver Building, with its rough limestone exterior and Romanesque Revival arches, housed the First National Bank of Northfield.[9] Across the alley from the bank stood two hardware stores owned respectively by J.S. Allen and A.R. Manning. On the eastern side of Division Street, opposite the bank in the Scriver Block, were a hotel and several stores. A young Northfield man, H.M. Wheeler, then a medical student at

Jesse James. (Courtesy of Erich Baumann)

the University of Michigan, stood in front of one of these build-ings at the time of the incident in question.[10]

About two o'clock on September 7, Charlie Pitts, Bob Younger, and possibly Jesse James, rode over the bridge, crossed Bridge Square, and dismounted in front of the bank. Tying their reins to hitching posts, they strolled lazily to the corner and seat-ed themselves upon some dry goods boxes in front of Lee & Hitchcock's store.[11]

Cole Younger and Clell Miller rode up Division Street from the south. In seeing the newcomers arrive, the trio seated in front of the store walked back to the front of the bank and went in. According to Cole Younger, the three were to enter the bank as soon as he and Miller crossed the bridge, providing there was not a crowd of people near the bank. "When Miller and myself crossed over the bridge, I saw a crowd of citizens about the corners, our boys sitting there on some boxes. I remarked to Miller about the crowd and said, 'Surely the boys will not go into the bank with so many people about. I wonder why they did not ride straight through the town.' We were half way across the square when we saw the three men rise and walk up the sidewalk toward

Scene from the 1982 Reenactment of the Northfield Raid. (Photo by Cathy Keller)

the bank. Miller said: 'They are going in,' and I replied, 'If they do, the alarm will be given as sure as there's a hell, so you had better take that pipe out of your mouth.'"[12]

Miller was convinced there was going to be trouble and, having lit his pipe just prior to crossing the river, remarked he was going to smoke through the entire robbery. As the three men before him entered the bank, Cole looked over his shoulder and saw his brother Jim and two other robbers crossing the river. Cole and Clell were to remain in front of the bank and sound any would-be alarm should the local citizens get suspicious and arm themselves. His signal to the trio in the bank and those riding up would be a rebel yell. According to Cole, none of the gang were to shoot anyone. Shots would be fired only to scare people off the the street.

Miller dismounted, walked to the bank entrance and closed the front door. Cole Younger stepped down from his horse in the middle of the street and pretended to tighten the girth of his saddle. Their awkward actions attracted the attention of some of the citizens. Many of these citizens had already heard that nine men had been seen coming out of the woods southwest of the city and the strange horsemen in and outside the bank were undoubtedly some of the same. Others laughed at their more suspicious brethren; their minds made up the men were merely cattle buyers conducting their business.[13]

The fact that nine men, not eight, were seen coming out of the woods would certainly add credibility to Los Angeles Bill Stiles' account. With the eight others in town, he would have been left alone to guard the escape route at the bridge and would not have been seen during the robbery or subsequent flight.

Steven Budd, an eyewitness in Northfield that day later recalled, "On the day of the bank robbery I was on the sidewalk opposite the door of the bank in front of Gress' store when two men on horseback rode up to the side of the street I was on and hitched their horses a little to the north of me. I went out to them as I had beef to sell and thought they were cattle buyers and, looking at them, concluded that was not their business and went into Gress' store again. Soon after three others came riding up and throwing the lines carelessly over the posts in front of the bank went back around the corner of Scriver's store north of the bank and stood there awhile talking. They remained there probably ten minutes until three other horsemen were seen coming across the bridge when they turned and went quickly into the bank."[14]

Another citizen, Norman Van Buskirk, was sitting in his shop on the west side of the river when he saw three horsemen riding across the bridge into town. Shortly after, Van Buskirk recalled five more horsemen cantering across the bridge. He wondered about the linen dusters they wore, which appeared to him as if the men wore some kind of uniform.

Mrs. E.P. Kingman also witnessed three men riding south through Division Street but, supposing they were cattle drovers, paid little attention to them. "I was on the side of the street opposite the bank near the end of the block," she later recalled. "They halted for a minute or two directly in front of Thorson's store, which was about four doors south of the bank, and then went towards the bank. My attention was then taken up with customers, and I lost sight of them probably for a minute or two."[15]

But at least a few citizens were suspicious. Francis Howard was standing at the west end of the bridge when the first three horsemen came riding abreast over the river. "They attracted my attention by their dress and general appearance, and I turned and followed them across the bridge, probably a rod or a rod and a half behind," remembered Howard. "I followed them until about forty feet to the east of the bridge, where I met Elias

Stacy, who stood on the sidewalk, looking at them. I was so near to them that when I spoke I had to speak very low so that they would not hear me. I said, 'Stacy, those gentlemen will bear watching,' and he replied that he thought so too."[16]

Howard and Stacy followed the riders up the street but remained on the sidewalk. The riders proceeded to the corner where the bank was and tied their horses. The Northfield pair watched their movements from the opposite corner. The robbers then walked around to a store at the north side of the bank and sat down on a dry goods box. Two more riders soon rode up in front of the bank followed by three others who stopped in the center of the square on the north side. As soon as the trio stopped, the first three men got up from the dry goods box and entered the bank.

J.S. Allen and two other Northfield citizens were standing on the corner talking. Howard stepped up to them and said, "There is a St. Alban's raid." Allen quickly left the men, walked to the bank door and attempted to look in. Immediately, Clell Miller stepped out of the doorway and grasped Allen by the lapel of his coat. Miller quickly drew his revolver, and in swinging it over his head, began shooting a volley of shots into the air and shouting, "Get out of there, you sons of bitches."

Allen jerked free from Miller and ran towards a store around the corner, shouting, "Get your guns, boys. They are robbing the bank."

Citizen H.B. Gress saw Allen break free and knew immediately what was transpiring. "Up to that time I had no idea what was to occur," said Gress. "I hollered at once, 'they are robbing the bank.' And it was taken up from store to store until the whole business part of the town was aroused to the situation."[17]

Meanwhile, H.M. Wheeler, who had been sitting in front of his father's drugstore on the east side of the street, had grown suspicious. He had witnessed General Adelbert Ames with his daughter leave the bank and walk toward the mill. After seeing three strangers go into the bank and two more in front of the building, he walked down to the bank. When he saw Allen struggling with Miller, he began shouting, "Robbery! Robbery!"[18]

Cole Younger and Clell Miller sprang into their saddles and shouted at Wheeler to get back. One of them shot at him as he ran back to the drugstore to get a gun. Unable to find the weapon, Wheeler left by the back door and ran up the alley to the Dampier Hotel on the corner. Rushing through the lobby, he grabbed the clerk's rifle and ammunition and took up a position in a third floor window.

Cole fired his gun in the air to let the riders coming up from the bridge know that the alarm had been given. In seeing

Scene from the 1984 Reenactment of the Northfield Raid. (Photo by Cathy Keller)

Miller firing at Wheeler, he shouted, "Don't shoot him; let him go." The other three horsemen rode up at a full gallop. Chadwell also saw Wheeler running away and was about to shoot, but Cole yelled for him to let the man go.[19]

The two outlaws began riding up and down Division Street shooting in every direction while shouting for everyone to "get-in." The three riders who had come up from the bridge employed the same tactics shooting at any window where a head appeared. The robbers meant to frighten everyone away. As bullets sent glass shattering and terrifying shouts filled the air, the street took on almost an circus-like atmosphere.

There was to be a show in town that evening, so many of the people thought initially they were witnessing some sort of street exhibit. In the excitement, Nicholaus Gustavson, a Swedish immigrant who did not understand English, was mesmerized by the spectacle. He remained in the street watching the events after being warned several times by the outlaws to leave the scene. One of the robbers shot him, and he died several days later.[20]

Gustavson had emigrated to the United States from Smaland, Sweden, and had been living on a farm with his brother, Peter, three miles west of Millersburg. He had come to Northfield on the day of the robbery to purchase supplies with some of his neighbors, Peter Youngquist, Mrs. Peter Gustafson, Mrs. Carl Swanson, and Mrs. Swen Olson. The Swedes always purchased their supplies in Northfield; it was closer than Faribault and had more to offer than Dundas. When the shooting began, Gustavson was in a store south of the bank, and he apparently dashed outside to see what was happening.[21]

A Northfield citizen, John Olson, witnessed the death of Gustavson: "As I was working in a cellar under the building on the corner south of where the First National Bank then stood, I heard shooting. I immediately ran up to see what was going on and went to the crossing on Fifth Street, which intersects Division Street one block south of the square. Immediately, a man came up to me and, pointing a revolver and cursing me, ordered me to get away, calling me all kinds of names."[22]

As the outlaw pointed the revolver at Olson, the Northfield man noticed a neighbor's little boy standing in the street weeping, and, as the father ran up and clutched his child, the outlaw turned away from Olson and began threatening the father of the boy. Just then, Olson saw a man fall on the other side of the street, and as the outlaw was distracted, he bolted down Fifth Street and returned to the cellar.

"As I turned to run in, a Swede named Gustafson [sic] came running up, and we met right half way between the corner and the stairway to the basement," said Olson. "The stairway is about twenty feet from the corner. Just as we met, a ball struck Gustafson and he fell backwards, striking me on the leg and staggering me. I kept on running to the stairway, however, but, on reaching the door, which was two steps below the street, I found it locked, so I squatted right down by the door. I began to think about the man who was shot and concluded I ought to help him down. I looked up and as soon as my head was above the sidewalk the robber caught sight of me and told me to 'sit right still where you are, or I'll kill you too.' I squatted down again, and the next thing I saw was Gustafson, who had been shot, run down towards the river."[23]

Olson ran to assist the injured Swede who was washing himself in the stream, and helped him get to a doctor at the Norwegian Hotel. The physician found that Gustavson's skull had been fractured and the brain pierced by the bullet. According to Olson, Gustavson lived another four days while he and a friend cared for him.

Olson continued : "From the position in which Gustafson was when he was shot, it was physically impossible for him to have been killed by a ball from the guns of any of those defending the bank. The ball would have had to turn the corner about ten or twelve feet. The building was a stone one. I believe he was shot by the robber guarding the corner. He was there the entire time I was out of the cellar and was shooting all the time in every direction and was evidently set there to guard the corner."[24]

Dr. D.J. Whiting also witnessed the shooting of Gustavson after seeing riders pass his office window in the north end of the bank building: "Soon I heard firing and saw doves fly-

ing. I thought the boys across the street were shooting and went
to the doorway at the head of the stairs and saw several men on
horseback riding up and down the street firing revolvers, swear-
ing and yelling in the wildest manner. Some man, apparently a
foreigner, was coming up the sidewalk. They wanted him to run
but he only took a natural gait, which seemed to enrage one of
the horsemen as he rode up near to him firing and ordering him
off the street. About this time some of them saw me and sent a
shot at me, ordering me back."[25]

Dr. Whiting was unable to grasp the situation. Earlier
that day, a lady in his office had told him an Indian show was
planned for that evening that promised a great deal of excitement. But before he could gather his thoughts, attorney A.O.
Whipple, whose office was located in the south end of the same
building, rushed in with the news a gang of outlaws was robbing
the bank.

Inside the bank, the first three robbers were negotiating
with three bank employees: A.E. Bunker, teller; J.L. Heywood,
bookkeeper; and F.J. Wilcox, assistant bookkeeper. Since the
cashier, G.M. Phillips, was out of state, Heywood was serving as
acting cashier. At the time, the bank was located in temporary
quarters. A "store-type" counter stretched across two sides of the
interior between the lobby and the room's interior. A tall railing
with glass panels ran the entire counter length, but there was an
open space, totally unprotected, where a man had ample room to
pass through.[26]

F.J. Wilcox recalled that afternoon when he was suddenly startled by a noise at the door, only to look up and find
three men with pistols in their hands. One of the robbers commanded, "Throw up your hands. We are going to rob the bank."
The outlaws jumped over the counter and demanded the three
bank employees get down on their knees with their hands in the
air. The bankers were then told there were forty robbers outside,
and it was a bad idea to think of resisting.[27]

Wilcox believed the outlaws did not see Heywood when
they came in, as he was sitting off to the side at a desk with a high
front that partially concealed him. When they demanded the
cashier open the vault, Heywood jumped up and was promptly
ordered to his knees with his hands up. According to Wilcox, the
three outlaws were Bob Younger, Charlie Pitts, and probably
Frank James. Wilcox was sure the men had been drinking
because the smell of liquor was very strong.

While demanding the opening of the safe, the robbers
went through the pockets of the bank employees, looking for
weapons. When Bob Younger's hand struck a large jack knife in
Wilcox's hip pocket, he remarked, "What's that?" Assured it was

only a jackknife, Bob left him alone. The outlaws searched the office for a cash drawer but found only an open till on the counter, from which they appropriated a handful of small currency. The money was put in a grain sack, which was left on the floor.

Their attention was then drawn to the vault. One of the robbers stepped into the open vault, when Heywood, protective of the contents, jumped to the vault door and partially closed it. He was quickly seized and dragged away from the door. Bob Younger noticed Bunker had edged to the counter, and the outlaw jumped in front of him after noticing a small revolver on the shelf. He commanded Bunker to keep silent, and placed the revolver in his pocket. Bob bellowed, "You couldn't do anything with that little derringer anyway."

Grabbing Heywood, the outlaws insisted he was the cashier. Said Wilcox: "As they stood over him, one pulled out a knife, drew Heywood's head back, and said, 'Let's cut his throat.' I think the knife was drawn across his throat leaving a slight scratch. Then to further intimidate him a shot was fired over his head. About this time the leader ordered one of the others to go into the vault and try the safe. I believe it was Pitts who replied, 'All right, but don't let him [Heywood] lock me in there."[28]

The recollections of A.E. Bunker differ slightly from those of Wilcox. According to Bunker, Frank James and Charlie Pitts both grabbed Heywood when he attempted to close the door of the vault and pointed their revolvers in his face. He was told to "Open that safe, now, or you haven't a minute to live."[29]

Recalled Bunker: "Heywood replied, 'There is a time lock on, and the safe can't be opened now.' 'That's a lie,' retorted James and Pitts, and repeatedly demanded that he open the safe, coupling each demand with a threat, and commenced hustling Heywood about the room. Seeming to realize they were desperate men, Heywood called 'Murder! Murder! Murder!' whereupon James struck him a terrible blow on the head with his revolver, felling him to the floor. Some think this would have killed Heywood had no other injury been inflicted. He fell perfectly limp, and could not have been fully conscious after receiving the shock, as no word escaped his lips. Pitts then drew a knife from his pocket, and, opening it, said: 'Let's cut his damned throat,' and drew the edge of the knife across poor Heywood's neck, inflicting a slight wound while he was lying helpless on the floor."[30]

The outlaw pair then dragged Heywood inside the vault and again ordered him to open it. At the same time, revolvers were leveled at Wilcox and Bunker, and they too were ordered to unlock the safe. The robbers did not know that the safe was not locked at the time. With the door closed, the bolts thrown in place, the outlaws could not tell the dial was still tuned to the correct combination.

Growing angry, Pitts placed his revolver to Heywood's head and fired. The bullet struck a tin box of jewelry and valuable papers in the vault. While Pitts and James were intimidating Heywood, Bob Younger again turned his attention to the other two bankers. When Bunker had first thrown up his hands, he was still holding the pen he had been using when the robbers entered the bank. When he went to set it down, Bob Younger leaped at him and stuck his revolver into his face, telling him to keep his hands up or he'd kill him.

Younger then ordered the two bank employees to get on their knees behind the counter. Bob shifted his revolver from Bunker to Wilcox, then fumbled through papers on the counter top or in drawers. While on his knees, Bunker remembered the Smith & Wesson .32-calibre pistol on the shelf.

"I turned to see if I was near enough to reach the weapon, while Bob's back was turned to me, but Pitts happened to be looking my way at the time, and rushing across the intervening space, secured the revolver himself and coolly stuffed it into his pocket," recalled Bunker.[31]

Bunker stumbled to his feet, thinking he must try and make some kind of defensive action or at least break away, get outside and sound the alarm. Bob Younger turned to him again and barked, "Where's the money outside the safe? Where's the cashier's till?" Bunker pointed to a box with partitions in it sitting on top of the counter, which contained less than $100 in nickels, pennies, and a little silver. He replied, "There's the money outside."

Below the box, underneath the counter, was a drawer containing about $3,000 in currency. Bunker did not mention that money nor did Bob Younger find it. Again, the outlaw ordered Bunker to get back down on his knees and keep his hands up. Reaching into his linen duster, Bob pulled out a grain sack and began transferring the money from the cash box to the bag. After dropping in a couple of handfuls, it suddenly occurred to him, according to Bunker that, "the claim he was working panned out but little."

Seeing Bunker still on his feet, Bob yelled, "There's more money than that out here. Where's that cashier's till? What in hell are you standing up for? I told you to keep down." He then grabbed hold of the banker and pushed him to the floor. Bunker did not resist. In doing so, Bob felt a large pocket book in Bunker's pocket. "What have you got here?" the outlaw shouted. After looking it over, he placed it back in the pocket, pressed his revolver to Bunker's temple and pushed him to the floor, again bellowing, "Show me where that money is, you sonofabitch, or I'll kill you."

Bunker was sure his time had come. Thoughts of his wife, his mother, and God flashed through his head as Bob continued to grip his shoulder. Seeing the banker was too frightened to answer, the outlaw released him and began another fruitless search for money outside the safe. Bunker stood up once more and noticed blood trickling down Heywood's face and neck from the wounds inflicted by Pitts. Since Heywood was prostrate, Bunker supposed the bullet had entered his head and killed him.

As Bob re-examined the contents of the drawer, Bunker started an escape move, despite the outlaw's gun pointed directly at him. The banker reasoned if he could get to Manning's hardware store, located west of the bank, across the alley, fronting Mill Square, the rear door of which was at right angles to the bank's rear door, he could sound the alarm. Of course, what was happening in the street might present another problem.

Wilcox was on his knees between Bunker and the door. Bunker motioned to him with his hand to move a little forward so he might be able to pass by. Suddenly Bunker dashed by him and, as he approached the doorway, Pitts, with a whoop, fired at him from the side of the vault. The bullet whizzed past Bunker's ear and through the blinds on the door. Bunker dashed out the rear door through what he later called, "the best opening for a young man I have ever seen." The weight of his body sprang the blinds as he crashed against them. Turning to the left outside, he descended some steps to the alley. But Pitts was in hot pursuit.

Bridge Square during the James-Younger raid on the Northfield bank. (Courtesy of the Minnesota Historical Society)

65

Bunker pivoted again at the bottom of the stairs when a second shot from Pitts ripped through his shoulder as he ran opposite the rear entrance of Manning's store.

The shot had been fired from twenty feet away. It hit the fleeing banker's shoulder, barely missing the joint. The bullet passed through the shoulder blade and exited just below the collar bone, within half an inch of the subclavian artery. Dazed, Bunker remained on his feet. Unsure as to his condition, he did not jump into Manning's, but continued west instead through an open lot to Water Street and another block south to the home of a Dr. Coon.

"By the time Bunker started, I had heard shots outside, and from my position could see men riding up and down the streets shooting," recalled F.J. Wilcox, who had been still on his knees during Bunker's break to freedom. "Very soon after Mr. Heywood was struck down and then dragged toward the vault, the call came, 'Come out of the bank' followed by 'For God's sake come out; they are shooting us all to pieces.'" Pitts, re-entered the bank, then dashed back outside, followed by Bob Younger.[32]

Out in the street, Cole Younger saw his brother Bob rush out of the bank. Assuming his other confederates were out of the bank, he jumped on his horse and started north to the corner of Bridge Square. At the square, he encountered a man upstairs across the street with a gun. To scare off this adversary, Cole fired a warning shot through a pane of glass above the man's head, and the man retreated out of sight. Cole later said he thought this man was Dr. Wheeler.[33]

Cole then fired into the corner of the building to frighten away some people who had gathered by the outlaws' horses. They quickly ran around the corner out of sight. Cole saw Bob run down the sidewalk to get to his horse, and seeing that his brother was the only one to come out of the bank, he rode back to the bank and yelled again. His "For God's sake, come out," was the call Wilcox had heard from within the bank.

The last robber left the bank. Turning to go, he fired a shot at Heywood. The cashier staggered behind his desk and sank into a chair. Heywood's desk sat at right angles to the counter, and he sat sideways to the opening in the front with his back to the wall. As the robber leaped over the railing, he turned, placed his revolver against Heywood's head and fired. Heywood staggered forward, the bullet lodged in his head, and fell behind the counter leaving a pool of blood on the matting.[34]

The blotter on Heywood's desk was smeared with blood and particles of brain, as was his desk. When the town's citizens entered the bank, they found the murdered man prone upon his face, blood and brains oozing from a hole in his right temple.

Joseph Lee Heywood left a wife and child to mourn his loss. Working in the place of Mr. Phillips, it had been his intent to leave with his wife for the centennial. He was formerly of Minneapolis where he was in the employ of Captain John Martin. When the bank in Northfield had opened four years earlier, he had accepted a position there, serving also as city treasurer of Northfield and treasurer of Carleton College. Heywood had accomplished these positions after being diagnosed as a hopeless consumptive ten years earlier.[35]

But who had killed Heywood? Frank James, if he was indeed in the bank, had had his gun in his hand, and the cashier had deceived him. But Frank was known as being bitterly opposed to killing anyone during a robbery and later fought with his brother because Jesse was so ruthless. It could have been Bob Younger because he was drunk. When drinking, he was known to be too quick on the trigger. Cole would not let Bob stand guard outside the bank that day because of his inebriated state, and had ordered his younger brother to do no shooting inside the bank.[36]

A Faribault attorney, who later visited the Youngers in Stillwater Prison, pointed a finger at dead outlaw Charlie Pitts as the murderer of Heywood: "I also heard them [the Youngers] say that Pitts was the man who shot Mr. Heywood as he lay on the floor. Pitts went into the bank with Cole, but he had been drinking quite heavily just before the raid."[37] (This account of Cole Younger being in the bank contradicts several others.)

As Heywood lay dying inside, the streets of Northfield had turned into a battleground. Norman Van Buskirk was among those who answered the call of, "Get your guns, they're robbing the bank." Van Buskirk, who was then crossing the bridge, recalled: "One of the robbers came riding down the square, shouting, 'Get back you sons of bitches,' and shooting so close that I could hear the bullets whistling. I got back, making far better time than I did going over. When I got out of range I turned and saw that they were preparing to go away . . ."[38]

Gilbert Onstad heard shots being fired and looked out his window. "I saw my little boy with another child walking along the sidewalk on the other side of the street," he recalled. "I ran out and when I was about in the middle of the street, a fellow on horseback rode up to me, and, calling me names and firing a revolver over my head, ordered me to step back. I ran by him and over to my boy and ran into the corner store in Scofield's building."[39]

By then, the whole town was aroused. Guns were already loaded and ready because it was hunting season in that part of Minnesota. Guns popped out from upstairs windows and from

Joseph Lee Heywood, killed during the Northfield Raid. (Courtesy of the Minnesota Historical Society)

Frank James. (Courtesy of the Minnesota Historical Society)

around the corners of buildings up and down the street, as the robbers shot back, trying to keep the town at bay.[40]

Said one historian, "The street at Northfield must have been pure confusion, terror, dust, smoke, yelling, shooting, horses running and jumping and neighing, people getting shot at, shooting at, dodging horses, perhaps dodging falling outlaws . . ."[41]

The surprised outlaws found hell to pay for the scant sum for which they had committed murder. The bank later stated that $280 was missing. The bag of nickels Bob Younger had compiled had been left behind when things got hot outside. A linen duster was found in addition to the grain sack marked with the initials H.C.A. (A newspaper published a week later in referring to the duster and grain sack said, "Probably the bank would send these by express, if they could get their address.")[42]

Dr. Wheeler, who had been one of the first to sound the alarm, had positioned himself in a second-story window when the fight began. Mr. Allen, meanwhile, had run to A.R. Manning at the hardware store and told him of the robbery in progress. Manning quickly grabbed a Remington rifle and some cartridges. Re-entering his own store, Allen shouted the news to his clerks. One citizen, Elias Stacy, who had been armed with a fowling piece from Allen, picked up a loaded shotgun and rushed to the corner where Clell Miller was remounting his horse.[43]

Miller, directly in front of the bank, turned to face him, and Stacy surprised him with a full load of bird shot in the face. Miller was knocked from his horse but was not injured seriously, and Stacy ran for cover. Miller quickly jumped back on his horse, but Dr. Wheeler shot him from the second-story window. The bullet severed the subclavian artery and killed him.

Five doors from the bank, J.A. Hunt watched from a jewelry store. "I went to the door, and a man, Jim Younger, as I afterwards learned, rode up to within ten feet of me, firing with pistols in both hands, shouting and cursing, and ordered me back into the store. There were then three or four others riding up and down the street and one man still further south. As I went into the store, I saw one of the robbers shot and fall off his horse close to the sidewalk on the opposite side of the street. One of his companions, who was at the corner and whom I have since learned was Cole Younger, dismounted almost as soon as he fell and took the pistols from the body."[44]

Only seconds before, Dr. Wheeler had taken a shot at Jim Younger who had raced by, but his aim was high, and the bullet missed the outlaw. Jim looked around to see who nearly hit him, but by then Dr. Wheeler had espied another target, Clell Miller. This time, he did not miss. Wheeler's third cartridge had fallen to the floor; useless because the paper used in part of its

Scene from the Reenactment of the Northfield Raid, 1982. (Photo by Cathy Keller)

Bob Younger. (Photo by Jacoby's of Minneapolis. Courtesy of the Minnesota Historical Society)

manufacture was torn. But Dampier, the hotel owner, came to his rescue with fresh ammunition. This time Dr. Wheeler hit Bob Younger in the right elbow as he rushed from the bank. But Bob was a seasoned outlaw and utilized the "border shift" in tossing his revolver into his left hand, ready for use.[45]

Cole Younger later said he was with Miller and his own brother Bob when all hell broke loose. "Just then Miller called to me, saying he was shot, and, looking at him, I saw the blood running down his face," recalled Cole. "The firing by this time had become general, and as the two men in the bank had not yet come out, I was forced for the third time to ride to the bank and call to them to come out. And this time they did so. In the meantime, Miller had been shot again and had fallen from his horse. I jumped from my horse, ran to Miller to see how badly he was hurt, and, while turning him over, was shot in the the left hip."[46]

Cole said he took Miller's pistols, remounted his horse and, along with brother Jim, rode to Bob, who was standing near the stairway. At that moment, Bob was shot. Cole, seeing his brother switch his gun from right to left, knew Bob's limp arm was broken. "Bob ran up the street, and Jim helped him to mount," Cole continued. "I then called to Pitts to help me get Miller up on my horse in front of me. On lifting him up we saw that he was dead, so (I) told Pitts to lay him down again and to run up the street out of range, and I would take him up behind me."[47]

Captain French, the town's postmaster, looked out on the once sleepy street that had come to life with a flurry of bullets breaking windows and ricocheting from stone buildings in long mean whines. French quickly locked his doors, closing the post office, and frantically searched for a gun. Unable to find a weapon, he stepped into the alley, picked up an armful of sizable rocks, and began heaving them at the robbers. Soon Elias Hobbs and Justice Streeter joined him.[48]

Also heeding Allen's call, A.R. Manning, who had been waiting on a customer, looked out his door as shots rang out. He saw a pair of horsemen galloping by firing their pistols. The hardware merchant quickly grabbed a rifle out of the window of his store, pulled the cover off, took a handful of cartridges and headed for the bank. As he ran, he loaded the gun.

"Very soon A.R. Manning came around the corner," recalled H.B. Gress. "Others were with him but he seemed the leader and displayed more real nerve than all the robbers put together. He stood on the corner after the citizens had driven them south on Division Street and faced them all, not knowing but they might attack him from the rear. The robbers at that time were hollering to each other, 'Kill the white-livered sonofabitch on the corner,' referring to Manning."[49]

Manning later recalled: "As I turned the corner going to the bank, I saw two men on the opposite side of their horse, which was tied to a post. I knew they were robbers the minute my eyes struck them. I drew my gun on them, and as I did so they doubled right down behind the horse. Without taking my gun from my face I lowered the muzzle and shot the horse."[50]

The shooting of the horse was witnessed by W.H. Riddell. "Two of the robbers laid down behind the dead horse and commenced shooting north down the street while one of them was under the bank stairs," recollected Riddell. "One of those behind the dead horse jumped up and ran to the bank door and shouted, 'For God's sake, boys, hurry up: It is getting too hot for us.'"[51]

Manning quickly jumped around the corner to reload. In doing so, he found he could not pull the shell from his gun. He ran swiftly back to his store and chucked a ramrod through the rifle, releasing the shell. R.C. Phillips, another local citizen, had an explanation for the shell problem: "On the day of the Northfield raid, I was in the shop working for A.R. Manning. My shop opened directly on an eight-foot alley from the back door of the bank. The first thing I heard was some loud talking in the bank, and then I heard a shot. When I heard the shot, I started for the front of the store where Manning was working on his books. I asked Manning what that shot was and he said, 'I think it's that show that's going to be here tonight. I started to go up around the corner where the steps were, when I met John Tosney and John Archer who shouted, 'They're robbing the bank.' At that time five men whom I saw on the bridge started to drive rapidly across the square, firing right and left and shouting, 'Get in, you sons of bitches.' I ran back into the store, took the guns and revolvers we had and threw them out on the showcase, handing at the same time a single shot Winchester to Manning. In doing so, however, I made a mistake and gave him the wrong size shells, so that after he went out and attempted to load his rifle he found he had to come back to get new shells."[52]

But Manning returned to his position at the corner, again reloading as he ran. Seeing two or three robbers in front of the bank facing him, he fired a shot. The bullet hit a post that supported some stairs, but, in passing through it, it hit Cole Younger in the hip.

Manning was far from finished. Peeking around the corner, he found Bill Chadwell perched on his horse doing sentry duty some seventy to eighty feet up the street. More cautious now, he jumped back, reloaded and peeked around the corner. Taking deliberate aim, Manning fired. The bullet ripped through Chadwell's heart. The outlaw fell dead from his saddle, and the horse ran around the corner to a nearby livery stable.[53]

James Law witnessed the shooting of Chadwell. After hearing shooting that sounded like "firecrackers on the fourth of July," he rushed up to the corner. "Then I saw Manning in front of Scriver's store in the rear of which the bank was, with his rifle pointed around the corner," he later remembered. "Immediately one of the robbers came riding down the street past the corner, and, seeing Manning with the rifle pointed, turned and shot at Manning while making the turn. Manning did not move but leveled his rifle, fired at the robber when he was near the corner. The horse carried him up the street for about 140 rods where he fell to the ground in front of Lockwood's store. That was all I saw; I came back to the west side of the river and gave the alarm, and when I got back they had gone. All the while I was on the street, the robbers were shooting and shooting right and left."[54]

H.B. Gress saw the bandit fall: "A bullet from Manning's rifle struck him," Gress recalled. "He dropped to the side of his horse and turned and started back from whence he came, but soon fell off in the street and died there. The shooting produced such a concussion that frame buildings shook like trees would on a windy day. Anyone not being present could not imagine what an excitement the raid created and how people were terrorized."[55]

Still another, A.H. Bjoraker, witnessed the demise of the Chadwell. Bjoraker watched as confused riders rode in a circle shooting and shouting. Taking a closer look, one of the robbers screamed, "Get in there, you sonofabitch, or I'll kill you." Jumping behind a pillar, the frightened Bjoraker continued to watch one of the men on horseback. "When he was right southeast of my store about in the middle of the intersection of Division and Fifth streets, I saw him drop his lines and the horse made a big jump and went north until he came to about the fourth store from the corner, where the man fell to the ground. I ran right over to him."[56]

Manning then saw a man in the street halfway up the block who was staring at the opposite side of the street. Manning fired, the robber winced, and dashed around the corner. Then he saw a man on the sidewalk running toward him with a revolver in the air about to fire at him. Manning aimed his gun at him but the outlaw darted behind some boxes under the stairs.[57]

Two or three times the men dodged each other. At this point, Dr. Wheeler fired from the upstairs window hitting the robber in the elbow. The robber, of course, turned out to be Bob Younger. Manning, however, did not know Younger had been shot by Wheeler, so he rushed back through his store and out the other side in an effort to come up behind the robber. By then the people of Northfield were coming out of buildings and Manning could not get off a shot at the fleeing Bob Younger who had sprang from his hiding place and mounted behind his brother Cole. The band, with two of its members dead in the streets of Northfield, turned and galloped out of town on the Dundas Road. They left $15,000 behind, still secure inside the bank.

Among the first citizens to reach the bank was M.W. Skinner who later recalled: "Looking over the counter, I saw Mr. Heywood lying there dead, his head resting about where the paying teller usually stood. I helped carry him home to his wife. I then went to the telegraph office to telegraph to Dundas, in which direction the robbers had gone, what had been done here and ask them to intercept them, but the operator at Dundas was not in and the message could not then be sent. When I went home at night my wife said to me that before she knew what to make of the noise; it sounded more like the popping of corn than anything else."[58]

Ironically, among those with Manning during the gun battle was General Adelbert Ames, co-owner of the Ames mills, a stockholder of the bank, and a man despised by the James-Younger bunch. He just happened to be in town at the time and stood at Manning's back sharing the danger and advising his friend. Fifty-three years later he admitted his part in the Northfield affair: "Yes, it is true. I was with Manning while he, with his gun, was shooting at the murdering robbers who became, apparently, heroes. I was going over the bridge to the mill and met the James crowd going in the opposite direction. Shortly after reaching the mill, I heard someone shout, 'They are robbing the bank.' Returning, I saw Manning with his gun and joined him."[59]

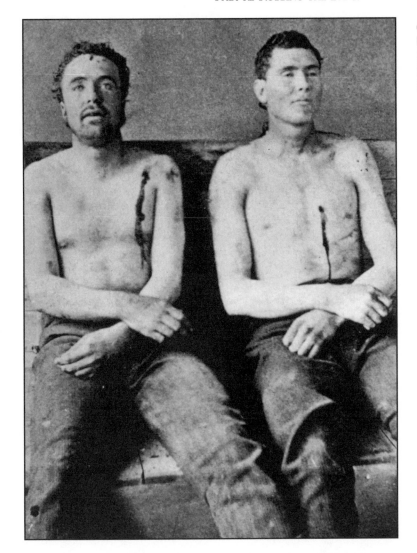

Clell Miller and Bill Chadwell, killed in the Northfield Raid. (Photo by Jacoby's of Minneapolis. Courtesy of the Minnesota Historical Society)

Ames downplayed his own role in the affair and gave Manning full credit: "Manning had a trembling hand but took deliberate aim and shot the moving horseman, nearly a block away, thru (sic) the heart and dropped him dead to the street."[60]

In front of the bank lay the dead horse, the first to die. Near the horse was the body of Clell Miller, and only a half-block away on the opposite side of the street, reposed the body of Chadwell. Only the death of the horse moved the citizens who viewed the aftermath of the battle. On each side of them, shattered windows served as a grisly reminder of what had only moments before transpired; hitching posts, doors, window frames and store-fronts were riddled with bullets.[61]

A woman who witnessed the scene later recalled: "I saw the bodies of three men lying in the dust of the street. Near them lay the body of a horse, one of those ridden by one of the robbers."[62]

The scene inside the bank was no better with the bloodied body of Heywood on the floor. His wife learned of the death quite by accident. She overheard a neighbor shout the news to another across the street. Although pained, the courageous lady in hearing the grisly details of her husband's death, said, "I would not have had him do otherwise."[63]

A friend referred to Heywood as a shy, well-liked young man and was deeply moved by his passing. She later recalled: "I don't think there was such a thing as an ambulance in town at that time so they came for Mr. Heywood's body with a regular buggy. It was drawn up at the rear entrance of the bank. I saw the men carry out the body of poor Mr. Heywood and lay it in the buggy. Then they covered it over with a sheet."[64]

The bodies of the two dead robbers were taken to be photographed in the studio of Ira E. Sumner, long time Nothhfield photographer.[65] Both the dead robbers showed splendid physical development, and initially, it was thought they might even be brothers. One was six feet, three inches tall and appeared to be about twenty-five years of age. The other was five feet, eight inches, somewhat older than the other and more stoutly built. Both men had blue eyes and darkish, red, curly hair. A map with a route marked through LeSueur County was found on the body of the younger man. About $5.50 was found in their pockets as well as two gold watches.[66]

Cole Younger later blamed the deaths on a quart of whiskey, which he concluded one of his men had concealed on the way to Northfield. Three of the men drank the whiskey in the woods during their separation the morning of the robbery. He said if he had known the men had been drunk, he would not have entered Northfield, since he was not a drinker and had no confidence in a man who was.[67]

During the ride out of town, the last man to leave the bank conveyed to Cole what had happened to Heywood. As the outlaw jumped the counter in leaving the bank, he saw Miller lying in the street. At that moment, one of the clerks jumped up and ran towards a desk. The outlaw thought the clerk was going for a pistol, and he ordered him to stop and sit down. When the banker persisted and jumped from the counter, the killer leveled his pistol and fired.

"Cole Younger told me that the most unfortunate thing that could happen [was] that some people were getting rather suspicious of their being in the town, and that night six of the group managed to purchase a two-gallon stone jug of whiskey and

stay drunk and noisy, which only increased the suspicions of their being in that town," recalled Cole's friend, Todd George. "Cole, at that time, was known to avoid drinking. Cole further said that

Artist's interpretation of Jesse James. (Drawing by John Stevens)

75

the group with him was in no condition to successfully rob the bank. In an attempt to rob—when the discharge of arms was heard from the outside Cole made every effort to hurry them out of the bank and get out of the town, but they were rather slow in moving and just as they were leaving one of the group turned and shot the cashier. . . . I have been asked so often if Cole Younger ever tole [sic] me who in the group committed the murder. On a number of occasions when I asked Cole if he could ever tell me who did this, his answer was always, 'Frank James knew who did it.'"[68]

Cole knew his brother Bob's arm was broken at the elbow, but during their hasty retreat, he also learned Jim had been shot through the shoulder. Concern was for his brothers, not for the money they did not get at the fat bank in Northfield. They had been thwarted at other robberies, and as Frank James had once said, "We sometimes didn't get enough to buy oats for our horses. Most banks had very little money in them."[69]

But this bank did and many, if not most, questions remained unanswered. Historians disagree as to who was really involved in the raid, which robbers were actually in the bank, and who pulled the fatal trigger. Jesse may have been in the bank for practical reasons. It was rumored he was not a good shot and he did not like shoot-outs. He had once fired six shots at a man and missed every time. Thus, he may have preferred being in the bank, rather than remaining in the street.[70]

One historian believes both Bob Younger and Jesse James were in the bank. She feels Bob was usually placed outside, but since the Northfield affair was co-planned by him, he decided to be in the bank. If so, Bob would not have been drunk, his post would not have been changed to "protect" the others—the robbery would have instead been called off or a drunken person left out of it. The bandits would not have taken a chance; they were professionals.[71]

Jesse perhaps went into the bank for the moral protection of Bob and because he felt he knew more about the situation. If Pitts went in, it would have meant that both Frank and Cole were left outside, which would not have agreed with the two leaders. Since Cole did not like to be in the banks, it was probably decided Frank would go in.

As this same scholar points out, it is curious indeed why Pitts was identified as being one of those in the bank. It was possible that one of the cashiers recognized Jesse (the only one who could probably be recognized) and was afraid of being a witness against him. Or, because of everyone being excited, it may have been a case of misidentification. Nor was Frank identified. If it were not for the many references to a dun horse, people would still be assuming it was Jesse who shot Heywood. If it were Jesse who shot Heywood, Cole would not have kept the secret of the rider of the dun horse as he did.

Although Pitts was well liked by his confederates, he may not have had the trust or prestige to be an inside man on such an important robbery. Of course, the egos of Frank and Cole would not have allowed them to both remain outside. And, since Bob was making such a big play of showing off his independence and importance, he probably would have strongly resisted Cole being in the bank.

Jim Younger once said: "The one time Bob listened to outside influences, firmly insisting that he was a man and could lead his own life, resulted in the Northfield affair. He was led to believe the subtly drawn picture by that master artist the crafty Mephistopheles, Jesse James, that there was a way of quick revenge on the North for our father's financial losses and the recovery of a huge sum of money. I never saw him so blindly enthused. Neither Cole or [sic] I could reach him. . . . Bob asked so many times if we forgave him for being so headstrong, both Cole and I assured him we were more at fault; being older, we should have found a way to prevent the whole thing."[72]

Despite the horrible tragedy that crippled Northfield, and with the robbers still running free in their attempt to return to Missouri, the *Faribault Democrat* was able to inject some humor through one of its editorials: "The *Pioneer-Press and Tribune* has not yet charged directly that the Northfield bank robbers were led by Tilden [a presidential candidate] and Hendricks, but it says: 'Tilden lost two devoted followers when the brace of highwaymen fell dead at Northfield.' If the *Pioneer-Press* believes that it can make votes for Hayes by such vile and brutal insinuations as that, it has mistaken the temper of the people. It is expected in every issue of the *Pioneer-Press* to see that the robbers were Democratic Ku Klux engaged in the work of intimidating Republican voters. In its reports it constantly keeps before its readers the assertion that they were Democrats, and colors every circumstance with a partisan hue. But what else can be expected from the *Pioneer-Press?* It is quite as honorable as any of its campaign work."[73]

In another section of the same issue of the *Faribault Democrat*, ran the following blurb: "The Northfield bank robbery is a sweet morsel to the *Pioneer-Press* who sees in it a chance to make votes for Hayes and Wheeler."[74]

Notes

1 Copyright © 1982, Blue Meadow Music, All rights reserved.

2 *St. Paul Sunday Pioneer Press*, August 28, 1966, Six Second Section under "Eyewitness Recalls Attempted Bank Robbery by Jesse James."

3 *Minneapolis Tribune*, July 21, 1860, "James' Holdup Witness is 100."

4 *St. Paul Sunday Pioneer Press*, August 28, 1966.

5 Mrs. Robert E. Fosdick letter to author dated February 24, 1982.

6 Grace Sumner Northrop letter to author dated February 12, 1982; Grace Sumner Northrop letter to Emily Buth, Curator, Buckham Memorial Library, Faribault, Minnesota dated July 18, 1978.

7 *Northfield News*, Saturday, July 10, 1897, p. 1.

8 *Northfield When, A Guide to Architectural History in the Downtown Historic District of Northfield, Minnesota*. A brochure sponsored by the Northfield Heritage Preservation Commission.

9 *Northfield News*, Saturday, July 10, 1897, p. 1.

10 George Huntington, *Robber and Hero: The Story on the Raid on the First National Bank in Northfield, Minnesota*, Ross and Haines, Inc., Minneapolis, Minnesota, 1962, p. 11-12.

11 *The Northfield Saga*, No author given, published for the Fiftieth Anniversary of the Northfield Bank Robbery, Collection, Northfield Library, p. 6.

12 *The Madelia News*, Thursday, November 25, 1915, "Cole Younger's Story of the Northfield Raid."

13 *The Northfield Saga*, p. 6; George Huntington, *Robber and Hero*, p. 13-14.

14 *Northfield News*, Saturday, July 10, 1897, under "The Northfield Raid, What Some of Our Citizens Saw 21 Years ago."

15 Ibid.

16 Ibid.

17 Ibid.

18 *The Northfield Saga*, p.6; Lester E. Swanberg, *Then and Now: A History of Rice County*, under "Bank is Raided," pp. 181-182; *Faribault Democrat*, September 15, 1876.

19 A.E. Hedback, M.D., 1897 Prison Physician Stillwater Prison "Cole Younger's Story of the Northfield Raid in His Own Handwriting," Minnesota Historical Society.

20 *Webster* (South Dakota) *Journal*, July 17, 1930 under "As Boy and Man;" Northfield News Inc., *The Northfield Bank Raid*, Northfield, Minnesota, 1933, p. 9.

21 B. Wayne Quist, *The History of the Christdala Evangelical Swedish Lutheran Church of Millersburg, Minnesota*, Small World Press, Dundas, Minnesota, 1994, pp. 19-21.

22 *Northfield News*, Saturday, July 10, 1897.

23 Ibid.

24 Ibid.

25 Ibid.

26 George Huntington, *Robber and Hero*, pp. 17.

27 *Northfield News*, Saturday, July 10, 1897.

28 Ibid.

29 *The Madelia Times*, November 20, 1896, A. E. Bunker, "Recollections of the Northfield Raid," p. 6.

30 Ibid; *Minneapolis Tribune*, Sunday, April 4, 1982, "A Century After His Death, Jesse James Still Good Copy" by Mark Peterson, p. 13A.

31 Ibid. The revolver was found on Pitts' body following the robbery attempt and taken by an identified person as a souvenir.

32 *Northfield News*, Saturday, July 10, 1897.

33 *The Madelia News*, Thursday, November 25, 1915, "Cole Younger's Story of the Northfield Raid."

34 *Minneapolis Tribune*, Friday Evening, September 8, 1876, "Northfield's Sensation," p. 1.

35 *St. Paul and Minneapolis Pioneer Press and Tribune*, Saturday, September 9, 1876, "The Dead Cashier," p. 2; *The Northfield Bank Raid*, p. 4.

36 *Kansas City Star*, Sunday, February 16, 1936, "The Inside Story of the Northfield Bank Robbery."

37 *Northfield Independent*, Thursday, November 25, 1948, "Pitts Named as Heywood Slayer in Notes Left by G.W. Batchelder Dictated to His Wife."

38 *Northfield News*, Saturday, July 10, 1897.

39 Ibid.

40 *Kansas City Star*, Sunday, February 16, 1936; *The Norborne* (Mo.) *Democrat & Leader*, Friday, January 3, 1936, "The Younger Boys Last Stand," by Harry Hoffman, ex-marshal of Jackson County, Missouri.

41 Chuck Parsons letter to author dated December 16, 1996.

42 *Rice County Journal*, Northfield, Minnesota, Thursday, September 14, 1876, "Robbery & Murder!" p. 1.

43 *The Northfield Saga*, p. 9; In the *Madelia Times*, November 20, 1896, a clerk, Joseph B. Hyde was given credit as being the birdshot marksman.

44 *Northfield News*, Saturday, July 10, 1897.

45 Carl W. Breihan, *Younger Brothers*, the Naylor Company, San Antonio, 1961, pp. 178-179; *Mankato Free Press*, Wednesday, September 19, 1979, "Northfield Robbers Left State in an Uproar" by John Stone, p. 12.

46 Stillwater Prison Affidavit signed by Cole Younger in 1897.

47 Ibid.

48 *Minneapolis Sunday Tribune*, January 18, 1948, "Northfield: The James Boys' Downfall" by Stewart H. Holbrook, p. 11.

49 *Northfield News*, Saturday, July 10, 1897.

50 Ibid.

51 Ibid.

52 Ibid.

53 George Huntington, *Robber and Hero*, pp. 32.

54 *Northfield News*, Saturday, July 10, 1897

55 Ibid.

56 Ibid.

57 Ibid; *The Northfield Saga*, p. 10; *Minnesota Monthly*, September 1981, Vol. 15, No. 9, "The James Gang Rides Again," p. 41.

58 *Northfield News*, Saturday, July 10, 1897.

59 *Northfield News*, August 2, 1929.

60 Ibid.

61 George Huntington, *Robber and Hero*, p.38.

62 *St. Paul Sunday Pioneer Press*, August 28, 1966, "Eyewitness Recalls Attempted Bank Robbery by Jesse James." The third body referred to by Mrs. Maude Ordway was that of Nicholas Gustavson.

63 George Huntington, *Robber and Hero*, pp. 39-40.

64 *St. Paul Sunday Pioneer Press*, August 28, 1966.

65 Grace Sumner Northrop, letter to Emily Buth, Curator, Buckham Memorial Library, Faribault, Minnesota dated July 18, 1978.

66 *Faribault Republican*, September 13, 1876, "The Dead Robbers," p. 3.

67 Stillwater Prison Affidavit signed by Cole Younger in 1897.

68 Todd M. George letter to Owen Dickie dated February 22, 1968, Nicollet County Historical Society, St. Peter.

69 Len James letter to author dated March 3, 1983.

70 Carl R. Green and William R. Sanford, *Jesse James*, Outlaws and Lawmen of the Wild West series, Enslow Publishers, Inc., Hillside, New Jersey, 1992, p. 32.

71 Marley Brant letter to author dated November 22, 1982.

72 A private letter written by Jim Younger in Stillwater Prison in August 1898 in collection of author Marley Brant.

73 *Faribault Democrat*, September 15, 1876.

74 Ibid.

Chapter 4

Flight into Hell

THE ROBBER HUNT

This is the bank at Northfield.

This is the malt, that lay in the vault,
That was in the bank at Northfield.

This is the eight, that smelled the bait,
That is, the malt, that lay in the vault,
That was in the bank at Northfield.

These are the men, that mounted then
To chase the six, that got in a fix,
That's left of eight, that smelled the bait,
That is, the malt, that lay in the vault,
That was in the bank at Northfield.

This is Brissette, the capital pet,
Who swore, you bet, he'd have 'em yet,
That joined the men, that mounted then,
To chase the six who's got in a fix,
That's left of eight, that smelled the bait,
That is, the malt, that lay in the vault,
That was in the bank at Northfield.

This is Mike Hoy, that broth of a boy,
Who shouldered his little Winchester toy,
To beat Brissette, the capital pet,
Who swore, you bet, he'd have 'em yet,
That joined the men, that mounted then,
To chase the six, that got in a fix,
That's left of eight, that smelled the bait,
That is, the malt, that lay in the vault,
That was in the bank at Northfield.

And this is Dill, who went to fill,
With silvery speech, the deadly breach,
Between Mike Hoy, that broth of a boy,
Who shouldered his little Winchester toy,
And Johnny Brisette, the capital pet,

Who swore, you bet, he'd have 'em yet,
That joined the men, that mounted then,
To chase the six, that got in a fix,
That's left of eight, that smelled the bait,
That is, the malt, that lay in the vault,
That was in the bank at Northfield.

This is the Governor's right hand bower,
Who wavered his hand with majestic power,
And ordered, in words that might appall,
The prisoners sent to "ye great St. Paul."
O where was Dill, who went to fill,
With silvery speech, the deadly breach,
And where Mike Hoy, that broth of a boy,
Who shouldered his little Winchester toy,
And where Brissette, the capital pet,
Who swore, you bet, he'd have 'em yet,
That joined the men, that mounted then,
To chase the six, that got in a fix,
That's left of eight, that smelled the bait,
That is, the malt, that lay in the vault,
That was in the bank at Northfield.

And this is the Surgeon General, too,
Who probed with a telegraph wire, and knew
Better than Cooley and Overhott,
Whether the men could travel, or not,
Who backed the Governor's right hand bower,
Who waved his hand with majestic power,
And ordered, in words that might appall,
The prisoners sent to "ye great St. Paul,"
O, where was Dill, who went to fill,
With silvery speech, the deadly breach,
And where Mike Hoy, that broth of a boy,
Who shouldered his little Winchester toy,
And where Brisette, the capital pet,
Who swore, you bet, he'd have 'em yet,
That joined the men, who mounted then,
To chase the six, that got in a fix,
That's left of eight, that smelled the bait,
That is, the malt, that lay in the vault,
That was in the bank at Northfield.

And this is Glispin, who knew his "biz,"
And sat right down on the St. Paul "phiz,"
And when 'twas squelched, he upward rose,
And put his thumb to the end of his nose,
And this to the Surgeon-General too;
Who probed with a telegraph wire, and knew
Better than Cooley and Overhott,
Whether the men could travel, or not,

And this to the Governor's right hand bower,
Who waved his hand with majestic power,
And ordered, in words that might appall,
The prisoners sent to "ye great St. Paul,"
O, where was Dill, who went to fill,
With silvery speech, the deadly breach,
And where Mike Hoy, that broth of a boy,
Who shouldered his little Winchester toy,
And where Brisette, the capital pet,
Who swore, you bet, he'd have 'em yet,
That joined the men, that mounted then,
To chase the six, who got in a fix,
That's left of eight, that smelled the bait,
That is, the malt, that lay in the vault,
That was in the bank at Northfield.[1]

—"The Robber Hunt"
From the *Winona Republican*, September 1876

WHILE PANIC ERUPTED IN THE STREETS OF NORTHFIELD, Mrs. Ida Bennett Porter prepared a threshers' supper in her aunt's farm home. A horseman came galloping down the road shouting, "The bank's being robbed." The farmers, who were pooling their harvest, ran in from the field. Passing up the two kinds of meat being served, they grabbed pieces of cake from the table, harnessed horses to buggies and were off for Northfield.[2]

As a second rider hurried past the farm, he shouted, "Bodies all over the street." Mrs. Porter and her aunt, whom she was visiting during the harvest season, glanced at the bushel of potatoes they had peeled, considered the hours of baking they had done and went into action. Harnessing another team of horses, they rushed into town to see what all the commotion was about. Reaching Northfield, they found the town in an uproar.

Townsfolk were already forming posses to hunt down the escaping outlaws, but Mrs. Porter returned to the farm and went back to her baking. Said Mrs. Porter: "Nothing very exciting happened after that in Northfield."[3]

But for the James-Younger gang, they would experience nothing but excitement for the next few weeks. As they escaped from the city of Northfield, they had no way of knowing that the largest manhunt in the history of the United States, up to that time, was being formed to chase them down. Since the gang did not cut the telegraph wires as they rode west out of town, messages went through immediately. Soon over a thousand men would be hot on their trail.[4]

Quick flight was impossible. Jesse had been shot in the thigh on his way out of town. Frank also may have sustained a leg wound.[5] Charlie had been shot while waiting for Cole and Bob. And Bob and Jim had both been hit.

Just outside Northfield, Bill Revier was returning with his team of horses after making an ice delivery for John T. Ames. On a hill, he stopped at the Foster house, and its owner came out and asked him about the shots he heard coming from Northfield. "It was then that we saw six of the gang riding toward us, two of them riding double—hence their need for another horse," recalled Revier. "They came toward us, their horses on a slow canter and they were reloading their revolvers as they rode. As they neared me, I heard one of them say, 'Let's take a horse here,' while another said, 'No, no. Go on further.'"[6]

The robbers did not take Revier's horses because they were too near town and a pursuit was imminent. They had passed up some very good horses, however. The following summer the pair were sold for $450 by Mr. Ames to Governor John S. Pillsbury to be used as a driving team.

The riders headed for Dundas, three miles south of Northfield, the only place where they could cross the Cannon River; six men riding five horses.[7] Riding abreast, they took the entire road. They paused at the river to cleanse their wounds. While in hiding by the river, a local man, Philip Empey, who was hauling rails, happened along with a team of gray horses. Empey was immediately ordered to give up one of his mounts. Bob was placed on the horse and the robbers sped into Dundas with the "borrowed" horse.[8]

A slightly different account was reported by Mrs. Nellie Empey Odell of Sioux Falls, South Dakota, the sister of Philip Empey. Mrs. Odell, who had lived several years in the Northfield area, maintained that her brother Philip was at the Centennial exposition at the time of the robbery. She said a man whom she and her brother had hired came walking up to the house leading one horse. The hired man said while he was working in the field near the road, some men rode up and began stripping the harness from one of the horses. He told the bandits the horse did not belong to him, but they hit him on the head and took the horse.[9]

"It was Bob Younger who took our horse," recalled Mrs. Odell. "Some people recognized the animal as the robbers were going over the Dundas bridge and shouted at them, 'What are you doing with Phil Empey's horse?' They rode right on, and soon we all knew who they were, and there surely was great excitement. We got our horse back after a few weeks but he was never the same."[10]

Only ten minutes behind the robbers were two Northfield men, Jack Hayes and Dwight Davis. One of them was mounted on the horse of the robber Manning had shot, and the other on the horse the gang had left tied in the street near the bank. They were the first two men to leave Northfield in pursuit of the James-Younger boys.[11]

As the robbers were taking Empey's horse from the wagon, Hayes and Davis rode up. One of the outlaws shouted at them to halt. Fearing other robbers were hiding in the bushes, the pair backed off out of sight. When the robbers rode away, the pair slowly followed them, stopping to wait at Millersburg for reinforcements.[12]

George Taylor, four other men in a double rig, and seventeen others on horseback, caught up with Hayes and Davis at Millersburg. The entire party took up the trail together and rode into Shieldsville.

Other Northfield men were quick to respond as evidenced by a special telegram to the *St. Paul Dispatch*: "A party of horsemen is now organizing here and I start with them, having put away for the nonce the formidable weapon with which you armed me, the pencil, and taken the trusty breach-loading carbine which brought down one of the villains here. I hope to telegraph a successful issue of the enterprise before many hours have passed. It is raining hard, but groups of excited men have been talking at the street corners all the morning, and the excitement has increased immensely since the definite news of the assassins' whereabouts arrived. The men now going out are determined, and if they come up with the thieves, they will make short work of them. No quarter will be given. Chief King's men are still out and believed to be in the immediate vicinity of the highwaymen."[13]

A Minneapolis newspaper reported similar news regarding posses forming at Northfield: "A number of the citizens of Northfield lead be [sic] Dr. Wheeler, who did such good service, started, shortly after, in pursuit. They were well armed and equipped. Wheeler did not even stop to put on his boots. It was reported this morning that his horse had given out, and he would be obliged to return."[14]

While the robbers galloped full speed through Dundas, George Sexton and C.W. Brown stood in front of Sexton's store. Sexton supposed the men to be a party of drunken rowdies when he noticed one of the men slumped in the saddle. He then called out, "Haloo, are you a cavalry regiment?" According to a September 13, 1876, newspaper account, the riders pointed their revolvers at the pair, whereupon Brown, addressed one of the gunmen, and pluckily shouted, "Get off that horse and I'll whip you. I can whip any man who points a revolver at me." The men rode away, and when Brown learned the identity of the riders, he was pleased to have given the men "a lesson in good breeding."[15]

About a half-mile beyond Dundas, the men stopped at the farm of Robert Donaldson. Three of the men concealed their weapons beneath their coats while asking Donaldson for a pail of water. They explained that one of their number had fallen from his horse and broken his leg. The farmer asked them to bring the man into the house. The riders declined his hospitality but asked him to follow them to where their three friends were waiting. When Donaldson asked about the man's arm wound, he was informed the injured man had been shot by a blackleg [gambler] with whom they had had a row in Northfield and killed.

The men, who had previously stopped to bandage the arm, began pouring water on the wound. As they rode away, Donaldson cried out, asking the name of the man whom they had killed. One of the men quipped back, "Stiles."[16]

They had considered taking one of Donaldson's horses, but were not impressed with any of his mounts. They met several teams as they rode along and compelled every passing man to give them the road. The outlaws rode three and three with the wounded man, who was bleeding heavily, riding in the middle.

Three times that day, small detachments of pursuers nearly caught up to them. About the time they were stealing Empey's horse on the Dundas road, a squad of Faribault men had arrived in Shieldsville, fifteen miles west of Northfield. Because they had taken a shorter route, they were ahead of the robbers. They had, however, gone inside Haggerty's, leaving their guns outside, when the robbers rode into Shieldsville.[17]

The robbers rode up to Hanlin's Hotel, where they had stopped before the robbery, and asked Hanlin's son how long the men had been there. He informed them it was a Faribault team and had arrived only about five minutes earlier. One of the men then whispered, "They are after us; let's smash their guns." Riding over to the wagon, one of the men picked up a gun, just as its owner ran outside and attempted to take it back. The robbers leveled their guns at the men coming out of Haggerty's and ordered them back inside.[18]

Another account related the men drank from a pump by Haggerty's saloon and pumped water onto concealed rags under their coats with which they intended to use to treat their wounds. An old man in front of Haggerty's watched them with a suspicious eye, and when Bob fell from his horse, Jesse quickly explained that the man was a captured horse thief. Four men appeared in the doorway, but the gang drew their guns and told them to stay put.[19]

After watering their horses, the robbers fired several shots into the pump and rode off leisurely up the hill by a Catholic church. Here they proceeded down the Dodd road heading southwest through Morristown and into LeSueur county. The Faribault men, however, were right behind them. Five miles from Shieldsville the pursuers spotted their quarry ascending a hill near a ravine.[20]

The Faribault party, led by S.T. Seamans, J. McCann, and two Leo brothers, opened fire on the outlaws who wheeled their horses into the ravine and returned fire. Pitts was thrown from his horse and dragged a short distance when the animal stumbled and fell. He climbed back on his horse, but the saddle girth broke, and was again heaved to the ground. Leaving the horse, which had been taken in Dundas, he stumbled into the woods and jumped up behind Bob Younger on his mount.

A Northfield newspaper mistakenly thought Pitts had been shot, but it was only a case of a stumbling horse: "Latest.— 4:00 p.m. Frank Wyman, Kennedy, and Bush returned. They confirm the report of a robber wounded near Shieldsville last night. The main force are still pursuing. The horse stolen from Phil Empey at Dundas has been recovered."[21]

As the robbers retreated into the Big Woods, another small posse, led by two men named Buckham and Harn, came across from the Warsaw road, joined the other group and went in pursuit of the Missouri men. By then, a torrential downpour began, a hard rain which would last on and off for the next two weeks. The robbers turned right toward Cordova, followed the road a short way, then took a sharp right back into the woods.

The posse did not see their elusive move and continued on to where the road forked. Here they divided their force and scoured both roads. Once the posse had passed them by, the outlaws made their way back to the Dodd road. Tearing down fences, they moved slowly through the fields in a southeasterly direction until about dusk when they reached the farmhouse of Seth H. Kenney.

On the road by the farmhouse, they met a rider named Levi Sager, to whom they professed to be members of a posse trailing the men who had robbed the bank at Northfield. Sager related another posse had just passed down the road looking for the same outlaws. The men told Sager they must overtake the other party and ordered the farmer to give them his horse by virtue of their official authority. They also asked Sager to accompany them and show them the road to Waterville.

One of the robbers climbed aboard Sager's horse, but quickly dismounted in learning the mount was not used to the spur. Sager then rode along with them for a quarter mile and was allowed to go home after showing them the desired route. This was about seven o'clock in the evening. About three-quarters of an hour earlier, a trio of men, known only as Crocker, Pearce, and Jackson, passed over the Kilkenny road to Cordova, gave the alarm, and the roads were picketed. Meanwhile, a party led by Donald Grant, moving directly from Faribault to Waterville, had all the roads in the vicinity guarded by nine o'clock.

Back on the Dodd road, which, ironically, was named for a Union general, the outlaws approached the township of Kilkenny. Taking a dirt road, they followed it over a railroad crossing one-half mile south of town; a road that to this day is called Younger Crossing. Near here, they stopped at the farm of Daniel and Jane Walsh. The men asked Walsh if they could spend the night in his barn. The farmer remarked he had never seen such beautiful big black horses and in such good shape.[22]

The outlaws had passed through Kilkenny on their way to Minnesota and had remembered talking with Daniel Walsh and his neighbor, Patrick Shortall. Walsh and Shortall had moved to Kilkenny in 1855, leaving Ireland after a third potato famine. The gang spent the night in Walsh's barn, conveniently situated next to Calvary Cemetery. They paid him the following morning for their lodging.

Another account insisted that the men spent that same Thursday evening at the home of a Lord Brown in Kilkenny. Following the outlaw's stay in the township, a rumor began circulating that Ed Brown, son of Lord Brown, was one of the outlaws who had robbed the bank in Northfield. This allegation eventually fizzled when no proof could be found.[23]

Other rumors poured out of Kilkenny. Among them was a sighting of Jesse James and "the Langer boys" walking briefly into Dyne's Saloon, before making a hasty retreat in the direction of Mankato and Madelia.[24]

Friday morning the outlaws left Kilkenny and headed southwest toward Waterville and Elysian. En route they rode up a very steep wooded hill known locally as "the Klondike" and hid in a cave. While they slowly made their way up the hill, a posse appeared below and surrounded the Klondike. Members of the posse were certain they had the gang this time because it was next to impossible to descend the hill with horses. Instead of scaling the hill, the posse members merely waited. When the outlaws did not show themselves, the law members started up the hill. They were shocked to learn the outlaws had, in fact, slipped down the hill under cover of darkness and were by then miles away.[25]

According to one Waterville resident, the robbers stopped to water their horses at a farm near the Cannon River. Some neighbors were discussing the robbery while cutting wood when the riders rode up. One of the woodcutters sputtered, "I would sure like to get a look at them there fellers." One of the outlaws snapped, "Take a good look. You are looking at them now."[26]

One-half mile north of a lake west of Waterville, the robbers crossed the Cannon River where it was most fordable. Lawmen, led by Major A.B. Rogers, were guarding the ford above, and were positioned so near, they could hear the outlaws talking. Despite their position, which was quite advantageous since the robbers were unaware of their presence, the posse was reluctant to attack.

Word that the outlaws had broken through the picket line soon spread, and a new picket line was formed well in advance of the fugitives. With telegraph wires flashing every bit of available information and trains bringing in more posse members, the pursuit became more concentrated.[27]

With the manhunt growing by the hour and picket lines formed that had the gang surrounded, Minnesotans were certain the fugitives could not get away: "The Northfield robbers crossed at the west end of Waterville Lake at two o'clock this afternoon going south towards Okaman," reported a dispatch from Janesville. "They have been seen four times today, but the citizens could not get enough together to take them. They have them cornered, and will have them by morning, they think."[28]

Just outside Waterville, two men presumed to be Frank and Jesse James, leading a third mount, rode up to the farm of George James. Mrs. James approached the two men and was asked if she had seen two black mules and if there was a swamp ahead where the animals might be bogged down in mud. Mrs. James answered in the affirmative, the men thanked her and rode off in the direction of the marsh.[29]

On Saturday afternoon, the men stopped at a farmhouse and appropriated some fresh baked goods. A local newspaper reported: "All the roads through the woods are guarded night and day. Sunday the Winona & Sioux City roads run extra trains to assist in the chase. The robbers were in the woods in Waseca county between Janesville and St. Peter, during Sunday, and with such a force of men in pursuit that it seems impossible for them to escape their just desserts, yet the later reports indicate them as having eluded the pursuers."[30]

Another account was published in a Twin City newspaper: "The last trace of them was found in a field near Waterville, where their tracks were discovered in a meadow. Here they doubled their tracks, and the scent was lost in the Big Woods. Many have an idea that they got away during the night and pressed on to the Minnesota River. Their horses were good for it, probably, except the one that carried double. The general impression is that they did not know the road; that the wounded man could not hold out, and that they are concealed in the Big Woods. Every bridge and road was guarded through the night, and if faithfully done, they could not have passed."[31]

The heavy rain continued, and the swelling Cannon River was at near-dangerous levels. On the Cordova Road, the band of outlaws discovered some workers, mostly German, huddling in a shelter from the rain. One of the outlaws asked the men if they knew how they could get back across the river. They said they wanted directions to St. Peter, because they were looking for the robbers of the Northfield bank. One of the workers replied there was a bridge not too far down the road.

As the robbers sighted the bridge, they also saw the remnants of a posse led by Captain Rogers. Rogers and his men had ridden down the west side of the Cannon River, fourteen miles north of the bridge in two small parties. Passing the bridge, the fugitives rode instead around Tetonka Lake, and in reaching the opposite shore, came face-to-face with the entire Rogers posse. A shoot-out erupted and the outlaws dashed their mounts into the lake. Making it safely across Tetonka, one of the fleeing outlaws shouted, "Let us go into the woods." They rode swiftly into the underbrush and lost their pursuers.[32]

Briefly abandoning the labyrinth of lakes and dismal swamps, the robbers rode through cornfields. At the edge of Elysian township, the men came across two boys plowing a field with a team of horses. Quickly purloining the team, the robbers forced Wilhelm Rosenan (or Rosenau), one of the two boys, to guide them through the woods. Reaching the Elysian road about four p.m., the men freed the boy, giving him a horse that was disabled. The robbers continued south.[33]

Captain Rogers telegraphed the following report: "At last reports they [the robbers] are surrounded near the west end of our lake [Sovencek]. I have sent a man to Cordova to notify Hoy's party, and my clerk to Janesville, to telegraph to Waseca, Eagle Lake, Mankato, and St. Peter. This I get from an eye witness: The six staid [sic] at Lord Brown's last night in section 33, town 100, range 23."[34]

Three hours later, the riders stopped at another out-of-the-way pasture and ordered two boys to unhitch their team of plow horses and guide the men back to the main road. The robbers' tired horses were left at a farm near Waterville, where two of the outlaws who were not badly wounded, bought themselves a meal.[35]

Another dispatch was relayed from Captain Rogers at 7:15: "Emery is just in from the German church on the Cleveland road through Elysian township. He says the robbers have taken the road due west. Brissette of St. Paul and fifty men are in sight of and after them. Two are known to be wounded and another apparently wounded. George James shot at these men as they crossed the river at noon and thinks his man is wounded. Baxter and his crowd are with Brissette."[36]

That evening, the rainstorm grew worse with a wind coming in from the northeast. The rain did not let up through the night, and the showers continued until midway through Monday. The rain helped, not hindered, the robbers flight by obliterating their tracks. Although they were surrounded by 200 men, many of these were disgusted with their soaked condition and abandoned their picket posts, leaving roads and bridges unguarded. A party under the leadership of Officer Brissette of St. Paul tracked the robbers to a point south of German Lake but then lost them.[37]

But special telegrams continued to be wired to the *St. Paul Dispatch*: "Brissette and Baxter with about fifty men have followed the robbers to Lake Elysian, where they have them corralled. It is thought here that every one of the gang will be shot or captured before night."[38]

But the boys were not corralled, shot or captured. Another telegram followed with more frantic news: "A messenger just arrived, reports the robbers seen this morning a few miles northwest of Elysian, near German Lake. Reinforcements are now starting from here."[39]

The robbers spent that night on an island in a marshy area. Under cover of darkness, they abandoned their horses and continued their flight on foot. At daylight, they reached the town of Marysburg, and in fear of being seen, made a circle around the town, walked another four miles south and camped. Nine miles west of their camp, they walked up to a deserted farmhouse two or three miles from Mankato. The farmhouse, situated in a deserted forest, constituted a perfect hideout and they remained two days and nights.[40]

On September 12, some Faribault men—a Dr. Hurd, C.D. Harn, James Scott, Benjamin Roberts, Will Wilson, John S. McCarthy, and an unidentified posse member—brought two of the robbers' horses into that city. They had found the horses about five miles northwest of Lake Elysian, between two and three miles from German Lake. The two mounts had been tied to a tree. One broke when the posse arrived, only to be overtaken on the road. The other was still tied to the tree, and both mounts, nearly starved, had stripped the tree of its bark as high as they could reach. Neither horse was bridled and five saddles were also found.[41]

In the five days since the robbery, the outlaws had covered a distance of less than fifty miles. Even so, they had out-distanced their pursuers, who, on Tuesday morning found their half-starved horses and deserted camp of the previous Saturday. Many of the posse members saw the hopelessness of the situation. They abandoned the chase and went home.

But others pumped new life into the not-altogether-hopeless situation. A detective, L.M. Hazen of Cincinnati, arrived in St. Paul. Hazen was certain that the Northfield robbers were the same personnel who had robbed the Adams and United States Express safe on the Kansas Pacific Railroad on July 4, fourteen miles east of Sedalia, Missouri. Hazen said the men appeared to be the same because they all were mounted, heavily armed, and their first order to the frightened passengers was to "Throw up your hands."[42]

Hazen was able to identify most of the robbers correctly. His biggest headache was over one of the two men killed in the streets of Northfield. A relative of the deceased man journeyed to Northfield from Cannon Falls to view the body of his brother-in-law, Bill Yates. The relative said he could prove Yates' identity from a bullet scar under his left arm. The scar was found, just as the man said, but at this point, he suddenly refused to identify the corpse.[43]

Bill Yates, it was learned, was a former resident of Minneapolis and still had a brother-in-law living there. A desperate, bad man, Yates had left Minneapolis some time ago and gone to Texas. His sister had received a letter from him only days before the Northfield raid stating he now had lucrative employment and if she needed money he would send her some. He also said he would be up to Minnesota soon and would call on her.

But in the confusion, the *Dispatch* also stated that the dead man could be Stiles instead of Yates, or possibly Chadwell, or even Chadwick. But it was also stated that Yates or Stiles or Chadwell or Chadwick was also known as Raymond. If he was, in fact, one man, he used many aliases. But could one man pull off so many fake names and get away with it?

Hazen was not the only fuel to be added to the fire. A special train left St. Paul on the St. Paul and Sioux City Railroad carrying not only Detective Hazen and twenty-five to thirty well-armed men, but Chief of Police King as well. The train was in communication with the large posse at Janesville, and it would go to a point designated by them—probably stopping at St. Peter and scouting southward toward Lake Elysian or go directly to Janesville by way of Kasota Junction.

Chief of Police King's participation was to bring to the attention of local officers the importance of watching closely all approaches to the Minnesota River. It was also brought to their intention to watch the rail line of the Milwaukee & St. Paul Road; the Winona & St. Peter Road was already being picketed. The Winona & St. Peter had even offered a reward of $700 for the capture of the outlaw gang, to be added to the $1,500 already offered by Minnesota Governor John S. Pillsbury. The First

National Bank of Northfield promised a reward of $500 per out-
law, while the Adams Express Company declared a reward of
$1,000 per man.[44]

Law officials were becoming convinced that the capture
of the robbers was at hand. One Iowa sheriff, John McDonald,
took the train to Mankato with every intention of joining the
chase, but unhappy over the way things were being handled,
quickly returned to his native state. An Iowa newspaper reported: "After seeing how inefficiently the companies are organized
that are out on the hunt, and ascertaining for himself the exact
situation of affairs, he concluded he did not care to attach himself to the mob and so came back to organize a company of his
own and start out in a direction in which he believes he will run
across the brigands on their travel south."[45]

One Faribault man recalled being bitten by the robber-
hunt fever, and like most everyone else, felt it was his duty to
pursue the bandits: "A group of forty-seven started for Mankato
to join in the robber hunt. From there of course most every man
who was not a coward and could go had already been out since
the time it happened and had succeeded in harassing the robbers
and keeping them out in the cold rain."[46]

Although safe in the deserted farmhouse, the robbers
were well aware a picket line had been thrown around the entire
area.[47] Their presence in the vicinity was no secret as evidenced
by an Owatonna newspaper: "Yesterday, a dispatch went over the
line, signed by the mayor of Mankato, to the effect that the robbers had been seen one half mile north of Mankato Junction.
There were six of them and they all had bridles and rubber
coats."[48]

But the posse members could not pinpoint the location
of the robbers even though they believed them still to be in the
area. One Mankato resident recalled: "News at that time traveled slowly. No telephone, very few newspapers, so most of our
information was spread by word of mouth, from house to house,
etc. It was the wettest fall we ever experienced. All streams were
swollen, bridges were out, the entire country was a quagmire."[49]

Confusion was the result, and the militia suspected anyone on a horse. A local newspaper carried the following report:
"Yesterday at noon, two men were arrested at St. Peter on suspicion. It is now thought here that they are confederates of the robbers. They are mounted on gray and bay horses, small sized and
good animals."[50]

While the two men were eventually released, everyone in
the Mankato area was on guard that Jesse James and the
Youngers might be coming. "People were scared to death," said
one man who was there at the time. "They were afraid to leave

homes during the day, and equally afraid to stay at home during the night. Reports of all sorts were afloat."[51]

On September 13, about 6:00 A.M., the very real robbers walked up to the Henry Shabut farm. The men demanded provisions and issued dire threats if the requisition was not honored or if any word of their presence was divulged. The frightened farmhand gave them the food, but his plight was far from over.[52]

Another account said the farmhand, Jefferson Dunning, was out in the field with Shabut's cows. Six men, who said they were in pursuit of the robbers, accosted him. Within minutes, the men overpowered him and tied his arms.[53] Still another reported that Dunning had just come in with the cows and was grabbed at the back of the farm by the robbers. They all were wearing rubber coats, carrying blankets and bridles.[54]

Dunning later recalled that the men told him they were hunting for the robbers and suspected him of being one of them. They insisted he come with them. They tied his hands behind his back with a bridle and forced him to show them the way to Mankato along the Bluff Road. After walking close to a mile, the men told him they were the robbers and said they needed to get across the Minnesota River behind Mankato.

The frightened farmhand was asked if he thought the men could swim across the river. They asked several questions, then told him they would not have murdered Heywood if he had opened the safe, and during their next bank job, the cashier would open the safe.

As they neared Mankato, the robbers debated whether to kill their prisoner or let him go; knowing, of course, that Dunning could spread the word and bring a posse directly to them. After a long meeting, the bandits decided to set him free with assurances he would be killed if he told anyone. The prisoner swore he would not tell of seeing them or reveal where they were headed. They told Dunning he seemed to be a good man, and asked for his mailing address, so they could send him a present.[55]

The men sat down and watched Dunning until he passed out of sight. Dunning did not go home as promised but instead he rushed into Mankato and told his story to the sheriff. A posse was quickly raised and set out after the robbers, while more volunteers remained in the city to await further orders from the sheriff. The men were told by Dunning that one of the outlaws wore one of his arms in a sling, and that another called "captain" (Cole Younger), was about five-foot-six and wore a rubber overcoat with a blanket wrapped as a bundle. The big man, said Dunning, was very conspicuous with a beard grown all over his face. He said the man was Clell Miller, whom he confused with Charlie Pitts. This big man never spoke a word.

Cole Younger later recalled the incident: "In the vicinity of Mankato, between daylight and sunrise, we met a man whose name I forget. We compelled him to go with us for about a mile, and then, realizing the risk we took but not knowing what else to do with him, we turned him loose. We learned from this man, for the first time, that there had been one man [Nicholaus Gustavson] killed and two wounded at Northfield."[56]

From what Dunning had told him regarding the murdered Swede, Cole believed he and his brother Jim were innocent since they were both in front of the bank and the only shots they had fired went north over Bridge Square. Cole told Dunning he thought the fatal shot had been fired by a citizen who had aimed poorly, hoping to hit the outlaws.

Later, Dunning told Captain A. Barton at Faribault that Bob and Cole had saved his life. While the discussion continued as to what to do with Dunning, one of the outlaws proposed to shoot him. Cole intervened by saying, "No, we will not kill him." The man who wanted to kill him said he would leave the prisoner's fate up to Bob Younger. Taking Dunning to where Bob and Jim were sitting, the outlaw with an itchy trigger finger asked Bob what to do with him, stressing that if he were sent free, the whole country would be after them in twelve hours. With Bob's serious injury, there would be little hope of escape.

"I would rather be shot dead than to have that man killed for fear his telling might put a few hundred after us: there will be time enough for shooting if he should join in the pursuit," Bob snapped.

That same evening, following the release of Dunning, Mrs. Lyman Matthews, who knew Dunning, was awakened by a commotion among her chickens. Looking out her window, she saw several men chasing her chickens, and after catching all the birds they needed, they went into her melon patch and helped themselves again. She wisely offered no objection.[57]

While sauntering down the road, the outlaws were spotted by Sheriff Davis of Faribault County, who, with a companion, was on the same road heading into Mankato from Good Thunder. The men, Davis discovered, were in a clearing high on a bluff, away from the road on the opposite side of Indian Lake, where the lake was quite narrow. The men were only about eighty yards from the two lawmen whose suspicions were immediately aroused.[58]

Dismounting their horses, Davis and his friend concealed themselves in the bushes across the lake. According to a newspaper report, "they first saw four men and could hear them talk. They said something about horses. Davis slid into the bushes and saw five men facing him. They were well dressed; one, the very large one, had a white, stiff-brimmed hat, one a cap, and the others slouch hats. The man with the sheriff saw a sixth man in advance of the others."[59]

On their way once more, the fugitives came to the county bridge over the Blue Earth River, which they found well-guarded. About a quarter-mile beyond, however, they crossed the river on a railroad bridge and easily made their way in the darkness around the city of Mankato. But they had been seen crossing the river. The was alarm given and all available men in Mankato mustered. The pursuers, however, had to wait for daylight.[60]

The first party to take after the gang was led by Mayor Ames of Northfield, Detective Mike Hoy, and two other Minneapolis policemen. It did not take them long to locate the robbers that morning, when at about 6:00 a.m., they smelled smoke emanating from a dense wood near Minneopa Falls. Investigating at once, the men climbed down from their mounts. As they pushed through the heavy underbrush, they heard men scurrying up the other side of the ravine, although they could not see them through the bushes.

Meanwhile, a party of fourteen or fifteen men from Lake Crystal had come down on the early morning train and jumped off a mile or so west of Minneopa and had trudged through the thicket toward the falls, just as the Ames/Hoy party was on its way from Mankato. John Riley, one of the Lake Crystal party, later recalled: "The robbers were alarmed as they were getting their breakfast and left their camp, part of a roast chicken, some green corn, a hat, and a rubber overcoat."[61]

Another report reached St. Paul: "The very latest reports state that the Missouri and Kansas bandits are in the woods near Mankato. Hundreds of men are in hot pursuit and there is a fair prospect of the villains being captured."[62]

The robbers came out of the woods on the north bank of Bush Lake, but only after holding an important discussion. With Dunning probably spilling his story over the countryside, and with Bob and Jim still seriously wounded, although on the mend, the Jameses had decided it was best to split company. Not only would the two riders have a better chance of escape, but their flight would be heavily pursued, giving the other, more seriously wounded faction, a brief respite. Charlie Pitts and the Youngers agreed to remain behind.[63]

Leaving the others, Jesse and Frank stole a horse at the Benson farm and rode toward Loon Lake. A picket line had been organized between Lake Crystal and the Minnesota River, extending east of the Blue Earth River as well. A double guard had been posted on the road at Loon Lake but the boys passed undetected at the initial post. Reaching the second at a creek crossing, they found several guards asleep in a bed of straw. One of the guards near the H.C. Howard farm, home of Minnesota's first dairy commissioner, was not asleep. Just after midnight he saw two men approaching, riding double on a single gray mare.[64]

The guard fired his rifle into the darkness, and the horse halted, throwing the two riders onto the muddy road. Not able to catch their horse, the two men ran on foot into Mrs. Rooney's cornfield, southwest by the Cookson farm, and escaped their pursuers. In the early morning, these same guards trailed them to the Elrid Rockwood farm near Garden City. The robbers had forced Rockwood at gun point to turn over his fine team of draft horses, (which only a few days before had taken first prize at the Garden City Fair), cut up a harness for bridles and reins, and had long since departed into Watonwan County.[65]

The Younger boys and Charlie Pitts heard the gunshot fired at Loon Lake and turned back to Minneopa Creek (also called Lion's Creek), according to one source, and went into cover at a Welsh settlement for the next few days. The majority of the pursuers, as planned by the gang, had followed the trail of Jesse and Frank, giving the Youngers a little freer movement. The boys followed the Norwegian Road to the town of Butternut Valley, then continuing on to an empty log house, and from there to Matson Lake or Strom Lake. Whenever they met people on the road, they claimed to be hunters.[66]

Rumors as to the gang's whereabouts continued to spread throughout southern Minnesota. Several stories circulated that when the robbers left Mankato, they headed to New Ulm, where posses were searching southeast of town.[67] Just west of Mankato, as one account suggests, the robbers came upon a bridge over a river they needed to cross. But afraid that the bridge was in some way guarded, one of the outlaws threw a stone on it from the underbrush, thinking he might arouse any posse members waiting in ambush. There was no response and the men passed over the stream unseen.[68]

Charles Brust of New Ulm recalled the James boys stopping there: "After crossing the stream, they got as far as Judson, where the James boys stole a horse, and went back over the route, which Cole Younger and Pitts had laid out, before the Northfield bank robbery. Both times, coming and going, the James boys stopped off in New Ulm. They had a map of the route, and got back to Missouri without trouble."[69]

August Thiede, who lived outside New Ulm in Brighton township, also remembered the boys coming to the area and insisted that Jesse James slept at his farmhouse following the robbery. The Thiedes did not fall asleep that night as the outlaw continually watched them, forcing them to remain at home so the authorities could not be alerted. In the morning, they procured horses at the Fred Wellner farm several miles closer to New Ulm.[70]

Another account placed the boys in Freeborn County, which they had passed through on their way to Northfield. W.A. Spicer, who spent sixty-nine of his eighty-six years on Seventh-Day Adventist missions, recalled being visited by the robbers about this same time: "I have not forgotten the time when the

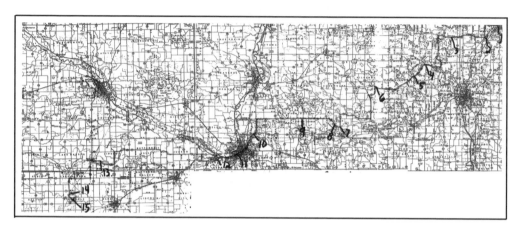

Jesse James' escape route from the Northfield Raid: (1) Northfield; (2) Dundas; (3) Millersburg; (4) Shieldsville; (5) Thursday Night Camp, September 7; (6) Killkenny; (7) Elysian; (8) Klondike Hill, Friday Night, September 8—left horses here; (9) Marysburg, Sunday Morning, September 10; (10) Dunning Capture; (11) Mankato; (12) Minneopa Falls, James boys depart; (13) Lake Linden, Sorbel Farms; (14) LaSalle; (15) Capture Site. (Courtesy Rex Macbeth)

men who came with the threshing outfit, and who lived upstairs in the old log-house, left us a rather exciting memory. It turned out they were the Younger Brothers [with Bob Cole] rather famous highwayman of those days. They had robbed a bank further north [Northfield, it seems to me] and in getting away had turned into threshers, renting the outfit and traveling among the farmers to thresh the new crop. Afterwards we understood how one of them was sick and they kept the lamp burning all night. Cole had lost one finger—shot off we learned later. Well, they did the threshing, and Mother fed them well."[71]

While most of the posses followed the trail of the two escaping James boys toward the South Dakota border, Hoy and his party continued searching along the tracks of the Sioux City Railroad near Linden. About daylight, they stumbled upon a light blue smoke rising out of the brush about ten rods from the tracks. Rather than encircle the robbers and send a man for additional help, Hoy's men dashed blindly into the woods, driving the fleeing bandits up a bluff known as Pigeon Hill.[72]

When Hoy's men attempted a pursuit, they found the outlaws had escaped once again through the dense underbrush. Returning to the outlaw camp, Hoy found some green corn and some nicely prepared chickens, which had been stolen nearby. In addition to the robbers' uneaten breakfast, the posse found two bridles, a linen duster, a handkerchief covered with blood stains, and parts of a bloody shirt. The men knew at once that at least one of the robbers was wounded. Lost and turning in circles, the fleeing bandits pushed on through the thick swampland seven miles north of Madelia.

A young man recalled the hysteria that spread through the Madelia area as circulating reports placed the robbers in the vicinity: "I was an orphan boy of nine years, living with relatives on a farm, three miles east of the town of Madelia. The news of the raid on the Bank at Northfield, the killing of the cashier, and the escape of the gang quickly spread, and I can remember vividly how terrified my sister, four years older, and I were because at the time we were alone on the farm and knew the robbers were being hunted. At night we huddled together in a big chair, fearing at every noise (once the prop under a window fell down) that the wicked men were at the door seeking shelter and meaning harm to us children."[73]

Meanwhile, Thomas L. Vought, owner of the Flanders Hotel in Madelia began putting two and two together. He recalled the two men who had stopped at his hotel a couple weeks earlier and said they were cattle buyers. They had certainly asked more than their share of questions about the lay of the land. With a friend, Vought started off for the country north and west of Madelia.[74]

The two men went to a growth of trees near a bridge that Vought remembered telling the "cattle buyers" about. Vought was sure the strangers would come out of the woods at the bridge, and he and his companion concealed themselves in the underbrush to await the passing of the fugitives. While concealed in the bushes, the two men were discovered by a young man of "about sixteen" who was herding cattle. The inquisitive boy, Asle Oscar Sorbel, refused to leave until they told him why they were in hiding and for whom they were waiting. When told they were waiting for the Northfield bank robbers, the boy's curiosity was satisfied and he left.

Oscar Sorbel. (Courtesy of the Brown County Historical Society)

The following morning, the outlaws were walking down a road along Lake Linden in Brown County. Passing a farm, they nodded at a boy milking cows. The boy was this same Asle Oscar Sorbel. Recalled Sorbel: "It was the 21st of September, just two weeks after the Raid. Mind you, it had been a steady drizzling rain for two weeks and it was early morning. The sun was up about twenty minutes. We had the cattle in the road as it was too muddy in the pen. Jim Younger and Charley [sic] Pitts came walking and they walked one on each side of pa. He was milking. I had come up to the gate, and as they were far enough so they did not hear me, I said to Pa, 'That was the robbers.' 'No,' he said, 'they was nice men.'"[75]

Oscar's father, Ole, was impressed by the way the two men had given him a friendly "Good morning," the pair all the while stroking the back of one of the cows in the road. When the strangers passed out of sight, young Sorbel stepped into the mud in the road and examined their toe prints. He found their boots to be very worn.[76]

"I walked over to the road, and their big toes showed in the mud," continued Sorbel. "I said, 'Come here. I will show you how nice men they are.' He said, 'You never mind. Go and milk.' I milked one cow, and then I set the pail inside the fence and started after them. There was a bend in the road and timber, so I did not see them, but they crossed the creek about eighty rods west. I could see where they had gone into the timber. I went to three neighbors and told them."[77]

The three neighbors to whom Sorbel spread the alarm were Anton Owen, Mads Owen, and Gutterson Grove. At the latter farm, he climbed onto the roof of the house and surveyed the road hoping to see the robbers. Unable to find them, he ran up a hill east of the Grove farm and studied the three roads to New Ulm, Madelia, and Lockstock but again could not locate the robbers. Returning to the Anton Owen farm, he instructed Anton Anderson, Jens Nilsson, and Armund Brustingen to run up the hill and watch the roads. Sorbel said he was going to ride to Madelia for help.[78]

While young Oscar was following the outlaw trail, a second pair of robbers returned to the Sorbel farm and turned in at the old log house where Guri Sorbel was busy preparing breakfast for her family. Immediately, she noticed one of the men was limping and leaning on his pal. In greeting her, they asked if they could buy some food, telling her they had baked some bread the day before but it had soured on them. One of the men put down some money from a roll of bills.[79]

The men informed Mrs. Sorbel that they were hunters and were very hungry. They asked for breakfast and were told the meal wasn't ready but they were welcome to wait while she cooked it. The two men said they could not wait. Taking some bread and butter, they thanked her and disappeared into the timber.[80]

When Oscar reached home and was told two more men had stopped, he instructed his sister to go tell the neighbors they were looking for four men rather than two. She was then to go to the big hill and watch the road with the others. Oscar mounted a horse and dashed seven miles into Madelia to report the news.[81]

On the way, he kept to the timber side of the lake so the robbers could not see him. "About two miles from Madelia, my horse fell flat in the mud, and I, too," remembered Sorbel. "Well, I jumped on again, and when I got to Madelia, I was all mud from head to foot. The first man I met did not believe me and asked who knew me. I told them I knew John Owen, and they went after him, and he said he would stand good for that I spoke the truth."[82]

100

Galloping down the street, he headed straight to the Flanders Hotel and Colonel Vought, who had first told him of the robbers' presence in the area. Vought ran to Sheriff James Glispin, and a posse of seven men was formed consisting of Glispin, Vought, Captain W.W. Murphy, George Bradford, Charles Pomeroy, Jr, Benjamin Rice, and Ole Severson. Word spread quickly throughout the county, and soon scores of other men were grabbing guns and horses and joining the chase.[83]

Meanwhile, the robbers had started southwest from the area of the Sorbel farm looking for horses. It was rumored that on the way to Northfield, they had visited the Doolittle horse ranch outside Madelia, and it was a good bet the boys remembered the ranch and were trying to get back there. But the Doolittles remembered, too, and had taken their fine horses northwest toward Comfrey.[84]

The robbers stopped first at the farm of a man named Anderson. The farmer, who was aware of the robbers' quest for horses in the area, quickly turned his mounts loose in seeing the men approach. The robbers then met two mounted hunters from the Twin Cities, but the men, very suspicious, fled on horseback.[85]

But the posses were closing in. Sorbel's group of farmers back near the farm were still watching from the hill. "When the boys got on the hill, the robbers were half a mile southeast heading for St. James," recalled Suborn. "The boys sent [a] man on horseback, telling us where to go. One of the [outlaw] boys went ahead on horseback to three threshing machines and had them unhitch their horses and strike for the prairie.[86]

From three-quarters of a mile away, Sorbel's neighbors could see the robbers riding stolen horses from the threshers towards the prairie. Said Sorbel later: "They had three horses on the prairie, but their hobbles were locked, and so they could not get them off for about four miles. North of town we met Einor Smisma, who told us to go west, as the robbers were heading southwest and after that, we met several men who told us where to go. So we got to the timber about seven miles from St. James, just as the robbers got there."[87]

Sheriff Glispin's party of seven rode toward the site given him by Sorbel, after leaving orders to his subordinates to form a large posse and follow him. Stores were boarded up and most males rode out after him. A few miles from Madelia, Glispin met a rider who told him the robbers had been spotted to the southwest about four miles. Glispin and his men galloped in the direction of the bandits and, only one hour after getting the news from Sorbel, overtook the fugitives as they crossed a slough south of Lake Hanska.[88]

"My oldest brother was driving Horace Thompson, then president of the First National Bank of St. Paul, his wife, and niece, who were vacationing and hunting," recalled T.L. Vought.

"They were on the prairie, while the robbers were down on the Watonwan River bottoms in a thicket of willows and plum brush, and it is presumed the robbers thought they would get out and get the horses and try to escape if possible."[89]

Other accounts stated that Thompson and his sons were hunting prairie chickens when they came upon some robbers. The outlaws planned to steal their horses from a wagon, but in confusing Thompson's shotgun for a rifle, they disappeared into the thicket, thinking they were part of the posse.[90]

Meanwhile, a posse organized by "Cap" Murphy was heading in the direction of Glispin's confrontation with the strangers. En route, they met Mrs. Valentine Schaleben and a neighbor lady who were driving to Madelia and warned them the bandits were nearby and would try and get their horses. Murphy and company caught up to the Youngers at a point on the north branch of the river where they had concealed themselves in the underbrush. The posse divided into small groups in pursuit of the trapped bandits.[91]

The horsemen in both Glispin and Murphy's parties found the swollen slough impassable by horseback. After seeing the bandits run to the river and disappear, Glispin was joined by four armed farmers, and the tiny group divided itself and rode the perimeters of the slough. As Glispin's men found their way on horseback past the slough, the Youngers and Pitts ran two miles to the south, about three quarters of a mile from the river. When Glispin and his men were within a hundred yards of the robbers, one of the fugitives bellowed, "What do you want?" Glispin answered, "Throw up your hands and surrender."[92]

As the robbers resumed their foot race, Glispin opened fire. The bandits fired back while in retreat, but their aim forced Glispin and his men to dismount and take cover in the under-brush. Just as the robbers disappeared into the brush, Cap Murphy's posse arrived from Madelia, and Glispin quickly had all the men dismount and form a skirmish line. Moving forward, the posse reached the river just as the robbers were scurrying up the bank on the opposite side.

Trapped in the thicket, wounded and wet, and with no chance for escape, Charlie Pitts saw the hopeless reality of their situation. Turning to Cole, he said, "We are entirely surrounded. We had better surrender." With a firm white face, Cole looked his friend in the eyes and replied, "Charlie, this is where Cole Younger dies." The faithful Pitts answered, "All right, captain. I can die just as game as you can. Let's get it done." Cole was impressed and never forgot those words.[93]

Meanwhile, Glispen asked for volunteers and seven of the posse advanced upstream following the outlaws. George A.

The Seven Men who captured the Younger Brothers. Left to right: Sheriff James Glispin, Captain W.W. Murphy, George Bradford, Benjamin Rice, Thomas L. Vought, Charles Pomeroy, Jr., and James Severson. (Courtesy of the Wantonwan County Historical Society)

Bradford, one of the seven, was shocked in learning that not all sixteen men had answered the call. The seven were commanded not to shoot first and, if they fired, to shoot low, in hopes the robbers would surrender. Glispin walked the edge of the river with the others spread out every fifteen feet: Murphy next to Glispin, followed by Bradford, Rice, Vought, Pomeroy, and Severson.

"We were to march to the river, then wheel to the left and march slowly until we could see them," recalled George A. Bradford. "Soon after we started up the river, I became convinced that we were getting away from the river and leaned down to look under the brush and told Mr. Glispin that I thought he was getting away from the river—when something drew my attention to the front and glancing that way saw some of the men we were after and just then one of them [Pitts] jumped up and fired."[94]

Youngers' capture site as it looked in 1997. (Photo by Matt Stoesz)

103

Jim Younger, after capture, September 1876. (Courtesy of the Minnesota Historical Society)

The dead Clell Miller. (Courtesy of the Brown County Historical Society)

Dropping to one knee, Glispin fired back, hitting Charlie Pitts. As the man fell, he was riddled by bullets from the men on the skirmish line.[95]

"I had raised my gun to shoot, when a bullet struck, or rather grazed, my wrist and disturbed my aim, so it was a second or so before I fired," Bradford said. "Several shots were fired from both sides and a volley from across the river, from parties there. They could not see us from there but fired, the bullets cutting the twigs over our heads."[96]

With rapid firing continuing from both sides, two of the posse men were hit in the exchange, although their wounds were not serious. Colonel Vought doubled up from a bullet that had struck him just above the waist. Clutching his lower vest pocket, Vought was surprised to find the bullet had shattered a large rosewood pipe he carried. The bullet itself was found in his cartridge belt.[97]

The Youngers continued firing. Bob, although seriously wounded, reloaded their guns. With the sheriff's men creeping closer, the brush was cut down by their bullets, leaving the brothers open. As Cole reached for the .45 colts still in the hands of the dead Pitts, a bullet clipped the extractor from the gun. But Cole kept shooting.[98]

Things went from bad to worse for the boys. Jim fell and lay unconscious, hit in the mouth from a rifle ball that knocked out all his teeth on the left side. In a matter of seconds, Cole took a bullet in the head that lodged above his right eye and rendered him unconscious as well. Then came a haunting lull in the fighting, and Bob could not resist his captors.

Bob yelled, "I surrender, they're all down but me."

Sheriff Glispin immediately ordered his men to cease firing. As Bob stepped forward, Captain Murphy ordered him to put up both hands but the outlaw insisted his one arm was broken and he could not lift it.[99]

Markers near younger capture site. (Photo by Matt Stoesz)

George A. Bradford recalled that Bob Younger walked slowly forward from the thicket holding high a white handkerchief in his left hand: "The ground along the river was quite undulating and the robbers had been in a low settle. Bob came up on to the higher ground when told to come to us, and a man shot from across the river striking Bob under the arm cutting the flesh. He stopped, and, when told to come on, he said he had been shot from across the river. Murphy then called to them to cease firing as the men had surrendered. As Bob had said, the rest were all down, but Cole first got up and then Jim."[100]

Bob was shocked that someone had shot him while he was surrendering, especially since Glispin and the others had promised him protection. Glispin, also in shock over one of his men disobeying orders, then shouted he would shoot the first man who harmed any of the prisoners. Slowly advancing toward the wounded outlaws, the posse men helped Bob to his feet.

A.O. Sorbel remembered how badly the Younger boys had been shot up: "Cole Younger had one bullet and some buckshot received at Northfield, besides ten fresh buckshot in his body, but he did not pray. He offered to fight two of our best men at once. He said he had been dogged for two weeks in the rain, with nothing to eat, but that he could lick two of our best men. Bob slung his left arm around him and said, 'Come, or we will be hanged.' But Cole said he did not care, and that he would just as soon hang today as tomorrow."[101]

As the badly wounded Youngers were helped out of Hanska Slough, they watched as the body of Charlie Pitts was being carried toward a waiting wagon. Bob Younger asked for a chew of tobacco and some of the posse men said he should not be given any. But young Sorbel was there: "I went over to Oke Wisty and got a ten-cent plug and handed it to Bob, who took about half of it in one chew, and was going to hand it back. But I told him to keep it."[102]

Two days later, Sorbel met the captured Youngers again and, this time, was recognized by them as being the same young man who had spread the alarm that had led to their capture. Recalled Sorbel: "Bob said, 'Why, that is the boy who gave me the tobacco.' Cole made quite a speech to me, saying I did my duty, but if they had suspected me, they would either have shot me, or taken me along."

Sorbel would later talk with them again at Stillwater Prison on two occasions, and Cole informed him that it was he and Bob who came to his father's house looking for food during their first meeting. He also confessed that during the visit to the farm, Bob had concealed his wounded arm in a sling beneath his

Cole Younger, taken after capture, September 1876. (Courtesy of the Minnesota Historical Society)

coat. Cole said he and his brother never suspected that the boy's father knew they were the robbers who were then being hunted.

The three outlaw brothers were taken up the hill. A lumber wagon pulled by a team of horses was driven into the bushes, and after Pitts' body was dumped in the bottom, the Youngers were placed on spring seats. Cole was greeted by Colonel Vought, who remembered him as the man who had registered at the Flanders Hotel under the name of J.C. King.

Vought later recalled, "He recognized me and held out his blood covered hand and shook my hand and called me landlord. Allow me to mention a little scene which made a deep impression on my mind. The bold desperadoes, horribly mangled, were under the care of seven well armed men who stood over them wearing sad faces. For a short time all was silent save the rustling of the leaves in the underbrush. The voice of Captain Murphy broke the silence, and in measured words he said, 'Boys this is horrible but you see what lawlessness has brought to you.'"[103]

Murphy had a surprise waiting for him when he returned to his own wagon. In his haste to chase down the robbers, he had failed to notice his seven-year-old son, Ralph, hiding under a blanket in the bottom of the wagon box. Murphy was shocked that his little boy, from a safe distance, had witnessed the charge of the posse under Sheriff Glispin and himself.[104]

As the slow-moving wagon carrying the Youngers began its journey to Madelia, Jim continued to bleed from his chin, at times holding his face over the side of the wagon. He had suffered five bullet wounds, his brother Cole eleven. Bob had sustained an elbow wound from Northfield and a hole in his chest from Hanska Slough. Suffering from exposure, the bandits had wrapped pieces of clothing around their feet. When Cole removed his boots, his toenails fell off.[105]

Cole Younger. Photo by Sumner Studios of Northfield. (Courtesy of the Minnesota Historical Society)

En route to town, the wagon was overtaken by the family of George Thompson. Cole remembered Mr. Thompson from a visit he and Charlie had made to his store in St. James on their way up to Northfield. Mrs. Thompson gave Jim her handkerchief to put on his chin. "I shall never forget the tender words of Mr. and Mrs. Thompson or the true, noble, womanly spirit of their nieces, three charming young ladies, who took their dainty handkerchief from their pockets and gave them for bandages for the desperados' ugly wounds," recalled Vought.[106]

Following the Thompson family, was an official escort from Madelia, which guided the outlaws into town. As the Youngers reached the streets of Madelia, the townfolk began cheering. Cole managed to get to his feet, despite eleven wounds in his body, and tipped his hat to the thronging crowd. "[Cole] may have been an outlaw," related L.M. Pomeroy, brother of Charles Pomeroy, "but many of us that day admired his nerve, for he was a man who could take it on the chin and still smile."[107]

The wagon stopped before the Flanders House, and the robbers were taken to the second floor where Cole and Jim were given beds on the east end. Bob was put in a room on the west side.

"I was placed with Bob and was with him all night," remembered George Bradford. "He was very careful what he said regarding their identity or of their movements. But I was told that Cole had told them who he and his brothers were, but would not tell the names of any of the men with them on the attack on Northfield, expect [sic] Pitts, the dead man."[108]

Cole talked openly about a man named Willis Bundy who had supposedly shot Jim in the mouth. Two posse men,

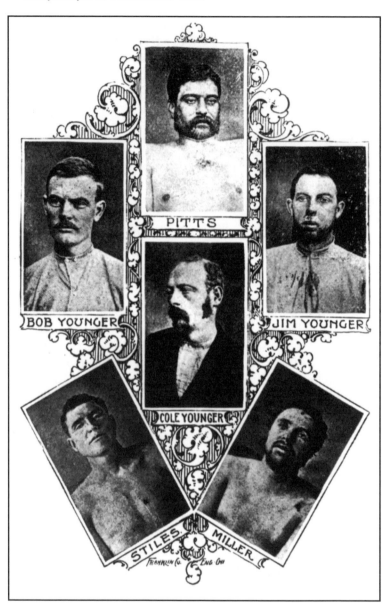

PITTS

BOB YOUNGER

JIM YOUNGER

COLE YOUNGER

STILES.

MILLER.

The six bandits killed or captured in connection with the Northfield bank robbery.

Bowne Yates and his brother George, had been posted on a steep hill overlooking the plum thicket, and when the posse advanced, it was Bowne who had in fact shot Jim.[109] But many persons swore it was Willis Bundy who had shot Bob Younger after the outlaw had surrendered with a white handkerchief.

Cole was furious even though he may have had Bundy's actions confused: "I want you to tell these people that I think your sheriff and the posse are brave men excepting one, who after we had surrendered and thrown down our guns and I was the only one standing, Willis Bundy, one of the posse shot my Brother Jim, who was lying on the ground, in the chin, a cowardly thing to do and if I live to be a free man, I will hunt that man down and kill him."[110]

At the Flanders, the outlaws' wounds were dressed, their wet garments exchanged for dry ones, and they were given what they craved most—hearty meals. Meanwhile, special trains rolled into Madelia on the St. Paul & Sioux City Railroad from Minneapolis, St. Paul, Mankato, and Sioux City. For two days there was a never-ending line of the curious going up the stairs to see the men they had heard so much about. The hired girls were too frightened to stay at the hotel all night, so Vought's mother stayed up making biscuits for the multitudes while a Mankato militia group guarded every corner, window, and door. Stories circulated that a lynching party from Northfield was on its way.[111]

"Sheriff James Glispin and Captain Murphy, in no uncertain language, said that the prisoners would not be taken unless it was over their dead bodies," remembered L.M. Pomeroy. "'These men are all badly wounded and have surrendered; no one is going to harm them while I live,' said Murphy." Cole, although weakened from loss of blood, maintained his fighting spirit when told of the lynching rumor and was quick to say, "You fellows just roll me over with my face to the door and give me back my gun and I can take care of myself for a while. You all met us in fair fight, and I do not want any of you to give up your lives for me."[112]

Judson Jones of Madelia induced Glispin to close all the saloons in the city so the mob would not get drunk. Jones then went into the jail and informed the Youngers everything was being done to protect them. Cole replied in a very dramatic voice, "Coming events sometimes cast their shadows before."[113]

When Edward Noonan heard the Youngers had been captured, he went to Madelia with his father and brothers to see the robbers. Said Noonan: "Arriving in town, my attention was attracted by quite a large gathering of people in the street directly in front of where the Farmers' State Bank is now situated. As I drew near to the gathering, I saw that Michael Fitzpatrick was the object of interest. Many of the people about him were from Northfield, Minnesota. Mike was telling the people that Cole Younger came near getting him. As evidence Mike displayed his hat, which had a hole through it resembling a hole made by a bullet."[114]

Because the following day was warm, the wet clothes of the outlaws were hung out on the clothesline to dry. Mr. Everett, a photographer, took off his coat and hung it on a line nearby. When he returned for it, he discovered his own coat, as well as those of the robbers, had been stripped of all buttons by eager souvenir hunters.[115]

Mr. Everett was assigned the task of photographing the captured desperadoes, and he had provided a chair on the hotel stoop to "shoot" them one at a time. A crowd gathered in the street hoping to get a glimpse of the robbers having their pictures taken. "After all had been taken, an officer who was minus one hand and who had decorated his linen shirt bosom with tobacco juice, seated himself in the same chair," recalled Colonel Vought. "A young lady standing up in a farm wagon raised her voice to a high key and said, 'Look, look, there is the worst looking one of them all,' and the crowd gave their approval in a hearty laugh, which greatly added to his chagrin."[116]

On September 29, a local newspaper reported the stay of the Youngers in Madelia: "The captured robbers all speak in praise of the good treatment they have received since their capture. They expected to be lynched when caught and are quite cheerful over the prospect of a civilized hanging bee. . . . Brave boys were they who fearlessly faced death and fought down the bandits near Madelia. They were worth a whole regiment of police officers and detectives such as pursued the crippled band of robbers about Mankato. Their rewards should be ample and their names should be printed in large capitals."[117]

But the rewards were not as ample as promised. Nearly one hundred applicants asked for a share of the reward money. Sorbel and the "magnificent" seven received equal cuts of state money with thirty-five others resulting in $46.25 apiece, but were awarded also $200 each of the bank's money. The other thirty-five men received ten dollars from the bank and another fifteen posse members were handed eight dollars each.[118]

A local newspaper reported: "The Madelians are now quarreling over the question of the robber bounty. Some of the brave fellows who sat on their horses near enough to scatter buckshot among the bandits are clamorous for a share of the reward, and think Glispin and his six don't deserve any more of the bounty than they."[119]

Payment of reward money took months of litigation and a reluctant court order as the men squabbled with their attorneys over collecting their shares. The attorneys set about to collect the money, but their clients called upon state officials to ignore the attorneys and send the money directly. Hans Frydenlund and Maddis Lee of Madelia, two of the captors, wrote the governor: "We do not want W.W. Johnson [one of the attorneys] to draw our share of robber bounty. He has no authority from us to do so. Let nobody draw our share less they got our own order."[120]

Another captor, George H. Overholt of Kenyon, urged the state auditor to "please send me by post office order the amount awarded me by Judge [Daniel A.] Dickinson of Mankato for my part in the capture of the Northfield robbers; send to Faribault and please write me at this place when to look for it."

The Youngers were to have been taken to Faribault on Friday, but Jim's doctors would not let him leave. His injury was not healing as expected. Glispin took the opportunity to visit Cole and asked him directly the names of the two robbers who had escaped. When asked if the James boys were involved, Cole clammed up. He did promise, however, to have a statement ready by morning. When Glispin returned the next day, he was handed a note from Cole that read, "Stay by your friends even if heaven falls."[121]

Note by Cole Younger. (Courtesy of the Minnesota Historical Society)

The trip to a jail in Faribault was challenged as evidenced by a report from a southern Minnesota newspaper: "A report passed over the wires last night saying that Gov. Pillsbury had ordered the robbers taken to St. Paul; but we are disposed to doubt the statement until it is fully confirmed. The prisoners properly belong in Rice county where the crime was committed, and as there is a better and safer jail in Faribault than in St. Paul, we can hardly see why the Gov should interpose. Unless it is absolutely necessary to prevent lynching, the State will undoubtedly allow matters to take their usual course, and Sheriff Barton will convey the noted prisoners to Faribault, so soon that they are able to stand the journey."[122]

But Jim's injury received only one additional day to heal as recalled by Colonel Vought: "The robbers were kept at my place from Thursday night until Saturday morning when they were put aboard the train and sent to Faribault. I shook hands with them and received their thanks for my kindness in their behalf, and that is the last time I ever saw them. I have been often asked if I would consider the captors safe if the Youngers were set at liberty. To this I have but one answer to make—Yes,

Warrant of Arrest, Rice County District Court. (Courtesy of the City of Faribault)

I have not a friend that would throw themselves between me and danger any quicker than would the Youngers if they had the opportunity."[123]

On Friday night, Sheriff Ara Barton and several deputies journeyed to Madelia to bring the prisoners back to Faribault. A movement in St. Paul, sent via dispatches, insisted that Sheriff Glispin, in the name of Governor Pillsbury, send the robbers to that city, but he, nonetheless, telegraphed Barton that the prisoners were at his disposal. At Mankato, Barton met two St. Paul lawmen who were also on their way to pick up the prisoners. Sheriff Barton, believing they should be tried in Rice County, asserted his power, and the pair returned to St. Paul. Picking up the prisoners, they arrived in Faribault about eleven o'clock Saturday morning with little fanfare.[124]

"When the prisoners reached Faribault, Drs. Rose and Wood were called and made an examination of their injuries, extracting such balls as they could reach and pronounced all the men in a fair way to recover," reported the *Faribault Democrat*.

"They are tough, well preserved, temperate men, of strong vitality, who will stand hard usage. They do not show any signs of suffering and express themselves grateful and satisfied with the treatment which they have received."[125]

During the afternoon, many people were in town to see a local favorite, Maggie, trot to victory in a popular horse race. But, it was a disappointing affair, when Maggie's legs went out after trotting only a half-mile. Many of these racing enthusiasts, dejected over Maggie's performance, left the track and went to visit the town's other attraction—the Younger brothers. But on Sunday, the jail was crowded with about 4,000 persons of all ages visiting the robbers. The first two days, the prisoners were permitted free use of the jail corridor, but then the three men were shackled and every precaution taken to prevent any possible escape.

That same afternoon, James McDonough, chief of the St. Louis police force, his assistant Officer Russell, and C.B. Hunn, Assistant Superintendent of the United States Express Company, dropped by to visit the prisoners with hopes of identifying them. McDonough carried photographs with him of several James/Younger gang members, and Russell had been a schoolmate for several years with some of the men. The St. Louis policemen immediately recognized Bob and Cole but they misidentified Jim as Cal Carter, a member of the gang who had been living in Texas. Carter had left Texas in August and was believed to be in on the raid.

A local newspaper was quick to pick up on the Cal Carter story: "It has been subsequently learned that the one calling himself Jim is no other than the infamous Cal Carter of Texas, if possible the vilest wretch of the party. It is not the purpose of *The Democrat* to repeat now, or at any other time, their conversation, as it is evidently little more than lies concocted to create sympathy in their behalf and surround them with a heroism to which they are little entitled."[126]

"Cal Carter" was described as a large, well-built man, with dark hair, eyes and complexion. His face was badly disfigured from the bullet wound, and his injury prevented him from speaking. Except for their obvious injuries, the three robbers looked like ordinary men, according to the same newspaper: "None of them exhibit special refinement or intelligence. Their appearance is docile enough, except when some remark is dropped that don't [sic] suit and then there is a light in their eyes that means anything but humiliation and penitence."

That same afternoon, the Hon. John L. Merriam of St. Paul and John F. Lincoln, superintendent of the St. Paul & Sioux City Railroad, visited the prisoners. The pair had been passengers robbed at Gad's Hill, Missouri, two years earlier. While seeing the boys at Faribault, they were convinced that it had been Cole Younger who had robbed them of their money and watches, especially after Cole asked Merriam if they had not met before. Merriam suggested they probably had, since he had been a passenger on the Gad's Hill train. However, Cole and Bob denied any participation in the robbery.[127]

One curious visitor discovered he had met one of the Youngers before: "I found I had played two games of pocket pool with Bob Younger in the basement of the Parcher House at Owatonna some time before the raid on Northfield. Later on a visit to them while in jail in Faribault, Bob mentioned our games of pool 'and said he liked the Parcher House.'"

Sheriff Barton became uneasy with all the people in the streets, and he put on additional guards. Afraid of a possible rescue attempt by the gang's confederates, Barton placed the men in irons; a decision they found humiliating but did not protest.[129]

On Tuesday, September 26, Justice John B. Quinn, of the police court, arrived at the jail with Judge Samuel Lord to read the warrants to the Youngers. Through their attorney, Thomas Rutledge, of Watonwan County, the Youngers waived an examination and were committed, without bail, to await trial. The official warrant charge read, "Whereas, J.H. Richardson has this day made complaint on oath in writing to the subscriber, City Justice of the City of Faribault, that Cole Younger, Jim Younger, Bob Younger, Jesse James, and Frank James of said County, on the 7th day of September A.D. 1876 in Northfield in said County, did without the authority of law and with malice aforethought kill and murder Joseph L. Heywood by shooting him with a pistol then and thus loaded with leaden bullets."[130]

A second indictment charged that the men had killed Nicholaus Gustavson. Shortly thereafter, Cole was charged with Gustavson's murder with Jim and Bob as accessories.

Citizen outrage was mirrored through a letter to the editor of a Faribault newspaper: "There seems to be many different opinions as to the crime for which the Northfield bandits can be punished. I think it can be clearly demonstrated that their crime is murder and should be punished as such." Later in the same letter: "How, then, are they to escape? Was not Heywood murdered? What was more probable than bloodshed in their unlawful act? Not only one, but all are murderers."[131]

Nervous guards patrolled the jail, but on October 2, the Northfield tragedy took another life. Warned by Chief McDonough of St. Louis and other detectives that a rescue might be possible, guards were doubled at night, posting two inside the jail and another pair outside. The outside guards had strict orders to stop anyone approaching the jail.

On Tuesday morning about four o'clock, guard Frank Glazier saw a person enter the jail yard. According to a local newspaper, "[Glazier] ordered him to halt, but the stranger continued to advance. Glazier asked, 'Who are you?' to which the person replied, 'Don't you know me; I am the city police,' at the same time putting his hand to his breast, which motion Glazier interpreted as an attempt to draw a revolver, and leveling his rifle at him he fired. The man fell heavily to the earth, and expired without a groan."[132]

An investigation discovered that the dead man was Henry Kapanick, one of the night watch. He had worn a police badge on the lapel of his coat, but with the coat buttoned, it could not be seen. Glazier testified that he had seen the man, to him a stranger, coming up the sidewalk, and he ordered him to halt. The man kept on coming: "I stepped back two paces. He got about halfway from the gate to where I was standing. I asked, 'Who are you?' I am sure he heard it; he still kept on. I had my gun all ready but had not drawn it on him when I spoke." It being dark, Glazier was alarmed. "Seeing he did not stop at my last call, I raised my gun and fired. When the smoke cleared away I saw him lying on the ground."[133]

An inquest was held, and, upon examination of the body, it was found the ball had struck Kapanick's left breast about four inches below the collar bone, and passed through the body, ripping apart the right shoulder blade. Some Faribault citizens felt the Youngers were to blame, but the majority believed it was the deceased who was at fault for disobeying an order. The inquest found Glazier had acted in self-defense.

But, during that first week of October, the Youngers had "real" visitors. Their sister, Henrietta (Retta) Younger and her brother-in-law, Richard Hall, husband of Belle Younger, came to the county jail. The family wanted to see if the prisoners were really Cole, Jim, and Bob. Their recognition ended the Jim Younger-Cal Carter controversy once and for all.[134]

Hall brought with him letters of recommendation from Chief of Police Spears of Kansas City for Chief King of St. Paul, and from other persons who lived in the Youngers' Jackson County area. Retta, the Youngers' youngest sister, was only nineteen years old, and the Northfield affair was kept from her until only the Friday before her visit. She maintained that her brothers were guiltless.[135]

Following an interview with Hall at the Barron House where he talked of family history with such anecdotes as Cole was not a Baptist as reported but a "furious Campbellite," the two family members were admitted into the jail. Several local citizens were present at the invitation of Sheriff Barton to maintain proper surveillance.

Jim was brought out first. Retta rushed to him, clasping him around the neck. While weeping heavily, she proclaimed in the sight of God that he was not a murderer. When Cole and Bob appeared, tears ran down the cheeks of all four Youngers. The boys also greeted their brother-in-law in friendly spirits although in a manner less demonstrative. Cole made it clear he wanted the family to know that the brothers had no one to blame for their situation but themselves.

The next day, Retta and Mr. Hall were given a second visit. Cole presented Retta, who was calmer than during her first meeting, with a small religious work that had been given him while in jail. On the fly leaves he had penciled some words to her to return to school and assured his relatives he was resigned to whatever his fate might be. She was also admitted inside the rails to see Jim, who still had difficulty speaking, and trimmed his fingernails.

According to one Madelian, Retta Younger also visited the scene of the Younger capture: "It was known that all the robbers had money and watches and other valuables, but at the time of the capture not a valuable was on them, not a cent of money. About two weeks after the capture a woman came to Madelia and asked for a livery rig to go out where the capture took place. She asked mother to go with her. When she came to the place, she asked to go down alone. Minutes spread into hours, but finally she came back and it was noticeable that the bag she carried was heavier than when she went down. Was she told something by someone? Was their stuff buried where she could get it when they knew the game was closed? She asked mother to say nothing about the trip, and it was years after that I was told that it was one of the sisters of the Younger boys."[136]

An article in the *Pioneer Press* blasting Sheriff Barton for letting people visit the Youngers moved him to deny any visitors unless they had recommendations warranting their admittance. But others, especially those sympathetic to the fate of the boys, praised the way things were being handled. Mrs. Fanny C. Twyman, the Youngers' aunt, and the person with whom Retta lived, wrote a letter to the editor of the *St. Peter Tribune* at the time Retta was in Faribault.

The letter began: "I received a copy of your paper, for which you will receive my heartfelt thanks, and though I would love to express my gratitude to Mr. Jones for the kindness expressed in his communication towards my unfortunate nephews, the Younger boys, I shall ever feel grateful to the people of Minnesota for their Christian charity. Only the brave know how to be magnanimous to a fallen foe. My nephews have broken the laws, and I am willing for them to abide by the law, believing, as I do, that the people of Minnesota will give them a fair trial and allow them counsel."[137]

One man who did have clearance to visit the boys was G.W. Batchelder, an assistant defense attorney working with

Rutledge. The young attorney was quite impressed with the kindness shown by the trio of outlaws. "They gave me their pictures, which are now in the files of the Rice County Historical Society, and many other little gifts, one of which was a small gold toothpick, that I have always kept," recollected Batchelder. "Cole told me when he bade me good-bye on leaving for Stillwater, that he hoped that my surroundings and upbringing would give me a better chance in life than they had had."[138]

On October 19, Edward T. Miller, brother of Clell Miller, stopped at the Arlington House with a St. Paul attorney, Samuel Hardwick. Miller said he had come to Faribault to recover some personal articles taken from the body of his brother, for their mother wished to preserve some mementos belonging to Clell. Ed was initially afraid to come to Minnesota because rumors circulated in Missouri that any relative of the outlaws would be lynched by the excited populace. He was given some keepsakes and the next day he was allowed to visit the Youngers in the company of officers.[139]

As the Youngers sat in jail awaiting trial, an attempt was made to sell their horses. Low prices were offered for all the horses. The local newspaper reported, "It is claimed that the Younger boys have sold their horses to different parties in the city, and it now looks as if the county won't get much booty after all."[140]

The Youngers spent over a month in the Faribault jail awaiting their court appearances. Retta and Mr. Hall returned on November 9 and discussed with the boys different legal options. Defense attorney Rutledge advised them to plead guilty to the charge of murder and they would not be hanged because of a Minnesota saving clause.[141]

On October 14, the brothers were arraigned in Rice County District Court. Four indictments had been handed down against them: the first charging them with accessory to the murder of Joseph Heywood, the second with attacking Alonzo Bunker with deadly weapons, the third for robbing the First National Bank, and the fourth charging Cole as principal, and his brothers as accessories, with the murder of Nicholaus Gustavson.[142]

Judge Samuel Lord presided over the court, with George N. Baxter, county attorney, assisted by Attorney General Wilson, conducting the prosecution. The Youngers were represented by Batchelder & Buckham, Faribault attorneys, and by Thomas Rutledge of Madelia. The defense opened by challenging the grand jurors, resulting in the removal of five of the twenty-three.[143]

The courtroom was filled with curious spectators, male and female, anxious to see the captured outlaws who were brought into the room in irons. All three men were clean shaven and neat, leaving some of the spectators disappointed since they did not look like the desperate men they were supposed to be. Sheriff Barton commanded silence in the court room, and County Attorney Baxter read the indictments. The prisoners entered no plea, having under the statutes, twenty-four hours to do so.

Four days later, Monday, November 18, shortly before noon, the Youngers went to trial. Again, the courtroom was filled with an enthusiastic, eager crowd who leaned forward to catch every motion and every word. Handcuffed and chained together, Cole in the middle, Bob on the right, Jim on the left, the Youngers were brought in through a side door. They were accompanied officially by Sheriff Barton, two deputies, and a guard, and by their sister Retta and their aunt, Mrs. Twyman. Both ladies were veiled and seated themselves with the prisoners within the bar.[144]

The court was called to order, and Sheriff Barton ordered everyone in the room to take their seats. County Attorney Baxter walked up to the judge's desk and read the indictments. Baxter also stated that he felt the prisoners' wrist irons should be removed, and following a brief discussion, they were removed. The Youngers stepped to the bench one at a time and all three pleaded guilty to the charges. The brothers were asked if they had anything to say in their behalf, to which they answered no. Judge Lord addressed each of the men and sentenced them to life imprisonment in Stillwater Prison, as Jim turned to Retta and put his arm around her.[145]

A local newspaper commented on the guilty plea: "By the plea of guilty, the prisoners saved the county the expense of a long and tedious trial; but it is exceedingly probable that by so doing they have saved themselves from the gallows."[146]

Wednesday morning, November 20, the prisoners were taken from the Faribault Jail and placed on the eight o'clock train accompanied by Sheriff Ara Barton, Fin Barton, Sheriff W.H. Dill of Winona, guards John Passon and Thomas Lord, Henrietta Younger, and Mrs. Twyman. A wagon was waiting in St. Paul to take the Youngers on the last leg of their journey.

A St. Louis newspaper was quick to write "Missouri surprised at Minnesota pluck," an article in which the state of Missouri thanked the state of Minnesota. The article began, "The fierceness, the intensity, and above all, the success, with which the bank robbers of Minnesota were pursued, day and night, ought to be a lesson to the people of Missouri, who, more than any others, have suffered from such outrages as the one which has been so fearfully avenged. To the people of Minnesota,

STATE OF MINNESOTA.

Office of PRISON WARDEN.

Stillwater, November 22d 1876

I HEREBY CERTIFY Ara Barton
Sheriff of Rice County, accompanied by John Casson, Thomas
Lord, WH Dill, Phinus Barton Guards, has this day delivered to me the persons of
Coleman Younger, James Younger & Robert Younger
convicted by the District Court in
said County, and sentenced for crime, as follows: of Murder and sen —
tenced to imprisonment for the term of their
natural lives

J.A. Reed.
Warden of State Prison.

Younger Brothers' transfer papers from Faribault to Stillwater Penitentiary. (Courtesy of the Wantonwan County Historical Society)

it seems that no time, no expense, nor pains are too much to be lavished in the punishment of an open and defiant act of out-lawry." The article goes on to state, "They have earned their reward, for it is safe to say that it will be a long day before a quiet village of Minnesota will be disturbed by a daylight murder and a fierce dash of robbers through its streets."[147]

Notes

1 This poem was reprinted in *The Northfield News*, Thursday, October 5, 1876. "The Capital Pet" is spelled both Brisette and Brissette, proba-bly not intentionally.

2 *Minneapolis Star* article, date unknown, author's collection.

3 Ibid.

4 Marley Brant, *The Outlaw Youngers, A Confederate Brotherhood*, Madison Books, Lanham, New York & London, 1995, p. 187; Chuck Parsons, "Madelia's Paul Revere-Nemesis of the Younger Gang," *The English Westerners Tally Sheet*, April 1977, Vol. 23 No. 3, p.2.

5 *Faribault Republican*, Wednesday, September 13, 1876, "The Pursuit," p. 3.

6 St. Paul newspaper, source and date unknown, "Revier Writes of Bank Raid." Author's collection.

7 *Worthington Advance,* Thursday, September 14, 1876, "The Flight."

8 Marley Brant, *The Outlaw Youngers,* p. 188.

9 Mrs. Nellie Empey Odell letter to *Northfield News*, date unknown. Printed in Northfield newspaper under "Interest Is Still Keen in Bank Raid Story," author's collection.

10 Ibid.

11 *Faribault Republican*, September 13, 1876, p.3.

12 *St. Paul Dispatch*, Sunday, September 10, 1876, "The Chase," p. 1.

13 *St. Paul Dispatch*, September 10, 1876, "The Chase Continued," p. 1.

14 *Minneapolis Tribune*, Friday Evening, September 8, 1876, "The Pursuit," p. 1.

15 *Faribault Republican*, September 13, 1876, p. 3.

16 Ibid.

17 *The Northfield Saga*, p. 10.

18 *Faribault Republican*, September 13, 1876, p. 3.

19 Marley Brant, *The Outlaw Youngers*, pp. 188-189.

20 *Faribault Republican*, September 13, 1876, p. 3; Marley Brant, *The Outlaw Youngers*, p. 189; *The Northfield Saga*, p. 10.

21 *Rice County Journal*, Thursday, September 14, 1876, p. 1.

22 Leo Stangler interviews with author December 20, 1996, and December 27, 1996, Burnsville, Minnesota.

23 *Faribault Republican*, September 13, 1876, p. 3.

24 Mae C. Zellmer Mach, *Remember When; A History of Kilkenny, Minnesota,* Sentinel Printing Company, no other information given, p. 207; Leo Stangler interview with author, December 31, 1996.

25 Leo Stangler interviews with author December 20 and December 27, 1996; Donna Fostveit letter to author dated August 27, 1982; Rex Macbeth telephone interview with author November 29, 1997.

26 Olive C. Dickie letter to author dated November 3, 1982.

27 George Huntington, Robber and Hero, p. 55.

28 *St. Paul & Minneapolis Pioneer-Press and Tribune,* Saturday, September 9, 1876, "Seen at Waterville Lake," p. 2.

29 Marley Brant, *The Outlaw Youngers*, p. 191.

30 *Windom Reporter*, September 14, 1876.

31 *St. Paul & Minneapolis Pioneer-Press and Tribune,* Saturday, September 9, 1876, "The Last Trace of Them," p. 2.

32 *St. Paul Dispatch*, Sunday, September 10, 1876, "The Pursuit Yesterday," p. 1.

33 *Faribault Republican*, September 13, 1876, p. 3; Kanne-Marzahn Minske Family Geneaology & History 1856-1980 complied by Leona (Kanne) Benson. Author's collection.

34 *St. Paul Dispatch*, Sunday, September 10, 1876, p. 1.

35 Marley Brant, *The Outlaw Youngers*, p. 191; George Huntington, Robber and Hero, p. 55.

36 *St. Paul Dispatch*, Sunday, September 10, 1876, p. 1.

37 *Faribault Republican*, September 13, 1876, p. 3.

38 *St. Paul Dispatch*, Sunday, September 10, 1876, p. 1.

39 Ibid.

40 *The Northfield Saga*, p. 11.

41 *Faribault Republican*, September 13, 1876, p. 3.

42 *St. Paul Dispatch*, Sunday, September 10, 1876, "Probably the Missouri Gang," p. 1.

43 Ibid.

44 Ibid.; *Faribault Republican*, September 13, 1876, p. 3.

45 *Sioux City Daily Journal*, Sunday, September 17, 1876, "The Northfield Brigands."

46 A.W. Henkel, "Dear Cousin William," September 29, 1876. Northfield Minnesota Bank Robbery of 1876. Selected Manuscripts Collections and Government Records. Microfilm Edition. Minnesota Historical Society.

47 *Mankato Record*, Saturday, September 16, 1876, "The Robber Hunt."

48 *Owatonna Journal*, Thursday, September 14, 1876, "Outlaws in Minnesota."

49 *Mankato School Spotlight*, Friday, February 14, 1941, Edward Noonan interviewed by Kathleen Lovett.

50 *St. Paul Pioneer Press*, Thursday, September 14, 1876, "Suspicious Characters."

51 *Mankato School Spotlight*, Friday, February 14, 1941, Noonan interview.

52 George T. Barr, "Account of Northfield Bank Robbery in 1876," unpublished manuscript, Blue Earth County Historical Society, Mankato, Minnesota.

53 *Mankato Free Press*, September 19, 1979, "Northfield Robbers Left State in an Uproar," by John Stone, p. 12.

54 *Faribault Democrat*, Friday, September 15, 1876, "Robbers Attacked While Eating Breakfast."

55 *Mankato Free Press*, September 19, 1979; Marley Brant, *The Outlaw Youngers*, pp. 192-193; *Faribault Democrat*, Friday, September 15, 1876.

56 *The Madelia News*, Thursday, November 25, 1915, "Cole Younger's Story of the Northfield Raid."

57 "James and Younger Gang Stopped for Rations Here: L.M. Demaray Recalls Story of Narrow Escape by T.J. Dunning and of Raid on Matthews Flock of Chickens," 1939 newspaper article, source unknown.

58 *Martin County Sentinel*, Fairmont, Minnesota, Friday, September 15, 1876, "In Pursuit of the Bandits."

59 Ibid.

60 *Mankato Free Press*, Wednesday, September 19, 1979.

61 *Mankato Free Press*, Monday, April 5, 1937, "Youngers Led Raid on Bank;" *Madelia Times-Messenger*, Thursday, July 4, 1957, "Capture of Younger Brothers," P. 1, Section 5.

62 *Martin County Sentinel*, Fairmont, Sept. 15, 1876.

63 *Mankato Free Press*, Monday, April 5, 1937; Marley Brant, *The Outlaw Youngers*, p. 193.

64 *Mankato Free Press*, Wednesday, September 19, 1979; *Mankato Free Press*, Monday, April 5, 1937; *St. Paul Dispatch*, Friday, April 27, 1962.

65 *Mankato School Spotlight*, Friday, February 14, 1941, Noonan Interview; *Mankato Free Press*, Monday, April 5, 1937.

66 Ibid.

67 L.M. Kellett, copied from notes found of Lydia Schilling, May 31, 1956.

68 "Charles Brust, Sr., Recalls James Gang's Visit Here," Brown County Historical Society, New Ulm, Minnesota.

69 Ibid.

70 *New Ulm Journal*, March 19, 1957, "Jesse James Slept in Brighton Township."

71 W.A. Spicer letter to Garlyn Johannsen dated February 28, 1949; Garlyn Johannsen O'Leary letter to author dated November 23, 1982.

72 *Faribault Republican*, September 20, 1876, "Blunder of Hoy," p. 3.

73 Charles Armstrong, "Recollections of a Nine Year Old Boy Concerning events Following the Northfield Bank Robbery." Northfield Bank Robbery of 1876; Selected Manuscripts Collections and Government Records. Microfilm Edition. Minnesota Historical Society.

74 Franklin L. Sorenson, "Story of Part Which Norwegian Lad Took In Capturing the Notorious Younger Bros," Undated *Blue Earth Post* article, Watonwan Historical Society, Madelia.

75 A.O. Sorbel letter to Carl Weicht dated August 19, 1929. Author's collection.

76 *St. James Plain Dealer*, October 16, 1924, "Sorbel of Webster, Iowa (sic-S.D.), Tells of His Work in Capture of Youngers, p. 4; Sioux Falls (S.D.) Argus-Leader, series of articles by J.A. Derome March 22 to June 4, 1924, "Webster Man Gives His Story of James-Younger Raid; Was First to tell of Gang's Hiding Place."

77 A.O. Sorbel letter to Carl Weicht.

78 *St. James Plain Dealer*, October 16, 1924; *Sioux Falls Argus Leader*.

79 *Hanska Herald*, Friday, March 18, 1949, "Hanska Community Centennial Memorial," papers of Inga Sorbel, p. 1; *Mankato Free Press*, Thursday, May 20, 1993, As told by Nettie (Sorbel) Asleson, pp. 13, 15.

80 Chuck Parsons, "Madelia's Paul Revere-Nemesis of the Younger Gang," *The English Westerners Tally Sheet*, April 1977, Vol. 23, No. 3, p. 2.

81 A.O. Sorbel letter to Carl Weicht.

82 *St. James Plain Dealer*, October 16, 1924.

83 "Captured at Madelia," Source unknown, Author's Collection.

84 Buster Yates, *Seventy-Five Years on the Watonwan*, Madelia, December 1986, p. 159.

85 "Captured at Madelia."

86 A.O. Sorbel letter to Carl Weicht.

87 *St. James Plain Dealer*, October 16, 1924.

88 *Mankato Free Press*, September 20, 1979, John Stone, "Shoot-out on the Watonwan, The Younger Gang Comes to Madelia," p. 6C-7C.

89 *Webster* (S.D.) *Journal*, July 17, 1930, T.L. Vought, "As Boy and Man."

90 Woodrow Keljik, "The 1st . . . Last of a Long Line," *Ace* magazine of the St. Paul Athletic Club, May 1984, Vol. 64, No. 5, p. 6; Christine Taylor Thompson, Cottonwood County Historical Society, Windom, letters to author dated January 6, 1997, and January 16, 1997; Jay

Donald, *Outlaws of the Border, A Complete and Authentic History of Frank and Jesse James, The Younger Brothers*, The Coburn & Newman Publishing Company, Chicago, 1882, p. 304.

91 Franklin L. Sorenson, "Story of Part Which Norwegian Lad Took in Capturing the Notorious Younger Gang."

92 *Mankato Free Press*, September 20, 1979.

93 *The Norborne (MO) Democrat & Leader*, Friday, January 3, 1936, Harry Hoffman, "The Younger Boys' Last Stand."

94 George A. Bradford letter to D.E. Hasey, January 20, 1924.

95 *Mankato Free Press*, September 20, 1979.

96 George A. Bradford letter to D.E. Hasey, January 20, 1924.

97 *Mankato Free Press*, September 20, 1979.

98 *The Norborne (MO) Democrat & Leader*, Friday, January 3, 1936.

99 *Minneapolis Journal*, Date unknown, "Last of Posse That Caught Younger Brothers is Now 83; Brother of Luther M. Pomeroy of Madelia Recalls Raid On Northfield Bank." Watonwan Historical Society.

100 George A. Bradford letter to D.E. Hasey, January 20, 1924.

101 *St. James Plain Dealer*, October 16, 1924.

102 Ibid.

103 *Northfield News*, Saturday, July 10, 1897. Account of T.L. Vought.

104 *New Ulm Journal*, January 12, 1939, "Old-Timers Remember Younger Gang; Captured Near Here After Robbery."

105 Marley Brant, *The Outlaw Youngers*, p. 203.

106 *Northfield News*, Saturday, July 10, 1897.

107 *New Ulm Journal*, January 12, 1939.

108 George A. Bradford letter to D.E. Hasey, January 20, 1924.

109 Buster Yates, *Seventy-Five Years on the Watonwan*, p. 157.

110 Charles Armstrong, "Recollections of a nine year old boy concerning events following the Northfield Bank Robbery." Northfield, Minnesota Bank Robbery of 1876; Selected Manuscripts Collections and Government Records. Microfilm Edition. Minnesota Historical Society.

111 *Rural News*, July 17, 1924, "Capture of the Youngers Recalled."

112 *New Ulm Journal*, January 12, 1939.

113 Owen R. Dickie letter to LeSueur County Historical Society dated January 30, 1971.

114 *Mankato Scool Spotlight*, Friday, February 14, 1941, Edward Noonan interview.

115 *Northfield News*, Saturday, September 18, 1897, "Capture of the Younger Brothers By One of the Captors," p. 7.

116 Ibid.

117 *Martin County Sentinel*, September 29, 1876.

118 *Madelia Times-Messenger*, Thursday, July 4, 1957, "Capture of Younger Brothers."

119 *Windom Reporter*, October 5, 1876.

120 *Madelia Times-Messenger*, Friday, April 29, 1938, "Record of Fight for Jesse James Reward Found in Files Reveals an Epilogue as Interesting as the Story Itself," pp. 8-9.

121 Marley Brant, *The Outlaw Youngers*, p. 206.

122 *Winona Republican* report published in *Faribault Republican*, Sep-

tember 27, 1876.

123 *Northfield News*, Saturday, July 10, 1897.

124 *Faribault Republican*, September 27, 1876, "Maneuvering for St. Paul;" *Faribault Democrat*, September 29, 1876, "Arrival of the Robbers."

125 *Faribault Democrat*, September 29, 1876, "Their Wounds;" *Sioux City* (IA) *Journal*, Monday, September 25, 1876; *Sioux Valley News* (Canton, SD), Saturday, September 30, 1876.

126 Ibid., "The Notorious Outlaws."

127 Ibid.; *Faribault Democrat*, September 22, 1876.

128 George A. McKenzie, "Reminiscenses of the Capture of the Younger Brothers." Northfield, Minnesota Bank Robbery of 1876; Selected Manuscripts Collections and Government Records. Microfilm Edition. Minnesota Historical Society.

129 Marley Brant, *The Outlaw Youngers*, p. 210.

130 Warrant of Arrest, State of Minnesota, County of Rice, City of Faribault. Copy of arrest warrants in author's collection.

131 *Faribault Democrat*, October 6, 1876, "What Constitutes Murder?"

132 *Faribault Republican*, October 4, 1876, "A Sad and Fatal Mistake, Policeman Shot Dead by the Jail Guard;" Thomas P. Healy letter to author (undated) 1982.

133 Ibid.

134 Marley Brant, "Bloodlines: The Younger Sisters," *Old West Magazine*, Summer 1996, p. 23.

135 *Faribault Republican*, October 4, 1876, "The Younger Brothers: They are Visited by Relatives."

136 *Webster (SD) Journal*, July 17, 1930, "As Boy and Man."

137 *Faribault Republican*, November 25, 1876, "The Younger Boys."

138 *Northfield Independent*, Thursday, November 25, 1948, "Pitts named as Heywood Slayer in Notes left by Faribault Attorney."

139 *Owatonna Journal*, Thursday, October 26, 1876, "Clell Miller's Brother."

140 *Faribault Democrat*, Friday, October 20,1876.

141 Marley Brant, *The Outlaw Youngers*, pp. 211-212.

142 *St. James Plain Dealer*, September 1926, "50th Anniversary of North-field Bank Robbers and Capture of Four of the Bandits in this County," p. 10.

143 *Faribault Democrat*, Friday, November 17, 1876, "The Robbers."

144 *Faribault Democrat*, Friday, November 24, 1876, "The Youngers."

145 Marley Brant, *The Outlaw Youngers*, pp. 212-213.

146 *Faribault Democrat*, Friday, November 24, 1876.

147 *St. Louis (MO) Globe-Democrat*, September 23, 1876; *Faribault Republican*, October 4, 1876.

Chapter 5

Hell and Beyond

A LEAP OF FAITH

Behind them Madelia, a Crimson flood,
Leaving a trail in lead and blood.
The Law rode, pursuing with panting breath,
But still Jess and Frank laughed at death.

The bold Youngers resigned to their sad fates
Like the noble cause and all the Confederate states.
Would ride no more, ironic yet sad,
Brave men—patriots, more good than bad.

Thundering posse, to avenge Heywood their hope,
Heavy with Colts and a well-oiled rope.
To make their mark on history's epic page,
By killing Frank and Jesse and quell their rage.

With Death pursuing, they were compelled to try.
They say it was an Angel that helped them fly
Over the grinning jaws of Hell
Two brothers, and with them Bill Chadwell?

—George Diezel II

NEAR LAKE CRYSTAL, IN A PELTING RAIN, the two outlaws believed
to be Frank and Jesse James, split from the Youngers and Pitts.
Soon the Jameses were fired upon by a young man named
Richard Roberts. According to a Mankato newspaper article,
Jesse's hat was shot from his head. "It was Roberts' shot that
frightened the stolen horse on which the brothers were riding.
They were thrown off, took refuge in a cornfield, stole two hors-
es that night, and began their trek to Missouri."[1]

Roberts later said he saw a horse splashing through the
mud, and as it approached, he noticed it was carrying two men.
The rear rider had a white bandage tied around his right leg.
When the riders refused to obey a command to halt, Roberts fired

his musket and the two were thrown off. That same day Roberts found the hat with a bullet hole in it.

"Subsequent events convinced me the hat belonged to Jesse James, and the rider with the white bandage on his leg was his brother Frank, for I learned that Frank James was badly wounded in the right leg by citizens at Northfield following the holdup," recalled Roberts. "The horse had been stolen near Garden City and that night two more were taken."

According to Sam Emerson of Mansfield Township in Freeborn County, a lone rider with two saddled, but rider-less horses in tow, approached his farm. Emerson related the dusty traveler had a hunted look, but the stranger did not say anything. He led the horses, who were three of the finest mounts Emerson had ever seen, over to the water tank, they drank their fill, and the man and horses rode off. "He went straight through," said Emerson, "not stopping for sloughs, groves, or anything else."[2]

Another report of the Jameses in Freeborn County was issued by Syvert H. Berkness. Berkness and a companion were riding in a wagon late in the afternoon when two horsemen rode up and asked for directions. The two local men in the wagon became suspicious of the riders, who did not look at them. Both riders turned their heads in every direction as if they were expecting someone. Berkness' companion told the men he was also a stranger in the area and could not tell them which way to take. The riders said nothing more and galloped away at top speed.[3]

Word quickly spread that the brothers were heading south or west in a mad dash to reach their Missouri haven, and every community dreaded the outlaws coming their way. Windom, in Cottonwood County, prepared to meet the robbers should they head west: "We managed to get up a little excitement about the robbers last Friday," reported a local newspaper. "A telegram came saying that two of the brigands passed Madelia at seven o'clock in the morning coming in this direction. Dr. Brown and our fighting editor prepared their cartridges with large shot and double charges of powder, bent on securing the $20,000 robber if he came this way; but he didn't come, and we are now looking for a fellow who wants to stand behind those charges and pull the trigger."[4]

Residents of Windom believed the fleeing brothers would cross the river at a bridge outside town, and Captain George, with several others, picketed the bridge just as darkness came. Captain George remarked that if the robbers attempted to cross, they would either be taken or killed. The *Windom Reporter* classified George and his patrol as a different class of men than those who had guarded the bridge at Mankato. George's men "had shot and been shot at."

Following their incident with Roberts, the outlaws, riding two large gray horses stolen from a Baptist minister, stopped at a

126

farm. In the farmhouse, Frank dressed the bullet wound in his right thigh which the watching farmer later called neither deep nor dangerous. The robbers purchased a loaf of bread and a hat, as well as two sacks. They then filled the sacks with straw and tied them to their horses, using them for saddles. One of the men took out a wad of bills, which according to the farmer, was as long as his arm. It consisted of mostly $100 and $50 bills, and they paid him a dollar and a half.[5]

On Friday night they stopped about five miles south of Lamberton, a station on the Winona & St. Peter Railroad, seventy-five miles west of Madelia. About sundown, they rode to the home of a German farmer, and producing a map of Minnesota, made extensive inquiries about the roads and rivers in the area. The farmer noticed both men suffered from leg wounds. They told the farmer they had been riding in a wagon and were injured when the wagon broke down. The farmer dressed the wounds of the older man but the younger would not show his wound. The brothers spent the night at the farm; both sleeping the full night in their clothes.[6]

That same night, Mike Hoy and his Minneapolis posse, camped at Three Lakes, thirteen miles south of Lamberton and only ten miles from where the Jameses were staying. Sheriff Barton and his party were at Big Bend, a little further west and three miles to the south. Sheriff Dill and his posse had crossed over to Lake Shetek by ten o'clock Saturday morning and were in direct line of the robbers' path only twelve miles further west.[7]

But at seven o'clock on Saturday morning, the Jameses rode north only a quarter-mile and turned into a cornfield, galloping full speed south across the prairie. Shortly after their departure from the farmhouse, all towns between Lamberton and the South Dakota border were notified, and a posse from Marshall, Worthington, and Windom headed west in pursuit. Dr. Hurd of Faribault rode to Sioux City and on to Yankton, Dakota Territory, to alert the people the outlaws were headed in that direction. Another Faribault man, Tom McDermott, went to Sioux Falls, Dakota Territory, to spread the alarm.

Sheriff McDonald and a half dozen men from Sioux City, Iowa, armed to the teeth, took the Dakota Southern train west hoping to intercept the two robbers should they turn south at the Missouri River. McDonald and his men disembarked at Elk Point and began guarding the ferries across the river. Sheriff Baker, with a contingent from Yankton, established communication with McDonald and began guarding the country between Yankton and Sioux City.[8]

McDonald says every person one meets on the cars along the St. Paul road is loaded down to the guards with firearms, resembling traveling arsenals," reported the *Sioux City Daily*

Sheriff John McDonald. (Courtesy of the Sioux City Public Museum)

Journal. "The greatest excitement prevails, and armed squads are moving to and fro continually. The hundreds of men engaged in the chase appear to have no head or organized leaders, and consequently the chances of catching the fleeing ruffians are growing fainter and fainter each succeeding day."[9]

As McDonald and Baker converged on the bandits, rumors began circulating that the fugitives had been seen in both LeMars and Sioux City, Iowa; another reporting they had crossed the Missouri River and were relatively safe, while still another claimed they had stolen a pair of black horses on the Jim River, some forty to fifty miles above the Missouri River.

Geography was not the only problem encountered by the McDonald-Baker force, as evidenced by a local newspaper: "The boys out after the robbers yesterday had a hard time of it. It rained steadily, and the traveling must have been very laborious on their horses. The robbers labored under the same disadvantages, still our sympathy does not spread thin enough to cover them, too. We shall expect to hear soon that the party who went out yesterday have [sic] caught the robbers, or that that [sic] the robbers have caught the party, either of which would be stunning news."[10]

One account states the Jameses may have spent a night outside Worthington on the banks of Lake Okabena. Worthington, founded only five years earlier, was a prairie settlement preyed upon by grasshoppers and surrounded on every side by seas of tall, waving grass. Julius A. Town, Nobles County sheriff, had formed a posse of ten to fifteen men, and the group was patrolling the area. Word reached Town that the James boys had been seen somewhere between Worthington and Luverne and had probably passed into Rock County.

"Suddenly there they were: Frank and Jesse James in full view of a posse from Nobles County," claimed Lewis Ellefson. "Sheriff Town shouted an order to pursue and a gallop chase across the prairie began. The horses broke through the tall grass and clattered over and around the stones of the Red Rock ridge . . ."[11]

Jesse James. (Photo by Sumner Studios of Northfield. Courtesy of the Minnesota Historical Society)

Another account from Nobles County tells of gunfire exchanged near Magnolia and the fleeing outlaws being chased across northwestern Nobles County on a pair of stolen gray horses. Fred R. Humiston recalled: "There was a posse organized at Worthington led by M.S. Twitchell. The party was armed with antiquated fire arms, old smooth bore rifles and shot guns. The posse was in sight of the fugitives a number of times, but as the James [sic] would stop on a ridge the posse was careful not to get in range. Near Canton they abandoned their horses and they were shipped back to their owner. I saw them in Worthington and they surely showed the effects of a hard trip."[12]

The *Faribault Republican* reported an account of two Worthington hunters who stumbled upon three members of the gang near the town of Bigelow, at Lake Ocheda in Nobles County. The outlaws went down on the grass, then arose, and when one of the hunters raised his gun to change positions, the outlaw, thinking he had been discovered, began running. He fell down three times, and his two companions helped get him to his feet. A posse from Worthington immediately took after three robbers, not two.[13]

The Republican states, "undoubtedly three of the robber gang came south of Heron Lake through the country northwest." They were trailed eight miles by the Worthington posse until the track was lost on a hill near Washington. A pelting rain destroyed any tracks. On Ocheda bridge, a blood-stained piece of the *Pioneer Press,* which had served as a bandage, was discovered.[14]

Eleven miles north of Luverne, near Magnolia and Battle Plain townships on the west bank of the Rock River, they stopped at the house of Charles B. Rolfe about 7:30 in the morning. Dismounting from their gray horses, the men went into the house, finding Mr. Rolfe away, but his wife at home. She asked them to take off their rubber coats, but they would not.[15]

Seeing that the men were lame and unable to lift their legs, she inquired if they were ill. One of the men answered, telling her their horses had broken their wagon and run away. He said he suffered from rheumatism and his friend had broken two ribs in a fall from the wagon. She noted the man with the bad right side could scarcely sit up to eat his breakfast. He turned down tea and asked for milk, and she noticed that, when they paid her, they did not unbutton their coats but reached up under.

The men had to climb on the fence and slide onto their horses to mount. Mrs. Rolfe said one of the men had a large tear on the right side of his rubber coat, and the other wore fine boots with small heels and square toes. The boots were wet from walking in the grass. She watched them ride away to the south, using straw for saddles and old ropes looped for stirrups.

Other accounts relate similar information, although Rolfe is spelled Rolph. (The Rolph spelling is probably correct since the name appears in Rock County historical records.) Charles Rolph was away at the time of the alleged James visit helping a band of Indians on a nearby reservation while his son's (Charles E.) new bride, Ella Phinney, "was emptying the ash bin in the farmyard. Frank and Jesse James had quite a climb from the level of the Rock River to the farmhouse on top of a hill. True to the custom of offering hospitality to travelers, Grandma Rolph made breakfast and fed the strangers. Only later in the day, and after the brothers had moved on toward South Dakota, did she learn the men were outlaws."[16]

Frank James. (Photo by Sumner Studios of Northfield. Courtesy of the Minnesota Historical Society)

The bandits continued west, stopping at the Davis house in Spring Water. Given bread and butter, they remained in the house about fifteen minutes before dashing off across the road northwest of Luverne. At three o'clock in the afternoon, they were seen by a Mr. Howard, who thought they were merely riding for pleasure. They rode out on a high knoll and leisurely surveyed the countryside. Shortly afterwards, Sheriff Rice and three others arrived in pursuit. The posse rode very near the outlaws, certainly within rifle range, but the posse was afraid of the fugitives and did not shoot. Rice's men followed the outlaws for seven miles, and lost the trail after dark, three miles east of Palisade, on Split Rock River, just into Dakota Territory.[17]

About a half-hour later, Rice met a boy who told him the robbers had passed. The boy said the robbers told him they were being pursued and gave him a "vulgar invitation" to report to the posse. When the robbers asked the boy for a good spot to cross the river, he led them to two crossings. They approached the lower crossing, but disappeared into the ravines and did not cross the stream.

But the Jameses were not the only sources of fear in the rocky ravines and prairie grass of the Dakota Territory that week. Tuesday, September 19, had been fixed as the day upon which the Indians at the various agencies along the Upper Missouri would be disarmed and their ponies taken from them by the military. Many persons feared the general disarming was imminent and would bring trouble and a massacre along the Missouri. Troops were sent to the most likely trouble spots, and the Twentieth Infantry from the Canadian border, with General George Crook and his cavalry, entered the territory.[18]

Crook was concerned about reaching Deadwood before Crazy Horse and his bands could stir up other tribes in the Dakota Territory. Knowing he was marching among hostile Sioux who had recently defeated General George A. Custer at the Little Bighorn in Montana, and, who were watching his every movement, Crook moved his column in a line so he could repel an attack within thirty seconds. With many civilians afraid to enter Dakota Territory in fear of Indian massacre, it was a good place for the Jameses to be, depending on how one looked at it.[19]

The brothers hid out in a cave on a farm north of Garretson, but, with the posse on their heels, they abandoned their hideout and rode into the Palisades, a stream bordered by red quartzite rock formations. Accounts vary as to which posse came in sight of the brothers—the St. Louis police force, a posse from Northfield, or Julius Town and his Nobles County group—but all agree the confrontation occurred while Frank and Jesse had split up to scout the area, each following one side of Split Rock Creek.[20]

Several accounts report that Jesse was approached by a posse, and in attempting to get away, he found himself at the edge of Devil's Gulch or Spirit Canyon, a deep fifteen-foot wide chasm with a red rock face falling 100 feet to the river, then rising sharply on the other side. Jesse stopped at the abyss, rode back a short distance and began coaxing his tired horse to leap the canyon. Just as the posse came up on him, Jesse rode toward the edge at full gallop, and at the narrowest point, leaped the canyon.[21] The sheriff's posse stopped at the edge; none of the officers considered the continued chase worth the foolhardy risk involved in leaping Devil's Gulch.

Serious scholars consider Jesse's courageous leap to freedom little more than folklore. The hard and rugged Sioux quartzite at the gulch would give a horse little chance of obtaining a firm foothold, and the distance between the two cliffs would be almost insurmountable. Yet, the Jameses were definitely pursued by a posse in the Palisades area, and many persons swear Jesse's leap is a part of history.

After slipping away from his would-be captors, with or without the leap, Jesse joined Frank in another canyon nearby. Discovering a small, narrow cave in the side of one of the canyon walls, with the opening little more than a crack between huge rocks, the brothers found the interior roomy enough for two men. While the posse surveyed the rocky countryside, the Jameses spent the night in the cave hideaway.

Just below the Palisades, the robbers stopped at the farm of a Mr. Nelson, between six and eight on Sunday evening, and inquired about the roads and fords in the area. Nelson, who was sitting on a fence, lit his pipe and began talking about other matters. One of the outlaws asked him if he was going to sit there all night. Seeing that the men were wearing revolvers, Nelson gave them the information they requested and went into the house.[22]

As soon as Nelson retired into the house, the outlaw brothers charged for his two black horses. What neither of them knew was, both horses were blind, one in one eye, the other in both. They rode the blind horses for about ten miles, changing them for a pair of grays, five miles north of Sioux Falls.

About five o'clock Monday morning, the brothers stopped the Yankton Stage and asked the driver where he was going. The driver answered and asked them the same question. The brothers probably intended to take the horses from the stage, but seeing they were poor mounts, rode away on their grays. The Minnesota posse was only five miles behind, and all the crossings of the Missouri River between Yankton and Fort Sully, had guards posted.

The Northfield newspaper printed an extra edition and included the following "report" from the Yankton area: "The two robbers seen eight miles south of here today. The previous night they stopped a squaw to inquire of her the road. It is reported that 150 Indians are in pursuit of them to see who they are."[23]

The *Sioux City Daily News* reported: "Armed companies, we learn, are watching the different roads through Southeastern Dakota, and it is hoped that the notorious robbers may fall into some of their hands and not escape across the Missouri. If they succeed in getting across the river, their chances for escape will be greatly increased. They know all of the country well from the Missouri south through to Texas."[24]

The same newspaper reported on September 21 that two men believed to be the robbers were seen about eight miles from East Orange, with a posse about two hours behind them. The posse caught up to the robbers six miles away, just as they were leaving the home of a Norwegian man named Swanson, where they spent the night. The Jameses had told the man they were laborers in search of work and complained of being extremely tired and lame after walking a long distance.[25]

As the posse approached, Jesse and Frank ran into a nearby barn where the owner, Andrew Shuelson, was feeding his horses. When the farmer protested the intrusion, one of the robbers held a revolver close to his eyebrows. When the coast was clear, the men rode away, crossing the Big Sioux River into Iowa. The sheriff's assistant and the Worthington party gave chase.

As the Jameses ascended a steep bluff on the opposite side of the stream, two of the posse charged. The outlaws stopped and dismounted. Several shots were fired at the two pursuers. One of the bullets struck one of the horses in the neck. The shots apparently frightened the Worthington lawman and his posse, who returned to Beloit, Iowa, for reinforcements.

The *Sioux City Daily Journal* for September 21was quick to comment: "The sheriff from Worthington, who is here, seems to think that the robbers will make back tracks for the Sioux and strike out for the Jim River country. A large force is scattered over the prairies between the Sioux and Rock rivers, and we are waiting anxiously for tidings from them. Had these men acted promptly they could have bagged their game this morning."

The *Journal* also made references to a third robber traveling with the James brothers: "The wounded man, who was with these two up to Sunday afternoon, has not been heard from since, and, as he was then scarcely able to stand, it is supposed that he probably died or has been left somewhere along the road."

Monday afternoon, the town of Canton, Dakota Territory, was thrown into a wild state of excitement by the arrival of an eight-man posse from Worthington and Luverne. The posse had pursued the fleeing outlaws to the Sioux River, north of town. The men said the outlaws had escaped through

Lyon County to Beloit, Iowa, and over to the Canton area. Three members of the Minnesota posse, with Will Miller of Canton, started south along the Sioux River to alert the people and cut off the robbers who were fleeing southward towards the Missouri River.[26] On Tuesday morning, the balance of the Minnesota party rode off for Sioux Falls but a driving rain aided the robbers.

The *Sioux Valley News*, Canton, Dakota Territory, reported that the robbers would find their way to Nebraska "where friends were waiting for them, to shelter and take care of them." Arthur Linn, the editor of the newspaper, believed the outlaws would cross into Nebraska somewhere between Sioux City, Iowa, and Springfield, Dakota Territory.

According to one account, the fugitives passed through the hills of the Big Sioux River and down into Joy Hollow, where they rested in a cave. On the Broken Kettle Road south of Milnerville, Iowa, one of the robbers stopped at the Prather farm and hastily devoured a plate of food. The second man waited outside watching the road. He, too, was given a plate of food. The outlaws then rode south through Stone Park.[27]

Another report stated that the James brothers never went near Canton but stopped at the farm of Reverend Krogness, a pioneer missionary and pastor of the Norwegian Lutheran Church, a mile and a half northeast of Beloit and two miles east of Canton. After the outlaws crossed the river, Reverend Krogness saw them on the bluff, and when they asked for food and lodging, he complied. The brothers looked fatigued, and Reverend Krogness was sure they were either the Jameses or the Youngers. He chose to cooperate. In the morning, they took one of the horses belonging to Krogness, apologized for doing so, and rode off, leaving one horse behind.[28]

As the robbers departed, Mrs. Krogness went to make the bed and discovered blood stains on the sheets. Reverend Krogness quickly rode to Beloit, while his son attempted to follow the robbers. Sheriff Dixon of Lincoln County organized a posse but could find no trace of the outlaws. The younger Krogness did not locate the robbers either, but he did find their horse near the town of Calilope, not far from Sioux City.

Still another report reached Sioux City that Sheriff McDonald and his posse had caught up with the bandits on the Missouri River in Dakota Territory in an area called Texas. One was reportedly killed, the other captured. The report ripped through the city like wildfire until noon when a second report received via a reliable courier disproved the story.[29]

At noon, on Wednesday, September 25, Dr. Sidney Mosher, Sr., of Sioux City, received a call to attend Mrs. Robert Mann, who lived some twenty miles northeast of the city. Mrs.

Dr. Sidney Mosher. (Courtesy of the Northfield Public Library)

133

Mann was urgently in need of a goiter operation, so Dr. Mosher hurried to the Broadbent livery stable and hired a horse for the trip. At Broadbent's, he discovered a gathering of local residents discussing the Northfield robbers, their subsequent flight, and the reward Minnesota Governor John S. Pillsbury had offered for their capture. Dr. Mosher then mounted a little bay and started out for the Mann farm.

As he rode along, he met two men on horseback near a bluff. Thinking they were locals, he raised his hand to them and called out, inquiring about the road. But the men continued on their way as if they had not heard him. Dr. Mosher, certain the men had not heard him, patted his horse and rode up to them. The pair wheeled their horses about, drew guns from under their coats, pointed them at his head, and ordered, "Hands up." No one said a word for several minutes when the smaller of the two strangers bellowed, "Well?"

The doctor informed them he was a physician on his way to attend a patient. The smaller robber called him a liar and accused him of being a detective from St. Paul out searching for the robbers. Dr. Mosher insisted he was no robber nor a robber hunter. The shorter man searched him while the other held him at gun point. But the doctor had recently purchased the new suit he was wearing and had failed to carry identification. The robber found only a pocket medicine case and a lancet in his pockets.

When the doctor told them he was unarmed, he was told he might have companions hiding near the bluff. To prove his identity, Mosher asked the robbers to ride back to the closest farm and ask the owner to describe Dr. Sidney Mosher of Sioux City and ask if there was a Mrs. Robert Mann in the area. Supposedly, Jesse rode back to a farm and confirmed Mosher's story. The outlaws assured the doctor they would not kill him, but they would have to detain him until evening. To make sure he did not make a mad dash for freedom, they exchanged horses, giving Mosher the worst spent of their two horses.

Jesse road in the lead, with Dr. Mosher behind him, and Frank bringing up the rear. As they rode along, Frank talked of the escape from Northfield and their "queer code of ethics." Dr. Mosher made a casual remark about the Civil War, which enraged Jesse, who, according to the doctor, bellowed, "Damn you, Doc. I'll kill you yet."

That afternoon, they stopped at a farm house and Jesse informed the owner that he was accompanying Dr. Mosher on his way to treat Mrs. Mann. Jesse said they had had a breakdown and the doctor desperately needed to borrow a saddle. The farmer was somewhat suspicious, but did not want to test the men's patience, so he gave up his saddle. At six o'clock in the evening, they stopped at another farm and ate some food.

It was not until evening that Dr. Mosher noticed Frank had been shot. They had ceased riding, and Frank admitted he could not easily get off his horse without help. Dr. Mosher lifted him down. Jesse asked Frank to have the doctor set his leg although the wounded outlaw made no reply. Frank, however, removed his clothing, and the doctor noticed the wound was a clean shot through the fleshy part of the thigh. Jesse ordered Mosher to remove his own clothing, tossed him Frank's, and the doctor put them on. Since he was a much shorter man than Frank, he had to roll up the legs of his trousers.

When it became dark, Jesse pointed to a light in a farm house a half-mile away and told the doctor to run toward the light and not turn around or he would kill him. As he started, he became frightened, thinking he would be shot in the back. He ran as fast as he could, but his progress was slowed by Frank's bulky coat flapping in the wind, the too-large shoes of Frank James, and the shaking of his own knees.

Entering the farm yard, a group of dogs began barking and growling. Without pausing to knock at the door of the house, he burst in to confront a woman rocking before the fire. She began shouting, "Robbers." Men came running from the barn, and the woman's husband carried a shotgun in his hand. Mosher quickly told his story, and a ten-year-old boy sitting by the fire recognized him as the doctor in Sioux City.

In the morning, the same boy found the little sorrel where Dr. Mosher had left her. Too tired to graze, she had dropped down and rested all night. When the farmer took Dr. Mosher into Sioux City that morning, the boy led the sorrel from the back of the wagon. Upon reaching town, he spread the alarm. Mosher said the Jameses had frankly told him they expected to be caught, but not alive and that they would fight to the bitter end and sell their lives as dearly as possible. He also carried their message to the Sioux City banks, "that when they gave this town a call, they [the bank officers] would do well to give up the vault keys peaceably, and thus avoid making martyrs of themselves."[31]

Dr. Mosher, after telling of his predicament, procured a fresh team of horses and rode off for the Little Sioux to treat Mrs. Mann. As he was leaving, Mr. Broadbent jokingly cautioned him to make a better trade next time, in case he was again held up and forced to exchange animals.

While Sioux City buzzed with excitement over Dr. Mosher's return, Sheriff McDonald and his company of scouts rode into town from their fruitless search of the countryside. But the never-say-die sheriff was off in the morning in hot pursuit, riding through Portlandville in a southeasterly direction. Only seven miles from LeMars, McDonald and company stopped at a farm where the robbers had breakfasted the day before. Realizing the robbers had a day on them, McDonald returned to Sioux City via the Floyd Valley for a fresh change of horses.

"During the balance of the afternoon there was nothing but a continuous stream of reports concerning the robbers," reported the *Sioux City Daily News*. "They had been seen in the city; they stopped and drank beer at the Greenville house across the Floyd in the morning; they had been seen at 11:00 A.M. at Sergeant Bluffs, and so on. The most probable conclusion finally arrived at was that the robbers had kept right along in their southeasterly course across the country toward Denison, and in this direction Sheriff McDonald expected to start with his party last evening."

An officer was immediately dispatched to the Greenville house to check out the story of the James boys eating there. The investigator returned with the news that the presumed outlaws were only a couple of herders who had some animals with them.[32]

About ten o'clock in the morning, August Pruist, a farmer living northeast of town, arrived and confirmed Dr. Mosher's story, saying he had seen the doctor in their company. Pruist took a measure of the imprint of the shoe of one of the horses the robbers rode and Broadbent recognized it as that of his stolen mount. Pruist said that after the robbers left Dr. Mosher, they turned and crossed the Floyd River at Hungerford's, heading in a westerly direction.

Pruist's report corroborated an earlier report of the boys being seen in the Broken Kettle bluff area. McDonald divided his party, sending one unit east toward Smithland, while he led another party to the Broken Kettle bluffs. Despite the attempted encirclement of the robbers, many Sioux City residents believed the robbers were hiding out within the city.

A local attorney, C.R. Marks, walked down Third Street in the vicinity of Pierce and Nebraska on business, after hearing of reports the robbers had taken refuge in the city. As he approached a vacant lot, he was startled in seeing two persons lying in the tall weeds. Marks was certain he had stumbled upon the robbers, and in pretending not to see them, he edged closer for a better view. As he did so, he became terror-stricken. He saw one of the figures raise an arm over the weeds. The man was clenching what looked like a navy revolver.

Marks rushed for reinforcements. Within minutes, the vacant lot was surrounded. As the party closed in on the presumed robbers, they found not Frank and Jesse James, but two Indians, one male, the other female, taking a rest. The extended hand clenching a revolver was nothing more than the man stretching his arms and yawning. The *Daily Journal* quipped, "Many reports circulated by parties who profess to have seen the robbers, would, if thoroughly sifted, turn out about the same way."

But more reliable news reached Sioux City when it was learned the robbers had stopped at the farm house of J.C. Thompson, near LeMars, about eleven o'clock Thursday morning. The strangers told Mr. Thompson they were hunting "the damned robbers"; that their horses, a dark bay and a gray, were badly worn out from the chase, and that they would pay him well to ride two of his horses to a spot eight miles away. Thompson agreed, and after putting their horses in his barn, hitched up two of his to a buggy. Thompson was told they would be back the same evening, but, of course, he never saw them again.

The *Omaha Bee* carried the story: "The two Northfield bank robbers who have been creating such excitement in the vicinity of Sioux City are still at large. The latest outrage committed by them occurred Thursday, when they went to the farmhouse of James Thompson, about ten miles northwest of LeMars, on the Illinois Central R.R., and said they wanted to go to a place called Broken Kettle, about twenty miles north of this city. Thompson had not returned home at a late hour, and fears are entertained that he has been murdered. Men are out trying to trace him and [his] team but at last account had not succeeded. The two villains are undoubtedly the notorious James brothers."[33]

A stranger also rapped at the door of the nearby Mason home after dark. Mr. Mason answered, but a voice from outside exclaimed, "Don't come to the door. I want to know where to cross the west fork." Mr. Mason told him where to cross, the stranger left, and Mr. Mason went back to bed.[34]

On the evening of September 23, Sioux City went into a state of frenzy when a man believed to be either Frank or Jesse James was captured on the west fork. About seven o'clock, the "James" prisoner was brought down Fourth Street in a wagon, surrounded by guards with pistols, and taken to the county jail. A mob of citizens followed. The prisoner was immediately locked in a cell as two to three hundred people took turns staring at him through the little wicket in the cell door.[35]

The prisoner was observed standing in his cell, his eyes surveying the tiny room into which he had been thrust. Sitting down, he began playing cards with two other prisoners, looking very unconcerned as if he had been brought up in prison. Most of the observers were sure the man was a James brother and, if not, certainly a proper subject for a prison cell.

Dr. Mosher was sent for and asked to identify the prisoner as one of the two men who had held him captive on Wednesday evening. Mosher took a good look and declared he had never seen the man before. Sheriff McDonald permitted sheriffs Finch, Davis, and Hurd, of Minnesota, all of whom were at the jail, to enter the cell and search the prisoner. Hurd immediately strip searched the suspect.

The prisoner was described by the sheriffs as a man of five feet nine or ten, 150 pounds, somewhat spare of built, sandy complexion, whiskers and mustache, long dark hair, thin face, firm resolute expression of countenance, and piercing gray eyes.

The prisoner insisted his name was William C. McFarland and that he lived near a Mormon settlement in Crawford County. He said he came to the west fork area looking for work and was arrested while in the employ of a man named Smith. When he had arrived at Smith's, he was told his services were not needed, but he refused to leave and was eventually given work. Deputy Ames, who arrested him, said when he nabbed his prisoner that the suspect warned that if he only had his guns with him, he would defy all of Woodbury County.

The incarcerated Youngers were told that one of the James boys had been killed, the other captured. Cole was considerably agitated and asked which had been killed, the larger or the smaller, and asked if anything had been said about him. When told about the experience of Dr. Mosher, Cole found the story quite amusing. Cole laughed and said, "Good boys to the last."

The capture of William C. McFarland, the suspected James brother, was initially a feather in Sheriff John McDonald's cap. One newspaper account published during his lifetime said he had the best record of any sheriff in the west, having captured and sent to the penitentiary more men than any sheriff west of the Missouri River. The account stated it was no easy job to be a sheriff. The lawman could only get his man by going after him, and to succeed, he had to be a good horseman. After getting his man, his job was only half finished, for he had to often protect his prisoner from self-appointed lynch mobs.[36]

While poor McFarland languished in jail, two deputies returned to the west fork and picked up the James' trail, following it to a site seven miles north of Correctionville, where the fugitives had eaten dinner. The lawmen were told the outlaws had inquired about the way to Denison. They followed in that direction, passing Willow Creek on the Maple River and picking up the trail again in Ida.[37]

The trailing lawmen were certain the Jameses had swum the Little Sioux River heading east, the Maple River above Silver Creek, and crossed the creek at a ford toward Sac City on the Coon River. Unable to pick up the outlaws' trail, and their own horses played out, they returned to LeMars. They felt confident, however, the Jameses were headed for Timber and planned to cross the Northwestern Railroad for Missouri.

The officers said the trail they were following was undoubtedly that of the outlaws. The gray horse one of the robbers was riding was shod with a shoe resembling a mule shoe in shape, and the taller of the two men was so lame, he limped badly. He had to step on the toe of his boot to walk. Stations along the Northwestern and Rock Island roads were alerted.

Upon hearing the officers' report, a local man, C.W. Hepburn, rode up to the river crossing, picked up the robbers' trail, and found they had swum with their horses across the river five miles above Correctionville at Jacob Bunn's farm. A posse was organized quickly and found the trail on the east side of the Little Sioux River, on the road leading up Moon Creek in the direction of Ida Grove. Farmers living along the road told the posse they had seen the two men pass by about noon on Thursday, riding at a gallop.

Near the Zupe farm, they discovered the robbers had stopped on the road to talk with one of the farmer's little daughters. They asked her what she was eating, and, when she answered raw potatoes, they laughed heartily, telling her they didn't want any, and continued on down the road.

The posse followed the outlaw's trail to within seven miles of Ida Grove, but, with night coming on, they stopped at a farm house. Here they learned that the sheriff of Plymouth County and a well-armed posse had passed only a couple hours before in the direction of Correctionville. The Sioux City party ate their supper, fed and watered their horses, and took off after the other posse. About midnight, they met the other group and learned that the Jameses had been tracked to the Coon River, but with a two-day start on both posses, the lawmen gave up the chase.

Meanwhile, a *Sioux City Daily Journal* reporter visited William McFarland in his jail cell and conducted an interview. The reporter was introduced to the prisoner by Sheriff McDonald and graciously received. "The first information the [prisoner] condescended to impart, after acknowledging the reporter's presence by a stiff nod of the head, was that he had 'a little matter to settle with the editor of that damned paper,' and that he should not 'go for him with a barrel stave either.'" McFarland added that his character and reputation had been seriously damaged because of the *Journal*'s branding him a James boy.[38]

The interviewer had come to the jail expecting to get a confession out of a cool, calm James brother who would admit to being a James in name and heart, spill how many men he had killed, and identify some of the other gang members. When he found McFarland in a very agitated state, he decided for his own safety to conduct a mild interrogation.

McFarland told the reporter he was not a James brother and he had never been arrested before in civil life. He admitted to being placed under arrest in the army for drunkeness and other minor violations of which he did not specify. When the interviewer said he was told McFarland lived in Crawford County, the prisoner replied, "I do not. Never was in Crawford County. I have a mother and brothers and sisters living in Davis County. I don't live long at a time anywhere but stop and work in one place a short time and hen [sic] move on to another place."

When asked if he ever lived in Missouri, McFarland said he had not but had traveled through the state several times. He stated emphatically he had not heard about the attempted bank robbery in Minnesota until he was arrested. McFarland talked of people he had worked for recently, remembering names but not faces, and told the interviewer he carried no extra baggage. He also said he was a veteran of the Civil War with the Second Iowa Regiment and the Eighth Michigan.

The reporter later wrote: "As regards the matter of his arrest, he says that he was pulling onions when the officer rode up unbeknown to him. On straightening up McFarland says he looked into the muzzle of the rifle in the hands of the officer, who ordered him to hold up his hands. Prisoner replied, 'Go to hell!' The officer said, 'Hold up your hands or I will shoot!' 'Shoot and be damned!' said McFarland. But he gave himself up."

The following morning, McFarland was released.

McFarland, however, would not be the only person arrested in the wave of James brother hysteria. On October 13, police converged on the home of Dr. William W. Noland, five miles from Independence, Missouri, and arrested a man believed to be Frank James. Dr. Noland and others insisted the man was John Goodwin of Louisiana, but since he had a leg wound similar to Frank's, he was taken into custody. Sergeant Boland, of the St. Louis Police Department, proposed that Dr. Mosher journey to St. Louis to identify the prisoner, and authorities in Northfield were asked to participate.[39]

"Chief McDonough is by no means certain that this man is Frank James, but feels certain that he is one of the band that robbed the bank at Northfield, and, if he is not Frank James, than he is Cal Carter," reported the *Owatonna Journal*. "He says his injuries were caused while hunting squirrels, but this story is very thin, and the police place no reliance on his statements. His wounds bear coincidence in location and time of connection with the Northfield raid."

Following the arrest at the Noland home, Dick Talley's place, only a half mile away, was also raided. The lawmen then paid a visit to the home of Widow Pettis, mother of desperado

Bill Pettis, who had been hanged some years earlier. Jesse was not found there either, but for a while police were confident they had his brother Frank.[40]

Another man, who professed to be Jesse James, strolled leisurely into the office of the *Leavenworth* (Kansas) *Times* and took a chair to wait for the editor. The impostor's shirt was streaked with tobacco juice, he was missing a collar, his eyes were glazed and his hair disheveled. "It could be said with truth, that Jesse was in some measure intoxicated, and this, coupled with the fact that he seemed unusually downcast and melancholy, might lead to the belief that he hadn't killed anyone that morning, and feeling that such diversion was necessary to existence, his intention was to see what kind of corpse he could make of an editor." This "Jesse" denied involvement in past robberies, attempted to borrow a quarter, then strode drunkenly toward the post office where he said he could write a check.[41]

Shortly after the abduction of Dr. Mosher, the trail of the very real Frank and Jesse James grew thin and eventually disappeared altogether. Numerous reports of robber sightings made headlines but the real outlaws left the area with nary a trace. G.W. Hunt, pioneer editor of the *Sioux City Democrat*, claimed to have the answers as to the whereabouts of the Jameses after the Dr. Mosher affair. His account, however, is not taken seriously; no copies of the *Democrat* exist today and almost no material on the *Democrat* can be found. Hunt's alleged story also ran no byline.

Hunt, who held a great admiration for the James brothers, contended that he interviewed Dr. Mosher upon the physician's escape to the city. Taking advantage of Deputy Sheriff Dan McDonald, brother of the sheriff, John, who let him read dispatches concerning the outlaws' whereabouts, Hunt decided to do everything possible to prevent them from being captured. This included his discouraging of a plan by Dan McDonald to patrol four skiffs on the Missouri River.

Hunt, whose undated article (with no byline) was found years later by Dan McDonald's daughter, wrote: "By this time we discovered that Sheriff McDonald and a well-armed party were on the fresh and well-defined scent of the James[es] and must capture them if not thwarted. Hitching up our team, we [Hunt and an unidentified companion] started out after the sheriff's party, soon overtaking them, and by a little strategy succeeded in turning them off in another direction."[42]

According to Hunt, he and his friend met the James brothers four miles from the village of Woodbury, on the Sioux City & Pacific Railroad. Hunt said as the brothers rode up, he identified himself, even telling them he knew who they were, and offered to strike up a deal. In exchange for their giving him an exclusive interview on the Northfield affair, he would help guide them back to Missouri. Although the brothers laughed, they consented. Leaving their horses behind to graze, the brothers climbed into the wagon, but when riders approached, they asked Hunt to lead them away by the shortest possible route.

Said Hunt: "That night we camped at a point adjacent to the Missouri River, nearly opposite the village of Sloan, not desiring to risk the chances of stopping at a house. During the night, they proposed and we acceded to an oath or pledge that we would not under certain circumstances reveal what facts they gave us until their safe arrival among friends, of which fact they could acquaint us either by telegraph or letter, and in addition, under certain other circumstances pending on the arrest and trial of the Younger brothers, we would not disclose certain other information given us . . ."

After sleeping in prairie grass that evening, the wagon proceeded down the Missouri Valley in the direction of Council Bluffs. Where the Little Sioux River runs into the Missouri, the strange party discovered a skiff moored to a stake by a small chain. Having procured provisions from Ed Haakinson's store in Sloan, the Jameses left their new-found friends and floated along the river at night until they reached Nebraska City. From that point on, they felt it safe enough to travel by day and reached St. Joseph, Missouri, within eight days of taking leave of Hunt.

James gang member, Dick Liddel, who later turned state's evidence, had a simple, but totally impossible, version of the escape. According to Liddel, the Jameses purloined a wagon and rode back to Missouri, with the more seriously wounded brother resting in the back. The hardly fleeing outlaws traveled sometimes through Iowa and at other times in Kansas and Missouri until they reached the home of an undisclosed friend. With men waiting all along the Iowa line, Liddel's fairy tale is hardly worth noting.[43]

Posse members, who expected the Jameses to swing south, placed a human noose around any would-be escape route. No one considered the robbers might travel north in the opposite direction. While General Crook and hundreds of troops poured into the Dakota, peaceful tribes in the eastern side of the territory prepared for winter. Many stories have been handed down how the fleeing James brothers swung north to evade their captors and entered the Lake Traverse reservation near Sisseton, which had opened in 1867. The brothers took Indian wives, then continued north to the Devil's Lake area where they spent the winter living in a dugout at Sweetwater Lake.[44]

Jesse may have been familiar with the Lake Traverse tribe through a chance association with the mother of Frank Cavanaugh just prior to the Northfield robbery. Jesse allegedly stopped at the Cavanaugh home in Faribault. Mrs. Cavanaugh, a teacher, kept her pupils singing several songs in succession when the suspicious-looking stranger entered in search of lodging. She directed him to the hotel boarding house run by she and her husband. They conversed later that evening, and Mrs. Cavanaugh may have disclosed information that her son, also a Frank, had taken an Indian wife and lived at Lake Traverse reservation as a farmer and post butcher.[45]

One story implies that Lake Kavanaugh, just north of Devil's Lake and where Jesse may have waited out the winter, was the homestead of Frank Cavanaugh's brother, but the two siblings disliked each other, so the brother spelled his name with a "K." Another version suggests that Frank Cavanaugh owned the homestead but the name of the lake was misspelled.

Tribal historian, Louis Garcia, Ph.D., interviewed a local missionary in 1983 and reported: "I talked to Father Dan and he said fifty years ago it was common knowledge among the Indians in the Dakotas of the relationship of Jesse James. He said all he can remember is that after they left Devil's Lake they went to Billings, Montana and he sent for his wife [and children?], but by then she had found out who he was and was afraid to go and so they split up forever." The Reverend Steven Spider of the Sisseton tribe is said to be a great grandson of Jesse.[46]

If the story is true, then Jesse's trail ends at Billings. Another consideration is the proximity of Devil's Lake to Grand Forks, where the father of Bill Stiles lived. The elder Stiles maintained his son had not died in Northfield, and whether true or false, the fugitives, with or without him, could have taken refuge in his home if they did indeed travel north into what is now North Dakota.

Other accounts relate the Jameses made their way to Fort Dodge, Iowa. Mrs. John Rolow was a seven-year-old girl when the Jameses allegedly came to her parents' door near Fort Dodge. The men arrived at sunset and were armed with knives and revolvers. The family was alarmed when the men said they were going to spend the night."[47]

This same courteous, soft-voiced stranger is supposed to have stopped at the George Armes home in the backwoods near Fort Dodge. Posing as a wealthy land buyer, he said he was seeking lodging while he negotiated for several farms in the area. He paid liberally for his board and helped with chores. The Armeses, however, wondered why he never removed his gun and cartridge belt, but since many men went armed, they gave it little more thought.[48]

Armes showed the stranger around and took him to local farms, several of which the newcomer agreed to purchase. When Armes agreed to take him to Fort Dodge to draw up the neces-

sary papers, the stranger gave his small-caliber pistol in apprecia-
tion of his services. At Fort Dodge, the stranger asked Armes to
wait at a corner while he met a friend to obtain some money. He
never returned. Armes moved his family to Saunders County,
Nebraska, in 1881 and several years later relocated in Oregon,
where he died in 1897, the pistol still in his possession.

During the Northfield robbery, one of the gang members
is alleged to have caught the cashier edging to a drawer. He
warned the man to step back, then opened the drawer and took
a small-caliber "hideout" (pocket pistol) gun which he dropped
into his pocket. If Jesse was in the bank, he could have been the
robber who pocketed the hideaway gun or it could have been
given to him by one of his confederates.[49] (It has not been established whether there was in fact a small pistol in Mr. Heywood's
drawer.)[50]

It is possible the Jameses left the heavily-guarded
Missouri River and turned eastward toward Fort Dodge. They
were aware that authorities in Missouri were watching for them.
They could catch a train in Fort Dodge for Kentucky where
they had relatives who would hide them, and they may have
been waiting for news of the Youngers whom they could possibly intercept at Fort Dodge. If news of the Youngers' fate did
reach them in the vicinity of Fort Dodge, they would most-
assuredly catch a train to Kentucky rather than ride into the
arms of Missouri officers.[51] The Jameses had lived in Midway,
Kentucky, and the Youngers had relatives there.[52]

Another account inferred that the James brothers, living
in barns and stealing raw vegetables from the fields, traveled only
by night during the three weeks after they left the Youngers.
Instead of rushing to Kentucky or Missouri, their destination may
have been Tennessee.[53]

Regardless of which direction the brothers followed, at
some point they must have crossed into Nebraska. One account,
and there are several, claims that the boys crossed near the John
Larson farm near Spinks Township, Union County. The somewhat shaky account reaches a ridiculous level when it alleges that
the brothers came in different rigs with several suitcases and
wearing fine clothing. Spending the night, the brothers gave the
Larson children stick candy and rode away in the morning. Spink
Township was located ten miles north of the Sioux River and
eleven miles east of the Missouri.[54]

A different account compiled by James scholar Emmett
C. Hoctor appears much more convincing. It had long been
rumored that the James brothers had a good friend in Nebraska
with whom they stayed while escaping posses in Minnesota, Iowa,
and Nebraska.[55] Near Council Bluffs, Iowa, the outlaws crossed

the Missouri River and rode directly south to Nebraska City to hide out with this old friend, Captain Logan Enyart. An October 4 edition of the Omaha newspaper reported a pair of horses stolen in the area by two men, one matching the description of Jesse James, concluding that the theft was probably the work of the fleeing bandits.[56]

Captain Enyart undoubtedly met the James boys some-time during the Civil War. When the war broke out, twenty-three-year-old Enyart enlisted in Company G, First Missouri Cavalry, quickly became captain, and fought with General Sterling Price until they were driven from Missouri to Mississippi. Present at the surrender of Vicksburg in July 1863, Enyart became a prisoner of war in Tennessee, Georgia, and Alabama. Upon his release, he retreated with General Joseph E. Johnston, seeing action at Lone Mountain, Kenesaw Mountain, New Hope Church, Peach Tree Creek, and the siege of Atlanta. He was recaptured at the Battle of Franklin in Tennessee. He was not released until June 17, 1865.[57]

It is quite possible that Enyart met Frank James and Cole Younger shortly before or during the Battle of Wilson's Creek in Missouri. General Price had gone to Lexington to organize vol-unteers just a few weeks after Frank had joined the Centerville Home Guards, not far from the James farm. Enyart, at the time, was with Price's army. Both Frank and Enyart fought at Wilson's Creek. Following the Confederate victory, Frank contracted a case of measles and was left behind at a Springfield hotel. Captured by Union troops, Frank took an oath to go home, but instead he responded to Price's "Proclamation to the People of Central and North Missouri and rejoined his army for the Battle of Lexington. Following Price's victory here, Frank joined Quantrill's irregulars and left the State Guard.[58]

When the war ended, Enyart, who had suffered three major wounds, crossed the Missouri River and started a success-ful freight business in Nebraska City, Otoe County. Jesse James visited the captain many times. In 1875, only one year before the Northfield affair, Jesse visited Enyart and had his photo taken at the Waldbaum Studio, which, presumably, had been recom-mended by the captain.[59]

On another occasion, Enyart and James together visited Paul Schminke, Nebraska City's only banker. Enyart introduced Jesse as his friend, "Mr. Brown," a traveling man, and it was not until several days later that Enyart told Schminke who his trav-eling friend really was. This same Mr. Brown "rode boldly down Central Avenue in Nebraska City with arms folded" with Enyart to Hawke's General Store where he and Enyart shook hands with various townsfolk.[60]

One of these local citizens, photographer Monroe W. Neihardt, who met Mr. Brown at the store, went to Enyart the next day and whispered, "Jesse looked pretty natural." Like Schminke, Neihardt was asked by Enyart to keep Jesse's secret. The following year, 1876, Neihardt, who had photographed prisoners for the Nebraska State Prison in Lincoln, purchased the Waldbaum Studio and discovered the tintype of Jesse. Neihardt knew it was authentic, having taken Jesse's picture and spoken with him in Hannibal, Missouri, in 1861 or 1862.

Frank James, too, visited Enyart in Nebraska City and was known to race horses in town. According to Neihardt, he had run across the James brothers six or seven times in Nebraska City between the years 1861 and 1882.

Enyart readily agreed to give both brothers a safe retreat or haven from the law on land purchased to the south of his large farm. One newspaper account reports that Enyart "bought ground to make another lane leading up to his house so that if Jesse had to leave in a hurry there would be several ways for him to go."[61]

Following the Pinkerton raid on the James farm in Kearney, Missouri, in 1875, Frank and Jesse are known to have hidden out on this farm. Later, when Frank was in jail in Alabama, he penned a letter revealing that Captain Enyart had been such a good friend while they were on the run from the law. And on their "return" from the Northfield bank, the James brothers were definitely on the run and in need of Enyart's safe retreat. Since Nebraska City is located on the Missouri River separating Nebraska from Iowa, and just a breath away from the Missouri line, it is quite possible Enyart was involved in their escape.[62]

The Jameses had another friend in Otoe County, James Henry Catron, who may have hidden the boys following their flight from Northfield. Like Enyart, Catron took an ox team to Nebraska City after the war and established a successful freight business. There he and Enyart befriended J. Sterling Morton, the originator of Arbor Day. They also maintained their friendship with Monroe W. Neihardt.

In 1928, Neihardt revealed his Jesse James secret and mentioned a hamlet known as Mt. Joy, located a few miles southwest of Nebraska City, where Jesse had stayed on several occasions. Mt. Joy was also the local haunt of other outlaws such as George McWaters and Quin Bohanan. It was later burned to the ground by locals hoping to rid the county of outlaw trash. Jesse was also seen in the river town of Old Wyoming where he later rented a house for his family.

Another area where Jesse felt comfortable in Nebraska was the site of the James Samuel family retreat in Rulo, Richardson County. There Zerelda had taught school, and her

Formerly a false-fronted building at 1541 Nebraska Street. The loft is alleged to have served as a hideout for the James brothers in Blair, Nebraska. (Photo by Emmett C. Hoctor)

husband attempted to establish a medical practice. In 1865, a wounded Jesse spent eight weeks in Rulo after being shot in Missouri while trying to surrender. Rulo, Nebraska, was close to home and rather safe compared to the Kansas-Missouri border. In addition, Zerelda's Cole cousins had been among the early settlers crossing into Nemaha County, Nebraska, from Missouri, and Jesse had been named for her brother, Jesse Cole.[63]

    While the Jameses were robbing the bank at Northfield, they may have headed for Brownville, Nebraska, some twenty miles below Nebraska City. The sheriff of Nemaha County was David Plasters, who had married one of the James' cousins, Anjalina Cole. Another cousin was a judge there. One rumor claims Jesse and Frank, pretending to be cattle buyers, stopped in Brownville, probably one year before Northfield, on their way to or from Nebraska City, and Jesse played a game of poker in a local saloon. The area between Nebraska City and Brownville would certainly have been familiar to them during their 1876 flight.[64]

The building on the right served as a Blair, Nebraska, livery stable where the James brothers left their horses. (Photo by Emmett C. Hoctor)

Omaha, a growing city of 25,000 in about 1873. (Courtesy of Emmett Hoctor)

There are several reasons why Jesse and Frank could have been in the Brownville area. Since Brownville was vying to become the capitol of Nebraska and held the first Nebraska state fairs, Frank would have been drawn to the track there with his race horses. That Jesse adopted the alias of Richard Brown, who had founded the town was more than coincidental, and, with relatives in the area, Brownville, like Nebraska City and Rulo, could have served as a safe retreat for the fleeing outlaws.[65]

The James were, in fact, familiar with all or most of the Nebraska country bordering the Missouri River. In 1873, Frank James and Cole Younger had spent time in Omaha while arranging to pull off their daring Adair, Iowa, train robbery. Their mission was to learn when the gold shipment was to reach Omaha, while Jesse and the others, including Bill Chadwell, waited in the hills of the Adair area.[66] Two years later, on June 6, Frank married Annie Ralston in Omaha. Missouri outlaw, Bad Jim Berry, was also living in Plattsmouth, Nebraska.

Another account alleges that the James brothers hid in a loft of a false-fronted building on Nebraska Street in Blair, Nebraska, during their escape from Northfield. Their horses were kept in a livery stable across the street and two doors west. Blair is located just north of Omaha, an area familiar to them. Presumably friends hid them in the "Blair hideout" until they were able to move on.[67]

The Jameses could also have taken refuge at the home of John O'Connor in Hastings. Believed to be a member of the James gang, O'Connor owned two farms near Hastings valued at $40,000 and three buildings within town worth about $30,000.[68]

The *Hartington* (Nebraska) *Herald* describes another hideout of the Jameses on the old Coon Ranch, about one and one-half miles north of Obert. In 1876, the trail to the hideout was partially obscured by timber, and the boys may have used the location because of its proximity to water.[69]

Still another account alleges that the Jameses spent time a few miles west of the town of Sumner in Dawson County.

148

George Mills, who lived about three miles west of Sumner, worked for a couple men later identified as Frank and Jesse James. Mills claimed he was paid every evening and that he was supposed to come to work after sun-up every morning and go home before sundown. One day, a woman on horseback arrived late in the afternoon, and both horse and rider looked worn from a long, hard trip. Mills was told that the brothers had to leave, and he should look after the farm. The work hand was paid in advance for six months, but the brothers never returned. Years later Mills opened a tool chest belonging to the brothers, and he discovered the names of Jesse and Frank James written on the lid.[70]

Finally, one area of Nebraska would have been geographically suitable for the escaping bandits, since it was located just below and between the Dakota Territory communities of Yankton and Ponca. Known as the Devil's Nest country of northern Nebraska, it has been claimed that Frank and Jesse James first came to the Nest in 1869 and started a trading post among the Indians. Using the names, Frank and Jesse Chase, the boys met and married lovely Indian sisters, both daughters of Thomas Wabasha. In 1870, Jesse's new wife delivered a son, Joe Jesse Chase, and Frank's wife bore a daughter, Emma.[71]

That same year, Frank and Jesse killed a French trader after a dispute and left the area. Although they wrote letters to their wives, the girls' mothers would not let them answer the letters. Jesse's wife later married William Good Teacher and Frank's wife disappeared into Minnesota. It is quite possible that there was a connection between Frank's wife who went to Minnesota and the Mrs. Frank Cavanaugh of Faribault, who directed the boys to the Cavanaughs at the Lake Traverse and Devil's Lake reservations.

The James boys did not officially marry until the mid-1870s. Historian Emmett C. Hoctor presents a good argument why the brothers could have used the Devil's Nest area for a hideout. The land is rich prairie with a sprinkling of timber, and the Missouri River runs through it into Missouri, providing the boys with an easy riding distance. Much of present-day Cedar, Knox, and Thurston counties of Nebraska was Indian reservation land in the 1870s, populated by the Santee Sioux, Omaha, Ponca, and Winnebago tribes.[72]

The legend of the Jameses at Devil's Nest also rumored that the brothers subsisted as cattlemen and occasionally paid the Santee to help them float timber from Cedar County down the Missouri River to Yankton. Another story states that the boys' mother once met them at Obert, Nebraska, only twenty miles from the Devil's Nest. It is also alleged that United States marshals stalked out the Devil's Nest area on three separate occasions, hoping to nab Jesse and Frank, and the Nest was given its name by one of the marshals who said the terrain "looked like a devil's nest."

The route of the James boys, following their kidnapping of Dr. Mosher, may never come to light. While scholars argue whether the boys retreated to Missouri, Nebraska, Tennesee, Kentucky, or even Montana, the outlaws simply voluntarily vanished until the heat was off. Even in December of 1876, the posses were still searching for the them as recorded in several newspapers:

"The attack was made on Wednesday night by Sheriff Groom, of Clay County [Missouri], and four men. It was very dark and rainy. The posse went to the home of the boys, four miles from Fearney [sic], knowing they were there. Frank was seen, and, as he saw the posse about the same time, he fired a shot in the air, as a signal for Jesse. The sheriff and one man fired at Frank, without effect, when he returned the fire, hitting the tree behind which the sheriff was concealed The boys then mounted their horses and then got away, shouting, 'come on, you — —.'"[73]

According to the report, the sheriff pursued and followed their trail to a friend's house fourteen miles from Liberty but could not overtake them. The account further stated, "Nothing has been seen of them since, though men are scouring the country. Ed Miller, a brother Clel [sic], who was killed at Northfield, and a man named Hoffman [Harry], are supposed to have acted as spies for the James boys, who are known to be working their way north."

Notes

1 *Mankato Free Press*, March 7, 1931.

2 *The Albert Lea Tribune,* June 1, 1949, p. 6; *The Madelia Times-Messenger*, October 29, 1996, p. 2.

3 *Heron Lake News*, November 9, 1961, S.H. Berkness, "My Life Story."

4 *Windom Reporter*, Thursday, September 21, 1876.

5 *Faribault Democrat*, Friday, September 22, 1876.

6 *The Madelia Times*, Friday, September 22, 1876.

7 *Faribault Republican*, Wednesday, September 20, 1876; *Faribault Democrat,* Friday, September 22, 1876; *The Madelia Times,* Friday, September 22, 1876.

8 *Sioux City Daily Journal*, Wednesday, September 20, 1876, "The Hunt."

9 *Sioux City Daily Journal,* Sunday, September 17, 1876, "The Northfield Brigands."

10 *Sioux City Daily Journal*, Wednesday, September 20, 1876.

11 *Worthington Daily Globe,* June 27, 1958, Raymond A. Crippen, "Did Jesse and Frank James Spend Night on Banks of Okabena?"

12 Fred R. Humiston, "Recollections," Nobles County Historical Society Newsletter, 1950.

13 *Faribault Republican*, Wednesday, September 20, 1876.

14 Ibid.

15 *Faribault Republican*, Wednesday, September 20, 1876; Rock County Biographies, Rock County Historical Society, p. 453.

16 Arthur Rose, *History of Rock and Pipestone Counties*, Rock County Historical Society; Mariella Hinkly, Coordinator of Correspondence, Rock County Historical Society letter to author dated April 27, 1997.

17 *Faribault Republican*, Wednesday, September 20, 1876; *The Madelia Times*, Friday, September 22, 1876.

18 *Sioux City Daily Journal*, Sunday, September 17, 1876, "The Missouri Indians."

19 John G. Bourke, *On the Border With Crook*, University of Nebraska Press, Lincoln & London, 1971, pp. 375-376.

20 *Brookings Daily Register*, Tuesday, July 29, 1975, "Jesse James Legend Haunts Historic Palisades;" *South Dakota Historical Review*, Date Unknown, "Jesse James in South Dakota;" Patricia Schmidt, South Dakota Division of Tourism, "Legend of Jesse James Haunts Historic Palisades State Park;" Jim Kranak, "Palisades State Park," two-page manuscript; untitled two-page manuscript from Palisades State Park; *Worthington Daily Globe*, June 27, 1958; Kay Hively, "Jesse James' Wild Flight Across Devil's Gulch," *Farmland News*, May 1931; Jan Jones, Assistant Naturalist, Palisade State Park, South Dakota Department of Game, Fish and Parks, interview with author June 11, 1983, Palisades State Park and Devil's Gulch, South Dakota; Arnold D. Alberts interview with author June 2, 1997, Devil's Gulch, South Dakota.

21 Some reports state both Frank and Jesse leaped the canyon with Frank going first.

22 *Faribault Republican*, Wednesday, September 20, 1876; *Faribault Democrat*, Friday, September 22, 1876; *The Madelia Times*, Friday, September 22, 1876.

23 *Rice County Journal Extra*, September 1876.

24 *Sioux City Daily Journal*, Tuesday, September 19, 1876, "The Robbers."

25 *Sioux City Daily Journal*, Thursday, September 21, 1876, "The Robbers Shot."

26 *The Sioux Valley News* (Canton, S.D.), September 23, 1876, "Northfield Robbers."

27 Charles and Vesta Knapp, signed affidavits, Plymouth County Historical Society, LeMars, Iowa.

28 J.A. Derome, "Canton Thrown into Wild Stage of Excitement When Report Was Given That Bandits Were Near," eighth in a series of articles.

29 *Sioux City Daily Journal*, Friday, September 22, 1876, "The Robbers."

30 Gertrude Henderson, "Dr. Mosher Makes a Call, Tales and Trails of Yesterday," Date Unknown, Northfield Public Library; "Sioux City Family Treasures Bullet Pierced Trousers Worn by One of James Brothers," Date Unknown, Northfield Public Library.

31 *Sioux City Daily Journal*, Friday, September 22, 1876, "The Robbers."

32 *Sioux City Daily Journal*, Saturday, September 23, 1876, "The Outlaws."

33 *Omaha Bee*, Saturday, September 23, 1876, "The Northfield Bank Robbery."

34 Mrs. Fred Wingert letter to author dated April 1982; *Kingsley* (Iowa) *News-Times*, 1981, Exact date unknown.

35 *Sioux City Daily Journal*, Sunday, September 24, 1876, "The Robbers."

36 Sheriff Russell H. White, Jr., Woodbury County Sheriff's Department, 1981, a two-page biography of sheriffs John and Dan McDonald, Sioux City Public Museum.

37 *Sioux City Daily Journal*, Monday, September 25, 1876, "The Missouri Bandits."

38 *Sioux City Daily Journal,* Tuesday, September 26, 1876, "Busted."

39 *Owatonna Journal,* October 19, 1876, "Arrest of a Man Supposed to be Frank James."

40 Nancy B. Samuelson, "How the James Boys Fled the Disaster at Northfield and the Capture of 'Frank James,'" *The Journal,* Vol. III, No. 1, Official Publication of the Western Outlaw-Lawman History Association, Spring-Summer, 1993, pp. 4-9.

41 *Omaha Republican,* Friday Morning, September 15, 1876, "Jesse James."

42 Scrapbook of clippings belonging to Mrs. H.C. Harper; *Sioux City Journal,* July 25, 1954, "How an Early Day Sioux City Editor Helped James Boys to Escape After Northfield Bank Robbery."

43 J.A. Derome, "James Brothers Stopped in Sioux Falls in an Attempt to Dodge Northfield Posse," Fifth in a series of articles.

44 Louis Garcia, telephone interviews with author, February 19 and 21, 1983.

45 Ibid; North Dakota Historical Collections (Collections of the State Historical Society of North Dakota), Vol. 3, 1910, pp. 195, 214, 236.

46 Louis Garcia letter to author dated March 2, 1983.

47 David Parker, executive director, Fort Dodge Historical Foundation, letter to author dated May 11, 1981.

48 *Omaha Sunday World-Herald,* January 22, 1995, "Café Owner Convinced Gun Was Outlaw's;" *Omaha World-Herald,* Date Unknown, "Nebraskan Refuses All Offers for Gun Jesse James Used in Famed Bank Raid."

49 Bob Shelburne undated letter to author, postmarked January 17, 1997.

50 Sue Garwood DeLong, Executive Director, Northfield Historical Society interview with author January 21, 1997, Northfield, Minnesota.

51 Bob Shelburne undated letter to author, postmarked January 17, 1997.

52 Louise W. Hampton, Scholl Family Research Association of America, letter to author dated March 7, 1983.

53 *Tampa Bay Star,* Wednesday, November 18, 1981, Paul Harvey, The Rest of the Story, "Jesse James Could Tell You Crime Just Didn't Pay."

54 J.A. Derome, eighth in a series of articles.

55 *Jesse James: The Life and Daring Adventures of This Bold Highwayman and Bank Robber; and His No Less Celebrated Brother, Frank James. Together With the Thrilling Exploits of the Younger Boys,* by One Who Cannot Disclose His Identity, Barclay and Company, Philadelphia, 1882; Emmett C. Hoctor, "His Best Friend in Nebraska," *NOLA Quarterly,* Vol. XVI, No. 4, October-December 1991.

56 *Omaha Daily Bee,* October 4, 1876, "Horse Thieves."

57 Emmett C. Hoctor, "His Best Friend in Nebraska;" History of Otoe and Cass Counties, Nebraska, 1889, pp. 706-709; *The* (Lincoln, Nebraska) *Daily Journal,* December 7, 1939.

58 Robert L. Dyer, *Jesse James and the Civil War in Missouri,* University of Missouri Press, Columbia & London, 1994, pp. 21-28; Albert Castel, *General Sterling Price and the Civil War in the West,* Louisiana State University Press, Baton Rouge and London, 1968, p. 61.

59 Emmett C. Hoctor, "His Best Friend in Nebraska."

60 Emmett C. Hoctor, "Rusticating in Nebraska: 1862-1882," speech presentation to the Friends of the James Farm annual meeting, April 11, 1992, Kansas City, Missouri; "Factoryville, A Nebraska Ghost Town," *Journal of Nebraska History,* Vol. XIV, No. 4, p. 259.

61 *Lincoln* (Nebraska) *Sunday Journal,* February 5, 1939.

62 Emmett C. Hoctor, "Rusticating in Nebraska: 1862-1882."

63 Ibid.

64 Dr. Hugh E. Black, "Did Jesse James Play Poker in a Brownville Saloon?" *Brownville* (Nebraska) *Historical Society Bulletin,* January, 1970, Vol. 14, No. 1.

65 Emmett C. Hoctor, "Safe Retreat Found," *NOLA Quarterly,* Vol. XV, No. 4, October-December, 1991; Emmett C. Hoctor, Letter to the Editor, *The Journal,* Official Publication of the Western Outlaw-Lawman History Association, Vol. 1, No. 2, Fall-Winter, 1991, p. 2.

66 Mrs. Jackie Wilson, curator, Jesse James Museum, Adair, Iowa, letter to author dated January 3, 1997 with enclosed clipping, "Jesse James Museum," source unknown, Summer 1992.

67 Emmett C. Hoctor, telephone interview with author, December 22, 1996; Emmett C. Hoctor, letters to author dated December 18 and December 31, 1996.

68 *Nebraska History,* Volume 71, p. 76, Nebraska State Historical Society Archives, Lori Cox, "A Comedy of 'Heirs': The Estate of John O'Connor."

69 *Nebraska History,* Volume 21, p. 115, Nebraska State Historical Society Archives, The Editor's Table, Hartington Herald—The History of Jesse James.

70 *Nebraska History,* Volume 19, pp. 400-401, Nebraska State Historical Society Archives, "Jesse James' Nebraska Home."

71 William A. Settle, Jr., *Jesse James Was His Name,* p. 167.

72 Emmett C. Hoctor, "Jesse James Revisted," *Wild West Magazine,* June 1994; Emmett C. Hoctor, "Rusticating in Nebraska: 1862-1882; *Lincoln Journal Star,* February 5, 1939.

73 *Faribault Democrat,* December 15, 1876, "The James Boys."

Chapter 6

End of the Trail

I am a bonded highwayman,
Cole Younger is my name,
Through many a temptation,
I led my friends to shame.

For the robbing of the Northfield Bank,
They say I can't deny,
And now I am a poor prisoner:
In Stillwater Jail I lie.

Come listen, comrades, listen,
A story I will tell,
Of a California miner,
On whom my fate befell.

We robbed him of his money, boys,
And bid him go his way,
And that I'll always be sorry of,
Until my dying day.

We started then for Texas,
That good old Lone Star State,
Out on the Nebraska prairies,
The James boys we did meet.

With guns, cards, revolvers,
We all sit down to play,
And drinkin' a lot of good whiskey, boys,
To pass the time away.[1]

Origin Unknown

IN JANUARY 1851, CONGRESS APPROPRIATED $20,000 for the con-
struction of a prison in the town of Stillwater, Minnesota. The
new prison was built in Battle Hollow, a site named for an 1839
battle that took place there between the Dakota and the

1874 view of old Stillwater Prison looking southeast. (Courtesy of the Minnesota Historical Society)

Ojibway. By 1862, the facility had reached its maximum capacity, and steps were taken to enlarge the grounds and erect more buildings. During construction, the walls were extended, enclosing nine and one-half acres, and a dry house and shops were added with a cost of $14,500. John A. Reed became warden on August 3, 1874, a position he would hold for thirteen years. It was during his administration that the prison received its most infamous prisoners: the Younger brothers.[2]

On November 22, Cole, Jim, and Bob entered Stillwater Prison.[3] Walking into the prison yard, they took a good look around, and one of the brothers was overheard to say he had found a home at last. Once placed in separate cells, they looked disappointed and were quickly told they were not caged curiosities fed with luxury and leisure. Bob with his wounded stiff arm was handed a paint brush.[4] Cole later wrote: "When the iron doors shut behind us at the Stillwater Prison, we all submitted to the prison discipline with the same unquestioning obedience that I had exacted during my military service."[5]

The brothers were bathed and dressed in "penitentiary stripes" of a third-grade prisoner. Prior to 1860, prisoners were identified by having their heads shaved, but when John S. Proctor had been appointed warden, he abolished the haircuts, believing clothing made for easier identification.[6] The men were

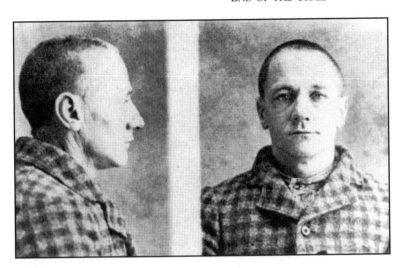

fingerprinted, given complete physicals and issued toiletries in their five-by-seven-foot cells.[7]

The Youngers, as well as any other incoming prisoners, were issued three tickets entitling them to certain privileges as long as they followed the rules. Each week they were given one ration of tobacco, and they were allowed to write letters under grade rules. They could have visitors—family and friends—once every four weeks. All inmates were required to bathe once a week in summer and once every two weeks in winter.[8]

Officers from Missouri who had come to Minnesota during confinement of the Youngers were asked to file charges against the brothers, but they refused. Cole was a wanted man there but Bob and Jim were not. According to the Missouri police, the Jameses and Youngers had been linked to several robberies, but they had never worked together.

"The Jameses are cold-blooded, deliberate murderers; the Youngers did hunt and kill the murderers of their father, who was waylaid, murdered and robbed of $5,000 by a party of Kansas jayhawkers," recorded a local newspaper. "They did not do this until after all efforts to bring them to justice through the law had failed. Since then Cole has been hunted like a tiger and has had no rest. He feels sorry for his brothers; but for himself he feels satisfied at being locked within prison walls."

Following a meeting with Warden Reed, the Youngers were given jobs making tubs and buckets in the prison basement. Reed felt it was a sound idea to place the brothers together at one work station where it would be easier to observe them. He had heard rumors that members of the James gang might try to break the boys out at any time, so, by putting the convicts together, he could concentrate key guards in one area.[9]

157

Soon, the Youngers advanced to second-grade prisoners, were issued different uniforms, permitted to grow their hair to any preferred length, and allowed to visit with each other once a month. Assigned new jobs in the thresher factory, Cole made sieves and Jim made belts. Since Bob could not straighten his injured arm, he was given the therapeutic job of painting walls. In their free time, the boys were given access to the prison library, and all three became enthusiastic readers.[10]

The prison library boasted about 6,000 titles with an emphasis on history, biography, science, art, fiction, poetry, and bound magazines. Works of fiction were most popular among the inmates, although they were carefully screened by prison personnel before being added to the library catalog. Thus, books of a sensational nature, such as the "Dead-Eye Dick" variety were considered in poor taste and were excluded from the library collection.[11]

By good behavior and adherence to prison regulations, prisoners could advance all the way to first-grade status in only six months. If any prisoner received two demerits in a single month, however, he would be sent all the way down to third-grade. He would then be required to keep a clean slate for three consecutive months before returning to second-grade status. A typical meal at Stillwater called for boiled corn beef, mashed potatoes, two kinds of bread but no butter, and cabbage usually cut into slaw. The prisoners ate in long rows and were not permitted to speak to one another. Should a prisoner want an additional slab of corn beef, he had to raise his hand. Once they were finished with their meal, they were required to sit up and fold their hands.[12]

Every cell, as well as the corridors, were scrubbed and whitewashed every day. Most of the pictures hanging in the prisoners' cells were gaudy and cheap, but occasionally an inmate displayed a picture of Christ, a priest, or a boy at prayer.

During an 1883 legislative tour of Stillwater Penitentiary, the Younger brothers were visited, and a reporter from a Twin Cities' newspaper interviewed the brothers. "Of the prison celebrities, those life-term convicts, the Younger brothers, came in for a large share of attention. . . . Their cells, which are on the ground floor in the second corridor, were surrounded continuously by a crowd of visitors. The chief interest to those familiar with the story of their crimes was in seeing how they bear their imprisonment, which has now ended the sixth year of their sentence for life."[13]

The reporter was quick to note that the Youngers received no special privileges. Cole was the only brother in his cell when the journalist and others passed through the cell block as Bob and Jim were working. Cole appeared to be in poor health, his close-clipped hair sprinkled with gray. When the reporter told Cole that he looked more than age forty-five, he was told by him that he was only thirty-nine.

"I was shot quite to pieces," remarked Cole. "Here in the face, in the neck here, behind the ear, and through my shoulder. There is a ball still in my head, and one in my breast." A visitor out of sight snapped that Cole did not like to be addressed by simple curiosity hunters, but Cole answered, "Someone says he doesn't want to look at me just out of curiosity. Oh, I don't mind that. I'm used to it, and I used to go see curiosities myself when I was a boy. . . ."[14]

A visitor in the crowd pushed his way forward and asked Cole the length of his prison term. Cole told the man he was serving a life term. "There isn't a requisition for me in existence, that I know of," said Cole. "There was, I believe, an indictment or two against me at Northfield, but they found that two clerks were the only persons in the bank where the cashier was killed . . . I never had a trial except in name. I was sentenced without a real trial. . . ."

Just then the dinner bell rang, and the prisoners filed in from the shops. Among them were Bob and Jim Younger. Bob sat with his back to the crowd of visitors but Jim did not touch his meal, preferring to talk instead: "The shot here in my mouth, and the one in my neck, is what's the matter with my voice . . . I got twelve different shots." Jim went on to explain he had once weighed 165 pounds but was down to 149 in prison.

The reporter noted that the prisoners' meal consisted of bread, coffee in a tin cup, meat (probably corn beef), baked beans, and a single raw onion. But the reporter added, "The Younger boys, if not other prisoners, seemed to have an addition of some nicely browned potatoes."

During the fall of that same year, Lee Morgan, a former Quantrill man and friend of Cole's, visited the Youngers at Stillwater. Morgan had informed relatives in Carlisle, Iowa, that he and others were planning to liberate the three brothers. When Morgan returned to Iowa, he told his brother the boys wouldn't be in Stillwater long. Morgan's brother, a former Union man from the Twenty-third Iowa Infantry, was angry and told the conspirator, "Lee, if you and those Southerners try to liberate those killers and bank robbers, I'll tell you those Minnesotians [sic] will just shoot all kinds of hell out of all of you and there won't be enough of you left to ship back in a pine box." Shortly thereafter, the plan was called off.[15]

But near disaster came not from an attempted prison break, but through fire. On January 8, 1884, at about 10:45 P.M., flames were discovered in the sash, door, and blind shop. Within minutes, the fire spread through the hard wood and wagon shops, boiler room, engine, blacksmith, and cooper shops, all of which were totally consumed. Fireman fought to save a building containing a large amount of valuable moldings and manufactured lumber and an ironclad building full of casting patterns.[16]

Gus Lindahl, a watchman, responsible for monitoring the steam heating and water supply, discovered the blaze in the third floor glazing room of the wood shops. Another guard, John Walton, joined Lindahl in an attempt to put out the flames, but the two men met with no success and quickly sounded the alarm. By the time the St. Paul Fire Department arrived, flames were shooting out of the windows of the four-story building.[17]

A local newspaper described the blaze: "The gutters became babbling brooks, then increased to rapid streams and a few seconds later had swollen to rivers that carried everything before them irresistible at the speed of a mill race . . ."[18]

The fire did not reach the cell block, but there was a genuine concern for the prisoners when the flames spread to within fifty feet of the inmates. The convicts were not removed from the building, although Warden Reed had them taken from their cells and chained together in gangs. Reed then called out company K of the state militia, and fifty men under Captain Merry arrived to watch the prisoners. The inmates remained docile and did not panic.[19]

A problem occurred when the firefighters failed to properly connect the penitentiary hose with the city hydrants, and the valves originally opened by Lindahl and Walton reduced the pressure on the stand pipes on the inside of the prison yard. The wood-working shops contained a large amount of flammable materials, and, before the firefighters could get started, the shops were ablaze.

Prison officials believed the blaze was deliberately set by convicts, although no one was charged. Damages caused by the fire amounted to about $300,000 and 300 men lost their jobs.

On January 25, disaster struck again. About 11:45 P.M., O.A. Watler was passing by the prison on his way home from a professional visit when he noticed a bright light in the basement beneath the car company's offices. Watler immediately rode to the engine house and notified the watchman. The alarm was sounded and an engine, hose cart, and hook and ladder truck rushed to the scene. Initially it appeared that the fire would be contained, but before long it was apparent the flames were spreading, and the prisoners inside the cell blocks were in danger.[20]

Cole Younger described the situation: "My cell is on the ground floor, on the south side of the building. I went to sleep about nine o'clock and had just wakened when I heard the alarm whistle. I smelled a faint odor of smoke but thought it was gas escaping into the corridor. I looked out of my window, which faces south, but could not see any fire. I was wondering why the whistle had been blown, when the guard, Mr. Cayou, informed me of the fire and told me to hurry. I did not apprehend any danger, but he told me how bad the fire was, and I hastened to follow him."[21]

Cole was sorry he could not remove his pictures from the wall or take his books along to safety. A pair of worsted wristlets, given him by Mrs. Cayou, sister of St. Paul Mayor O'Brien, as a Christmas gift, was all he could salvage. Two books, *Wit and Humor* and *God's Book of Nature*, given him by General Henry Sibley, were the two possessions he regretted losing the most. Cole was thankful he had only two weeks earlier sent his book on General Sibley's military campaigns home to Missouri.

"We were taken to the store room, where it was very cold, but it is very comfortable here," recalled Cole. "I have nothing to complain of in my treatment here. It certainly isn't like stopping at a hotel, but it's not very bad considering the place. We are all sorry for Warden Reed. This fire is a terrible misfortune to him. I'm a little dubious also about the prospects for food and sleeping quarters tomorrow—or, today, rather. I wish they'd send me back to Rice County until they rebuild. Sheriff Barton always treated me excellently."[22]

About 12:45, an alarm whistle called out Company K, and at the same time a telephone message brought assistance from St. Paul firemen. Once Company K arrived, most of the prisoners were taken from their cells chained and shackled, and taken to a large lumber warehouse in the rear.[23]

Cole Younger may have been an exception. Said Cole: "Attempt to escape? Why? We are on our parole. When the guard opened our cells, he was going to take me down chained, but I told him to spare himself the trouble. I would give my word of honor to make no attempt to escape. No, sir. I have been here too long for that, and will never go out until I can go out honorably."[24]

By the time the prisoner evacuation had begun, the cell building, containing nearly 400 cells, was filled with a dense cloud of smoke. The flames had been sucked under the roof of the building, and quickly burst through the roof in every part, preventing any hopes of containing the blaze. As the prisoners were ushered into the foundry, the 350-by-sixty-foot building was consumed in flames.[25]

Guard Cayou, who was in charge of the Youngers, described the scene: "The last time I started down the south side of the gallery, the smoke had grown so thick that I had to grope my way on my hands and knees. I opened a number of the doors and sent the men back to the stairs where they were met by guards. I succeeded in reaching the front end and had just started back down the north side when, as I stood up to open a door, I lost the sponge which protected my mouth and nose. For a moment I was almost stifled, and fell prostrate upon my face. The smoke was not so dense within a few inches of the floor, and I managed to crawl along a few feet at a time."[26]

One of the prisoners, Con Riellen, insisted on being left behind, and, after most of the convicts had been evacuated, the guards returned to his cell and found him locked in. One of the guards took a crowbar and battered the door. Riellen was removed and dragged to safety. Fire Chief Frank Joy also had a narrow escape when he was knocked down by a hose stream in the basement and nearly smothered to death.[27]

Convict Henry Lempke was not so lucky. Several prisoners had heard cries for help during the evacuation but no one could tell from which direction the sound was coming. Warden Reed and two of his guards searched the passages beneath the hanging, ice-coated rafters to the upper gallery. They found cell 212 locked. Unlocking the cell door, they found Lempke's body covered with a coating of ice. The victim's head was resting upon the bed, eyes wide open glaring up at the rafters, one arm raised in an attempt to protect his face.

While the Youngers sat in a vacant room awaiting their removal from the prison, head guard George Dodd came by. Dodd was to select twenty-five trustees to help evacuate fellow prisoners. As Dodd entered the room, Cole asked if the brothers could be of help. Dodd decided to take a chance on the boys and handed Cole a revolver, Jim an ax, and Bob an iron bar. Dodd asked them to relocate the female prisoners and also the women's matron, Dodd's own wife. Although Dodd was criticized for his decision by Stillwater residents, the boys led the women to safety, returned their weapons, and were highly praised by Warden Reed and his staff.[29]

Dodd later stated, "I was obliged to take the female convicts from their cells and place them in a small room that could not be locked. The Youngers were passing, and Cole asked if they could be of any service. I said: 'Yes Cole. Will you three boys take care of Mrs. Dodd and the women?' Cole answered: 'Yes, we will, and if you ever had confidence in us place it in us now.' I told him I had the utmost confidence, and I slipped a revolver to Cole, as I had two. Jim, I think, had an ax handle, and Bob had a little pinch bar. The boys stood before the door of the little room for hours and even took the blankets they had brought from their cells and gave them to the women to try and keep them comfortable, as it was very cold. When I could take charge of the women and the boys were relieved, Cole returned my revolver."[30]

Following the prisoner evacuation, a reporter was allowed to enter the foundry and interview prisoners. In one corner of the three rooms was a group of ten or twelve black prisoners, some wrapped in blankets, others stretched fully on the floor, singing old time ballads under the leadership of a lifer. In the opposite corner was a smaller group consisting of the most well-known felons in the prison. Bob Younger sat on a box, his brother Cole leaned against the wall opposite him, and Jim was lying on the floor between the two. Lifer J.B. Coney, Faribault murderer L.M. Sage, and other less notorious convicts sat beside them as did guard Cayou.[31]

Sage related his story to the journalist: "I was in cell 236 on the upper floor, just over the Younger boys. The smoke was stifling. I had difficulty in breathing. The men near me were greatly alarmed and were pounding on their cell doors and crying for aid. I could hear the fire roaring below. The heat became unbearable. The atmosphere was stifling. As I was beginning to succumb, I heard a rattling outside, and my cell door was thrown open by Coney. A number of others were released at the same time I was. The smoke and heat in the upper gallery were terrible, and I don't wonder that many of the boys fell on their knees to pray. You fellows can smile at it now, but you would have smiled rather differently if you had been in that gallery."[32]

Newspapers argued the origin of the fire. The *Stillwater Messenger* in its January 26, 1884, edition, stated: "The origin of the fire is wrapped in mystery, but there seems little doubt that it was the work of a citizen incendiary. The room in which it originated was filled with hardware and advertising matter belonging to the company, and no convict could have gained access to it, as we are informed by Warden Reed."

The *St. Paul Pioneer Press* for January 26, 1884, expressed the opinion the fire was not set by convicts, but did state that there were several rumors suggesting certain inmates were responsible. Other sources suggested an insurance scheme. Total damage from the fire amounted to $20,000.

The day following the fire, many prisoners were temporarily sent to facilities outside the prison where they were to remain until the damage in the cell block had been repaired. The Younger brothers were taken to the Washington County Courthouse where they spent four weeks; the only time during their incarceration that they were outside the prison walls.[33]

Following their return to Stillwater Prison, Cole went back to work as a librarian. Only two prisoners were employed in the prison library, and it was their duty to circulate the various books and papers among the inmates. Cole was also in charge of the "exchange box," where all materials to which inmates subscribed could be exchanged for others. Papers would circulate ten days from the date of issue and magazines every thirty. Cole then

delivered the materials to the room numbers indicated.[34]

When Cole became a hospital trustee, Jim took over his position in the library and he eventually became head librarian. Always a voracious reader, Jim kept to himself and did not interact with other prisoners, with the exception of his brothers.[35]

On June 12 and 14, one year later, the community of Stillwater was devastated by a flood caused by heavy rains. The town's largest hotel, the Sawyer House, and another, the Pitman House, were hit with three feet of water in their dining rooms. At the former, a hundred-pound boulder crashed through the hotel's barber shop, landing on a stove in the next room. Although the Stillwater Prison inmates were aware of the disaster around them, there was little to fear behind the protection of high prison walls.[36]

In the fall of 1885, Warren Carter Bronaugh of Clinton, Missouri, visited the Youngers. During that visit, Bronaugh learned that Cole Younger had been the picket whose warning had prevented him from being killed or captured in August 1862, by Kansas

Cole Younger in 1889. (Courtesy of the Minnesota Historical Society)

Jayhawkers and Redlegs. From the day of this enlightenment, Bronaugh made the cause of freedom for the brothers his own.[37]

Although Bronaugh carried a letter of introduction to Warden Reed from a St. Paul hotel owner, the warden was suspicious of anyone from Missouri. He did, however, allow Bronaugh to visit, but only on the condition he kept his arms bared to the elbow. A deputy warden presided over the visit, listening carefully to every word spoken. With the ten-year anniversary of the Youngers' incarceration coming up, a period that marked their eligibility for parole, the Missourian was determined to do everything he could to get the boys home. Although Bronaugh did not impress Warden Reed, he did receive support from Minnesota Governor William R. Marshall and Missouri Governor Thomas Crittenden.[38]

For some time, Cole had entertained the idea of establishing a prison newspaper, but he did not have the funds for such a daring enterprise.[39] But on August 10, 1887, his dream came

Bob Younger, two weeks before his death. (Courtesy of the Minnesota Historical Society)

true when on that day the first issue of the *Prison Mirror* rolled off the presses. With contributions from fifteen inmates, including twenty dollars each from Cole and Jim, and ten dollars from Bob, the first edition was distributed to 412 inmates and a handful of outside subscribers. The *Mirror* was unique for two reasons: it would become the oldest continuously published prison newspaper in the United States, and it was the only prison publication launched with funds from inmate shareholders. Since the Younger brothers were among the founders, the newspaper gained wide acceptance from its inmate readers.[40]

Lew P. Schoonmaker became the publication's first editor. The first masthead also included the names of two compositors, and, because of his outlaw notoriety, Coleman Younger was listed as printer's devil. It was not customary to cite a printer's devil since the position is nothing more than a shop clean-up per-

Henrietta Younger and her brothers Bob, Jim, and Cole taken in Stillwater Prison in 1889. (Photo by J.M. Kuln of Stillwater. Courtesy of the Minnesota Historical Society)

son, but Cole's name did attract subscribers.[41]

In the first issue, the *Mirror* ran the following information: "Cole Younger, our genial prison librarian, has received new honors at the hands of the *Mirror* by being appointed to the honorable position of 'printer's devil,' in which he will in the future keep flies off the gift of 'wedding cake,' and other editorial favors of like nature which may find lodgement in our sanctum sanctorum."[42]

The goals of the *Mirror* were to dispel rumors and to inform inmates on policies, procedures, and upcoming events. For its outside readers, the journalists hoped to present a correct understanding of the realities and problems of prison and prisoner. The negative headlines printed by outside news sources usually dwelled on sensational violence, reporting on escapes, beatings, killings, lockups, and riots. The *Mirror* was, and still is, a positive experience, reporting on realistic positive issues.

The investors who "funded" the venture would get their money back, but only at the rate of three percent a month. Once the men were paid in full, all claims upon stock, material, and shares would cease, and one-hundred percent of profits would be given to the prison library for the purchase of such books and periodicals that the warden selected. Treasurer of the *Mirror* was George Dodd, head prison guard who had helped the prisoners to safety during the fires two years previously.[43]

In 1888, a petition signed by several Missourians reached the office of Minnesota Governor William R. Merriam requesting parole for the three Younger brothers. During that year, Bob's health had begun to decline, and following examinations, he was diagnosed with tuberculosis. He was told by physicians that he was dying, and he accepted his fate, but he would not discuss his situation with anyone other than his brothers. Meanwhile, he continued to work toward a possible parole.

On June 12, 1889, an article appeared in the *Butler* (Missouri) *Times* stating that Bob's "former florid complexion had faded to an ashy paleness. His cheek bones stand out prominently, and his whole face is that of an invalid. He has lost much flesh, his arms and limbs are narrowed down almost to bones, and his hands are thin and shallow. He is but a shadow of what he was up to a year ago. As he speaks his voice is husky, and he once in a while coughs. His steel blue eye is yet bright and restless. He knows he is far from well, but his iron will, so the attendants say, does not for an instant weaken, and he says he is sure he will be better."[44]

On Sunday evening, September 15, he became suddenly ill. Unable to swallow, he could not take nourishment. His sister, Retta, as well as Cole and Jim, were at his side. The following evening, about six o'clock, Bob asked the trio not to leave because, he said, he had no more than four hours to live and wanted his family with him until the end. When Deputy Warden Jacob Westby entered the room three hours later, Bob asked him, since the official had been so kind to him, also to remain. Shortly after ten o'clock in the evening, on September 16, 1889, Bob passed away in the Stillwater Penitentiary.[45]

The *St. Paul Pioneer Press* carried the following: "Bob's account with the state is now fully settled, while his brothers Cole and Jim remain to drain the cup of expiation to the lees. A strenuous effort was made a few months ago by prominent Missourians, backed by ex-Governor Marshall and a few other sympathetic gentlemen of Minnesota, to secure the pardon of the Youngers, but Governor Merriam refused to exercise clemency, in which decision the popular sentiment of the state supported him."[46]

On the 18th, last rites were held over the remains of Bob Younger in the prison chapel. Reverend J.H. Albert, prison chaplain, conducted the services with all the prisoners and a number of visitors present. Retta Younger was accompanied by Mrs. Samuel McClure of Kansas City and several friends she had met in St. Paul during her visits to the prison. Ex-Governor Marshall was also in attendance.[47]

The *Prison Mirror*, of which he was a cofounder, eulogized: "He suffered with patience, and, when the hour of going came, he was the first to recognize it, and when grim death grew nigh, he looked it full in the face; and then, casting a last loving look at his faithful sister, Bob Younger died without a moan or quaver. Let us hope that ere the light of this world faded into darkness his eyes were greeted by the dawn of eternal day."[48]

A few days later, accompanied by Retta, Bob's casket was placed on a train and taken to its final resting place in Lee's Summit, Missouri.

Over the next few years, Cole and Jim continued their work in the library. Meanwhile, Captain Bronaugh waged war on the legal system, soliciting support from those individuals sympathetic to the Youngers' parole. On September 23, 1901, Peter Brennan, a St. Paul railway contractor and supporter of Bronough's efforts, penned a letter to Retta Younger. In the letter, he discussed a Bronaugh financial endeavor and the brothers' work. "I visited the boys on the 19th and saw Cole. They are well as usual. Jim did not come down. They are very busy just now covering the books over. Cole cuts the covers, Jim pastes and numbers them. All things are running smoothly just at present."[49]

In 1895, Honorable W.C. Masterman, chairman of the Senate Committee on State Prisons, accompanied his committee to Stillwater for its annual inspection of the prison. George T. Barr, state senator for Blue Earth County, recalled that, when he and his cohorts entered the prison library, they found Cole and Jim Younger in charge. The committee members passed quickly through the library, but Barr remained hoping to ask the brothers a few questions.

"I recognized the larger of the two men as being the one who had asked me for change back in 1876 in the bank at Mankato, and so lingered," remembered Barr. "He said he was the man when I asked and then volunteered the information that the original plan of the raiders had fixed on Mankato as the point they would strike and that the call on the Mankato banks, for they did visit both, was a survey upon which to determine which of them to choose."[50]

In 1897, Cole was assigned to help prison physician A.E. Hedback in his office. Cole occupied a cell in the hospital, recalled the physician. "At that time, the first effort to secure a pardon for the Younger brothers was made," remembered Dr. Hedback. "Warden Henry Wolfer, who I believe started, and certainly favored this action, advised Cole to break his silence of twenty-one years relative to the raid at Northfield and tell his own story of what took place. This he did, and later when he was about to throw the original into the waste basket, I asked for it and have kept it in my possession up to the present."[51]

According to Dr. Hedback, "Cole Younger had a charming personality, was a giant intellectually as well as physically and had a good command of the English language, frequently using quotations from Shakespeare in conversation. I shall never forget his admonition: 'You can run away from everybody else but you can never run away from yourself.'"[52]

On Monday, July 12, 1897, the Minnesota Board of Pardons held a meeting from two o'clock until five listening to arguments on the petition for pardon of the Younger brothers. The first two hours were taken up with the arguments for clemency by Younger supporters, and at 4:00 P.M., the Northfield delegation, which strongly opposed any pardon, opened their arguments. The Northfield representatives were still presenting their case at the time of adjournment, so the board met again the following morning at 9:00 A.M. to continue the hearing.[53]

Among those arguing for a pardon were Warden Henry Wolfer, all the members of the Board of Prison Managers, Minnesota State Auditor R.C. Dunn, ex-Sheriff Ara Barton of Rice County, Thomas Loyhed (a pursuing posse member from Faribault), and St. Paul Judge James McCafferty. Speaking for Northfield and Rice County against a pardon were F.W. Anderson of St. Paul, Mayor F.A. Noble, C.P. Carpenter, Professor Goodhue, Representative D.F. Kelly of Northfield, Mayor A.D. Keyes of Faribault, Attorney A.L. Keyes of Rice County, and W.R. Estes of Madelia.

James D. O'Brien of Stillwater, president of the board of prison managers, was the first speaker and delivered an effective plea for the Youngers before the fifty people who had crowded into the governor's office: "The board is unanimous in the opinion that these men have been exemplary prisoners. If freed, we believe they would make honest, respectable citizens. Their conduct has been beyond reproach, and I, for one, am ready to go on record as saying that if pardoned they will prove themselves good citizens. Our board considers that they have served time enough for the crime of which they were convicted. We do not believe that people should go beyond that in the consideration of this question. We unanimously recommend their pardon."[54]

Attorney General Childs asked O'Brien how many life convicts had been pardoned, and O'Brien replied that in the eight years he had served on the board, he remembered two such cases.

Warden Wolfer then read from a typewritten document he had prepared. Wolfer maintained that, normally, prisoners guilty of the kind of crimes committed by the Youngers should be locked up for life. But then the warden praised their character and blamed their fate on early bad association. He said he could not excuse any of their crimes, but, had they been given a chance as younger men, they would never have become criminals.

Wolfer ended his reading with a plea for justice: "I will not further trespass upon your time, but before closing I desire to say that, in justice to my own conscience and to these men, I could not say less than I have said. To have remained silent would have been cowardice, believing in the justice of their cause as I do."[55]

Judge McCafferty followed with an hour-long history of the Youngers' early life and presented several endorsements for a pardon from Missourians. The judge gave reasons why the boys should be pardoned. First, they were victims of their environment, and he placed the blame on the peculiar conditions of Missouri during the Civil War. "They were not naturally bad boys or possessed of criminal tendencies," he claimed.

Secondly, said Judge McCaffery, their punishment had been ample, and the law had been vindicated. "They had been grievously wounded in the affair at Northfield, when the people there took the law into their own hands, and had suffered intensely thereby for years," he said.

"You mean that they were injured by the people of Northfield while the latter were defending their property, don't you?" snapped Chief Justice Charles M. Start. Judge McCaffery admitted that the question presented a fairer statement of the case and went on with his argument.

McCaffery's third argument maintained that the prisoners' reformation was complete but he was again interrupted by Judge Start, who considered the statement misleading: "If that is the case," he said, "how is it in a case when the governor signs a warrant for execution? Is that done with the object of reformation? Reformation, as I understand it, is intended to apply to those sentenced for limited or definite terms. Is the principle of reformation intended to include life convicts?"

James O'Brien, president of the prison board of managers, suggested that the pardon board shift the responsibility of the boys' fate to the prison board, by commuting the sentence to a definite term of years, and the prison board "would do the rest."

The "rest" was granting a quick pardon. The chief justice and the attorney general, however, emphatically rejected the proposal, stating that the board of pardons would maintain responsibility over such cases.

State Auditor R.C. Dunn spoke next, stating he was speaking for the people of northern Minnesota. Dunn said he had traveled throughout the northern part of the state and interviewed the people there. Nine out of ten, he claimed, favored a Younger pardon.

Thomas Loyhead of Faribault, one of the pursuers of the robbers in 1876, also spoke in behalf of the prisoners. Loyhead said that he and his companions came too close for comfort when they stumbled upon the outlaws who were concealed in a thicket. Cole saved their lives by preventing Charlie Pitts from shooting them.

Former Sheriff of Rice County, Ara Barton, was the final speaker on the Youngers' behalf. Barton described the Youngers' "manly qualities" while they were his prisoners. He also stated that he had talked with the physician who had examined the body of Gustavson and was told that the Swede had been killed by a ricocheting bullet. Barton ended his argument saying he had interviewed 1,000 citizens of Faribault and four-fifths advocated a pardon.

Warren Carter Bronaugh, leading the fight for a Younger pardon, was much encouraged by his side's presentation on the first day. Bronaugh was confident that his group had a made a strong case for the prisoners and was hopeful they had been successful. Many others felt that the Youngers' cause was doomed, and believed that both the chief justice and the attorney general were opposed to the pardon. The general opinion was that the board would be reluctant to grant a pardon because of Northfield opposition.

The opposition voiced an opinion that the pardon would be a grave mistake and that such action would tarnish the state's legal reputation. The opposing delegation felt the boys had forfeited their lives to the state, and it was sufficient mercy to them, that they were allowed to live.

St. Paul's F.W. Anderson opened the case for the opposition. Anderson, a banker for years, spoke for the country bankers who were often the victims of outlaw raids. Anderson felt that if the Youngers were released, any protection for the banking institutions would be weakened. He then read a letter from Charles Parsons of St. Louis, president of the American Association of Bankers, who also protested any would-be pardon. "Their punishment should have been death," wrote Parsons. "I believe in the enforcement of the law and making the way of the transgressor hard. I hope the Youngers will be made to serve out their lives in prison."

Crossroads of the Chalk Level Road, site of the Roscoe Gun Battle. (Photo by Marley Brant)

Mayor F.A. Noble of Northfield then took the floor and attacked Cole Younger's statement that he had not killed anyone. "Those men were there in Northfield to kill," explained Noble. "Their record in prison has nothing to do with the case. Any fellow would be an exemplary chap there. You all know they were a gang of cut-throats and devils."

Noble then introduced R.C. Carpenter, an eloquent speaker who went right to work in his opening remarks. "These men turned hell loose in our streets," bellowed Carpenter. "The high tide of brigandage in this country passed away when they were put behind the bars at Stillwater. Their record since then has been so good that we believe it to their advantage to stay there. Indeed, they should be very grateful to the State of Minnesota for the chance it has given them to become such good men and make such exemplary records. Cole Younger is now seeking pardon through false statements and seeking public sympathy for misrepresentations."[56]

A number of affidavits were then presented by R.C. Carpenter from eye witnesses of the Northfield raid, all of which declared Cole Younger was the man who had shot and killed Nicholaus Gustavson. All the eye witnesses maintained they had actually seen Cole raise his revolver, fire at Gustavson, and the man then fell to the ground.

The first came from Dr. D.J. Whiting, the dentist who witnessed the raid from his office above the bank. Dr. Whiting said he saw Cole throughout the robbery attempt, and at no time did the outlaw order any of his men to stop shooting, as claimed by Cole. He said he did see Bob Younger take several shots at Anselm Manning, and he heard Cole shout to Bob that he should "charge upon him" and "shoot through the door." The dentist also said he heard Cole order another of his men to "shoot that man in the window."

Another man, P.S. Doherty said he saw Cole Younger shoot Gustavson. John Norton said he also witnessed the shooting of Gustavson and insisted that the man who took the pistols from the dead robber in the street was the one who did it. He added that he had seen Cole in jail and recognized him as the killer. Other affidavits were presented from Mrs. Ellen A. Ames, W.H. Riddell, and the bank clerk, Frank Wilcox. Professor Goodhue and Representative D.F. Kelly also voiced strong opinions against a pardon.

In addition to the affidavits, several protests to the pardon were filed by people who had known the Youngers before their incarceration. Three of the protests came from residents of Lawrence, Kansas, who had been victims of the Quantrill raid. Two others were from the wife and sister of Pinkerton Captain Louis J. Lull of Chicago, who, in 1874 with Pinkerton's James Wright and others, attempted to arrest the Youngers near Roscoe, Missouri. Lull and Sheriff Daniels of Osceola, and John Younger were all killed.

The closing speaker of the afternoon was Mayor A.D. Keyes of Faribault. "No doubt," said Keyes, "it is the best thing for the Younger boys themselves to pardon them, but they are a very small part of the people of the state of Minnesota numerically. What particular good, I would like to ask, will come to the people of the state by the pardon of these men, either now or in the future? It will either tend to prevent crime or it will promote it."

Keyes and other Rice County representatives felt that if Cole was really sincere, he should admit to the court that the killer of Joseph Heywood was Frank James. Warren Bronaugh was angered by this and wrote a letter to the St. Paul Pioneer Press the following day: "I do not understand why the people of Northfield should make this claim, inasmuch as it has been frequently asserted they are fully aware who these parties were, and that, acting upon reliable information, a requisition has been made by the governor of this state upon the Governor of Missouri, over twelve years ago, for the body of the prisoner who it was claimed was the only living person, aside from the Youngers, who participated in the bank robbery."[57]

Bronaugh went on to say that the Youngers were not the type of men who would turn informants to gain clemency for themselves. The Youngers, he said, felt they were responsible for their part in the raid and would suffer the penalty without implicating others. "I honor the Youngers for this position," said Bronaugh, "and I believe that every fair-minded man will do the same."

Alonzo Bunker, the bank teller wounded at Northfield, on the other hand, was angry over the possibility of a Younger pardon. In an interview with a Minneapolis newspaper, he especially took umbrage to Cole's remark that he had saved lives by not shooting during the robbery attempt and that a certain man on a buckskin horse had done the killing. Bunker said Cole had made these statements with the purpose of securing a pardon, he said, and he was shocked that some Minnesota newspapers favored a pardon.[58]

Bunker felt the statements made by respectable citizens of Northfield should take credence over those of a convicted murderer. He then added that, if Cole really tried to prevent the killings, he should prove it by naming the man on the buckskin horse and the last man to leave the bank. "Then I think he [Cole] overdoes the matter considerably in showing how many people's lives he saved by simply not shooting them," he explained. "He would have us believe he was at Northfield on that eventful day, very opportunely, for the purpose of preventing 'the boys' from killing law-abiding citizens."[59]

Bunker went on to debunk Cole Younger's story that he spared the life of Dr. Henry Wheeler by deliberately shooting above his head. If this were true, reasoned Bunker, why did he shoot a defenseless Swede?[60] He said the community of Northfield was safe as long as the Youngers were behind bars. "When I think of the murdering of poor Heywood in cold blood, and of the unprovoked assault in the law-abiding citizens of Northfield, to say nothing of other crimes committed by these men, I do not think they will live long enough to pay the penalty. I cannot interfere."[61]

But Bunker did not need to interfere, for on July 13, the board of pardons unanimously voted to deny their pardon. It was 3:30 in the afternoon when the board adjourned and began its discussion behind closed doors. When all members appeared to be in agreement, Chief Justice Start moved that the pardon be refused, and Attorney General Childs seconded the motion. Governor David M. Clough would have voted for the pardon had two board members been favorable, but since he stood alone, Clough did not vote.[62] An hour later, the decision was announced, but no explanations were offered as to how the decision had been reached and upon what grounds it was based. Later however, a board member consented to speak about it.[63]

"While under the law the board of pardons is not required to make a statement of its reasons in a case where a pardon is denied," said the board member. "It is perhaps just as well that the public should know the grounds on which the board based its refusal of a pardon to the Younger brothers. The petitioners in law and in fact were murderers. This proposition was established by a plea of guilty and the final judgment of a court of competent jurisdiction. It is the exclusive province of the legislature to prescribe punishment for murder—either death or imprisonment."[64]

The board member said his group did not buy the statement that the Youngers were forced into crime by the horrid Civil War environment of Missouri. Eleven years had passed since the surrender at Appomattox, and still the boys had refused to accept the "magnanimous" terms offered by General Grant. If they had indeed reformed, the law would then have to require a pardon for anyone serving twenty-one years in prison.

Bronaugh and Harry Jones, a nephew of the Youngers, were waiting in the office of Minnesota Governor David M. Clough when the decision was reached. Warden Wolfer had already boarded a train for Stillwater, confident that the pardon attempt had failed. No one was surprised by the verdict, although the Youngers had thought they had a friend on the board.

"It was eleven years ago when we took up the work of seeking a pardon for my uncles," said nephew Jones. "I had some hope that we would meet with success this time. But after the hearing of yesterday afternoon I realized that we could not expect a pardon this time. It was perfectly plain to me that Judge Start was against us, and I had fears that the attorney general was also not favorably inclined. But I did think the governor [David Clough] would give us his vote."[65]

Warden Wolfer had prepared the Youngers for the situation, explaining to them that although he had left before a decision had been reached, he was certain there was no hope for them. Bronaugh and Jones delivered the bad news two hours later. Both Cole and Jim laughed pleasantly, neither at all surprised by the outcome.

"There is one mighty good thing about it all," remarked Cole in a newspaper interview, "and that is we know we have got some good friends left on earth. I feel more sorry for them than I do for myself. We are deeply grateful to all who have tried to assist us in getting a pardon, and in this hour of our disappointment we have not one unkind word or feeling for anyone. We have got to stay here, evidently, to the end of the chapter, and we will stand it as well as we can."[66]

Another life prisoner named Rose was called in and informed he had been pardoned. Rose laughed hysterically and almost went into convulsions. Rose, the official rat catcher of the institution, had been a Federal soldier. He and Cole had planned to walk out of Stillwater together—a mingling of the blue and the gray as Cole called it. "Well, the blue has beat us out again," Cole told Rose in congratulating his more fortunate friend.

One of the petitioners for a Younger pardon told the *Northfield News* that if the signers from Missouri had spent more time creating sentiment in Minnesota, the decision might have been different. Next time they would canvas the state thoroughly. However, no further efforts at a pardon could be made until after the expiration of the term of Chief Justice Start, which was December 31, 1900. Governor Clough and his attorney general would leave office at the end of 1898, but the Chief Justice would bar a pardon, even if the other two voted for it, since the vote had to be unanimous.[67]

In 1899, shortly after Governor Clough's term of office had expired, George M. Bennett introduced a bill to the Minnesota General Assembly calling for the parole of life prisoners who would have been eligible for release had they been sentenced to thirty-five years. Known as the Wilson Parole Bill because it had been supported by Senator George P. Wilson, the bill passed in the senate chambers by a vote of forty-eight to five, but it was defeated in the house.[68]

Letters for and against the Wilson Bill flooded the *St. Paul Pioneer Press*. The most controversial was a letter signed simply B.G.Y., which was thought to be the work of former Madelia resident B.G. Yates. But presumed-dead outlaw Bill Stiles had also been hailed by the name of Yates. Whoever the writer, B.G.Y. argued vehemently for a Younger pardon:

"There is now in prison at Stillwater only one life convict who was there when the Youngers were committed; all have been pardoned, only one having died, among them some of the most cold-blooded murderers known. It seems difficult to understand why there is such opposition to the pardon of the best prisoners we ever committed, while we raise no voice in protest when the most vicious are pardoned by the dozen."[69]

Outraged by the "Yates" letter, other citizens challenged the effort. One writer explained the circumstances of the lifer who had been there longer than the Youngers. The lifer was a poor man without friends or money, and the writer stated that if Yates was sincere about pardoning good men, he should also be asking for the poor man's parole as well. Most of the writers, however, were concerned that once the Youngers were paroled and sent home to Missouri, they would be forever free since Missouri always refused to recognize requisition papers from Minnesota.

On June 6, 1901, a bill introduced to the Minnesota legislature by C.P. Deming, calling for parole eligibility of life prisoners who had served at least twenty-four years, passed by unanimous approval. Bronaugh returned to St. Paul in time for the Youngers case before the Board of Pardons. A large number of documents were presented to Governor S.R. Van Sant including

Samuel Rinnah Van Sant. (Courtesy of the Minnesota Historical Society)

a petition to release the Youngers signed by many prominent men: Bishop Whipple, the late Bishop Gilbert, former Governor Alexander Ramsey, Archbishop John Ireland, Henry A. Castle, and General Flower. Among the signers were three survivors of the Madelia shootout—W.C. Murphy, George A. Bradford and C.A. Pomeroy—as well as Dr. Henry M. Wheeler, who had shot and killed Clell Miller during the Northfield raid. Letters from other prominent men such as the late Henry H. Sibley, the late C.K. Davis, and General Elkins were presented as well as affidavits showing the conduct of the Youngers during the prison fire.[70]

But Cole Younger, perhaps, helped his own cause by writing of his life story while still in prison and by writing as a man who had realized his mistakes: "There is little to inspire

Cartoon from the St. Paul Pioneer Press, Thursday, July 11, 1901.

WHAT IN THE DEUCE IS THAT, COLE?
BLESSED IF I KNOW. LET'S GET BACK INSIDE!

mirth in prison. For a man who has lived close to the heart of nature, in the forest, in the saddle, to imprison him is like caging a wild bird. And yet imprisonment has brought out the excellencies of many men. I have learned many things in the lonely hours there. I have learned that hope is a divinity; I have learned that a surplus of determination conquers every weakness; I have learned that you cannot make a white dove [in]to a blackbird; I have learned that vengeance is for God and not for man. . . ."[71]

On July 10, 1901, the *St. Paul Pioneer Press* announced, "Cole and Jim Younger will be paroled this morning, unless the persons who have carefully watched the proceedings of the pardon board are badly mistaken. The questions asked by the members of the board Monday indicated they desired only to be satisfied that the Youngers when released from the restraints of prison walls would be given suitable occupation."[72]

Because of some of the remarks issued by Chief Justice Start, the *Pioneer Press* painted an indefinite picture, but Justice Start was in complete harmony with his associates on the board. The parole was a conditional parole, and subject to careful restrictions as to place of residence, employment, and lifestyle. Details of the parole were not announced until later that morning, long after the early edition of the newspaper had gone into circulation.

Ironically, that same morning, the *Pioneer Press* announced that Colonel John S. Mosby, the Confederacy's "Gray Ghost," came to St. Paul under orders from President William McKinley as special agent of the general land office for Minnesota and Nebraska. Whether he met with the Youngers following their parole is not known.

Cole and Jim were paroled the following day, Thursday the 11th. Governor Van Sant, Chief Justice Start, and Attorney General Douglas stated in a published memorandum that they did not consider the question of the Youngers' guilt, nor whether they had been sufficiently punished. "The board carried out the wishes of the legislature that passed the parole bill," they said. "According to that bill the Youngers were entitled to parole. They had been imprisoned more than twenty years, their conduct in prison had been 'almost perfect,' and the board of state prison managers had recommended the parole."[73]

The boys had been outside the walls only three times during their quarter century of imprisonment. Twice they had been allowed to go to the warden's house; the third time was their 1884 transfer to the Washington County Jail following the prison fire.

Henry Wolfer, the warden's son, received the news from the state capitol shortly after noon. Fifteen minutes later he walked to the library and informed Jim Younger that he was being freed. Jim appeared unmoved but held out his hand and

Stillwater Prison Warden Henry Wolfer. (Photo by John M. Kuhn. Courtesy of the Minnesota Historical Society)

thanked the bearer of good news. "Of course, I'm pleased," Jim said slowly. "It's the difference between life and death."[74]

As Wolfer approached Cole in the library, the former outlaw looked up from his work as if he knew why the warden's son was coming to him. "Cole, you've been paroled," announced Wolfer. Cole stared a moment in silence, then answered softly, "That's the best news I've had for many a long day. And I can tell you Jim and I will work hard to merit the good will of the people outside. Nobody's going to regret this."[75]

Colonel Bronaugh was the first Missourian to congratulate the brothers. When the Youngers joined Bronaugh and others in Deputy Warden Jack Glennon's office, Cole shared his feelings with everyone present: "I feel like shaking hands with the whole world. As I stand here today, I ain't got a grudge against any human being alive or dead. Men, I'm happy."[76]

Jesse James Jr., son of the noted outlaw, was behind the counter of his cigar store in Kansas City when he received the news. "I'm glad of it," he said, looking happy but not surprised. "I think that twenty-five years in prison is ample amends to justice for almost any crime." T. Crittenden, Jr., son of the former governor, was in James' store at the time and told a reporter that ninety percent of Missourians had been in favor of a pardon. Crittenden also expressed a certainty that the Youngers would make good solid Minnesota citizens.[77]

Warden Wolfer immediately set out to find employment for the two brothers. Within one day of the parole announcement, twelve offers of employment were made to State Agent Whittier. Since the Youngers could not do hard physical work, their job duties would have to be limited. Wolfer also tried to find employers who were in earnest, eliminating those who would hire the boys merely to obtain publicity for their company.[78]

Wolfer told the press he had no personal interest in the final disposition of the prisoners, but he would protect the Youngers from any undue notoriety. He admitted it would be impossible to keep their movements hidden from the public, but he would do everything he could to partially screen those actions from the interested public gaze. He denied a rumor that he had sought employment for the brothers at a Hopkins, Minnesota, threshing plant.[79]

At ten o'clock Sunday morning, July 14, the Youngers officially walked out of Stillwater Prison. Following chapel within the walls that morning, the boys were called "down front." Supposing a visitor had come to see them, they were surprised by Warden Wolfer, who handed them a set of civilian clothes, and said, "Put these clothes on. And you won't have to go back."[80]

After putting on the clothes, they walked through the gates and into downtown Stillwater accompanied by several newspapermen. Surprisingly, few people recognized them. It was a warm day in Stillwater but the brothers preferred walking on the sunny side of the street. They walked a full block without saying a word. Then someone said, "What do you think of it, Cole?" Facing the man who had asked the question, Cole replied, "Well, I thank heaven for this and the friends who did so much to help us."

Jim spoke up: "I don't know what I thought. I've been keeping my feelings in check so long, ready to meet anything, that I'm afraid I didn't let myself out. But it didn't hurt me a bit."

Cole wore a dark blue serge suit, a blue and white shirt, a white turn-down collar, a gray silk four-in-hand tie, a black wide-brimmed felt hat, and calf shoes. Jim, the shorter of the two, was dressed in a dark gray suit, a pink and white shirt, a polka dot four-in-hand tie, and a fedora hat.

As they walked along the street, the boys passed a former prison guard who had seen them daily over many years, but the man did not recognize them. Nor did a physician, who had practiced in the prison hospital for ten years, working side by side with Head Nurse Cole Younger. Only when they entered a cigar store and someone muttered, "It's Cole and Jim," did a crowd of gawkers gather. The brothers hurried back to the prison to escape the crowd.

Following dinner at the prison office, the Youngers joined Warden Wolfer and others on a three-hour boat trip down the St. Croix River. Wolfer decided the boys could take a fishing trip for about a week before settling down to serious employment.

Making their headquarters at the prison until they were ready to assume work, the Youngers met with Warden Wolfer and State Agent Whittier on July 15 to discuss fourteen job offers. The boys were given the opportunity of expressing their preferences. Wolfer told the press the boys were ready to work, but it would be three or four days before a decision would be made.[81]

While Warden Wolfer maintained a good relationship with the Youngers, his friendship with Colonel Bronaugh began to break down. Upon hearing a rumor, Bronaugh became agitated and wrote Wolfer on July 16: "I learned in the city yesterday from a gentleman that you are thinking unkindly of me for some reason. I cannot imagine the cause. I have always looked upon you as my friend, and I have no recollection of ever uttering a word in regard to you that was not in your favor, and if there is such a thing existing, I think it due me that you should notify me and tell me what it is and who the author is." Bronaugh left for Missouri the following day.[82]

While waiting to begin employment, Cole visited some people who had backed his parole, including a Minneapolis attorney, George M. Bennett. Bennett wrote to Warden Wolfer, "Cole came over on Friday, and I suppose went back Saturday evening or yesterday. I left him at Kenwood late in the afternoon, and he rather expected to go over in the evening. I was with him the greater portion of the time while he was here, and went around to see those to whom a call seemed to be due, and in doing so he met of course a great many people, capturing them all, including those who had been his enemies."[83]

Jim had been having a tougher time of it. He wrote to Warden Wolfer that he was agitated by ex-convicts wanting to borrow money from him. And since he wasn't working, the bold requests irritated him all the more.[84]

On July 29, 1901, Cole and Jim went to work for the Peterson Granite Company of St. Paul, selling tombstones, for the pay of sixty dollars a month. Jim, troubled since his release from Stillwater, wrote Warden Wolfer on August 14: "There's a fellow traveling for Peterson named Bloom. A big ignorant duffer, and passing himself for Cole. Here in North Branch, he done so, and in doing so up at Duluth, where he now is, the papers said Cole, was in Duluth. Please call him down."[85]

Jim wrote Wolfer another concerned letter a few days later: "I left the horse and buggy at Cambridge, and came to St. Paul, Saturday evening at six o'clock, and will return in the early tomorrow. Someone here is trying to keep up this Younger howl, by starting the foolish report, that first Cole, and then Jim, were going to get married. Three men have been to see me, but I was not in, and I will not be, to answer foolish questions."[86]

Another Jim Younger letter, with a similar message, reached Wolfer the first week of September from Princeton, Minnesota: "I notice the St. Paul news is—going to marry me off, wheather [sic] or no. I do hope these fellows of the press, will take a rest soon."[87]

On August 31, a very enthusiastic Cole, unlike his brother, wrote Warden Wolfer from the Merchants Hotel in Wadena: "I am not selling as many stones as I would like to but this is a new country and the cities as yet have taken no interest in the graveyards and the people are mostly newcomers and need all their ready money to improve their little homes and leave this dead to wait. Have to travel great deal on frait [sic] trains to make time. Some of my days are eighteen hours long. But I don't care for that if I can sell enough stones."[88]

The same day, he sent Wolfer his monthly parole report. In his report he informed the warden he had used tobacco "with pleasure," but no alcohol; coffee being the strongest drink he had inbibed. He said in his spare time, of which he had little, he had read the works of the late Senator G.K. Davis, Shakespeare, and several newspapers. He said his greatest enjoyment came from attending a performance of Uncle Tom's Cabin and in going to a dance at a hotel in Stafils [sic—probably Staples]. Overall, the people were treating him with great kindness.[89]

Jim, in particular, had trouble with the long country drives he had to make for his employer, and his health went into decline. Following what doctors diagnosed as a "partial stroke of paralysis," he was hospitalized for several days. While Cole continued working at the granite company, doctors advised a change of employment for Jim, recommending indoor work where he would not be exposed to the weather.[90]

In addition to physical problems, Jim sank deeper into depression. Earlier in the year, while still behind the walls of prison, Jim had been interviewed by a female freelance writer from St. Paul, Alix J. Muller. Following their meeting, the two corresponded regularly. Before long, they had fallen in love and wanted to marry. Marriage, however, was only a fancy since it was illegal while on parole.[91]

Jim painted a dreary picture in a pleading letter to Warden Wolfer: "I have hoped for just a few years of married life, with wife and children to love and to make me happy—and to make them happy in return. But I cannot marry while on parole, and long for freedom, to enable me to take this step as soon as possible."[92]

On September 20, Cole wrote Warden Wolfer the following message from the Merchants Hotel in Perham: "I was in Cloquet Sunday and saw in papers where Jim had gone to hospital so I ran down that night. Spent Monday with him then Peterson sent me up here." Cole urged the warden to send someone to see Jim because he was getting quite depressed.[93]

Included with Cole's letter was his monthly parole report. Except for Jim's health, Cole had enjoyed a pretty good month, attending the Minnesota State Fair in St. Paul, a revival meeting in Cloquet, and a theater production of Kentucky Cal. In his closing remarks, Cole wrote, "I have been at peace with all of mankind. I am all O.K."[94]

Released from the hospital, Jim accepted a position as head of the cigar and tobacco department of Andrew Schoch's Grocery Store in St. Paul. Schoch was elated. "My offer of employment was among the first filed when the talk of paroling the boys commenced," Schoch told the press. "Last week I received a letter from the prison agent asking if my offer of employment was still open, and when I replied that it was, Jim Younger promptly reported to me with the statement that he was ordered to report for duty."[95]

Although Jim was enthusiastic about his new job, he again wrote Warden Wolfer complaining about a newspaper ad naming him as head of the cigar department, and he urged the warden to put a stop to the advertising campaign. On a brighter note, however, he explained he had made big sales from the start, and had he been on his own, he felt he could have cleared thirty dollars a day.[96] With the job going so well for him, he took "nice" rooms on the corner of Tenth Street and Broadway in St. Paul.[97]

In spite of the new employment and nicer apartment, Jim continued to be bothered by ex-convicts who pursued him with "nothing but foolish questionings." But, he maintained, he held his own."[98] Wolfer wrote back to Jim immediately: "Do not allow the ex-convicts to bother you. If they ask you to do anything that you think you ought not to do, plainly tell them. I do not think, however, I need to give you this advice as you are very thoroughly grounded in this particular, and I know you do not fear to speak up plainly and to the point whenever moral courage is in demand. I am satisfied that you will get along well and that you are sure to prosper."[99]

But Jim did not hold his own as he had implied, as evidenced in another letter to Wolfer: "This town is full of ex-convicts on the bum. There has [sic] been thirteen of them in here drunk or drinking, asking me to treat or give them money. One fellow, old Bob Brown, got mad because I did not give him money. I notified agent Whittier today. One fellow proposed beating my parole. They are truly disgusting to me."[100]

When Jim received a check for one hundred dollars from Cole, news spread quickly, and Jim was besieged by "tramps, crooks, of every tribe on earth." After giving one man a bowl of soup, another ex-convict came to Jim and said he was paralyzed. Jim replied, "blow your whiskey breath the other way—or I will be paralized [sic] also."[101]

Ten days later, Jim wrote Wolfer again complaining of being followed home from work in the evening by a "lone hungry looking individual." Jim reported the man to the police and instructed his landlord to turn away any strangers. He added, "Fast women, have tried their little games also, but all alike have, and will in future fail. For in truth, they have become disgusting to me."[102]

Five days later, and for no apparent reason, Jim was more chipper, and he told Wolfer his health was improving and he was in good spirits. His short burst of good cheer can probably be attributed to Alix, for in his monthly report, he wrote he had been enjoying "Sunday dinners with my best girl."[103]

While Jim's physical condition may or may not have been better, Cole's health began to slide. In October he wrote Warden Wolfer from Breckenridge, Minnesota: "I was real sick here one night and I think it was the alkaly [sic] waters the doctors gave me. About four fingers of brandy and I went to bed. I don't know whether it was the brandy I took that cured me." His greatest concern, however, was for Jim.[104]

Both his letter and parole report reflected a waning interest in the granite company. In his letter, he complained of rain and mud, which cost him many sales. Under "remarks" at the bottom of his monthly report, a somewhat unenthusiastic Cole penned, "I feel all right when I sell tombstones. Enough so I can look Peterson in the face."[105]

Throughout November and December, Cole was ill with gallstones and rheumatism, which greatly reduced his movements. He managed to attend a few theaters via complimentary passes and spent Sunday church with the Philosophical Society, but most evenings he remained alone in the boarding house. He also had tired of working for the Peterson Granite Company.[106]

January and February 1902 were months of change for the Youngers. Cole took a new job at the Interstate Institute, 412 Rosabel Street in St. Paul, a hospital of sorts dedicated to the cure of alcohol and morphine addiction. Although he commenced employment at a dollar a day, within thirty days, he was making fifty dollars a month as an assistant manager. Despite his quick raise, he looked at his employment at the institute as temporary, all the while looking forward to a better job promised him by State Agent Whittier. For relaxation, he attended a meeting of the Railroad Men of Minneapolis and a gathering of newspapermen at the Elks Hall.[107]

On January 29, Jim became ill from the wound in his mouth suffered at Hanska Slough. He was unable to work until February 18, and his sickness cost him his job at Schoch's. Cole, however, found him employment as a clerk at the James Elwin Cigar Store in the Fremont Hotel in Minneapolis for sixty dollars a month plus room and board. For enjoyment, he attended the Elicium Theatre in Minneapolis for a performance of John Philip Sousa's Band.[108]

In April, Cole left his employ at the institute and went to work for St. Paul Chief of Police John J. O'Connor at a salary to be determined later. He described his new position as one where he looked after the workmen at the O'Connor home. Cole spent his evenings at the chief's home or hanging out at the police station with a group of officers with whom he felt comfortable. He said he was disappointed about not getting to work at a cigar store O'Connor had promised to set up for him but concluded he would be working there very soon.

Cole's work for O'Connor kept him out of communication with many persons, including Jim. On June 26, Jim wrote the following to Warden Wolfer: "I am asked daily what Cole is doing and I do not know, which leaves me in an awkward and foolish position. Please let me know and oblige."[110] Wolfer replied the following day: "In reply would say that Cole is working for John

O'Connor, Chief of Police, St. Paul. He is in charge of a cigar and fruit stand down near the Union depot. I supposed you were fully posted as to Cole's whereabouts and what he is doing."[111]

Jim had seen an article in the *Minneapolis Times* stating that Cole had opposed an effort to secure an absolute pardon not made through the proper channels. The plan he vetoed had been originated by Mayor H.F. Bevans of Morris and Union Civil War hero Colonel William Colville during a reunion of the First Minnesota Regiment. Colville told Cole he had planned to circulate a petition among members of the regiment asking for a pardon, but Cole was adamant about his refusal.

"We don't want to be in a hurry about this matter," he told Colville. "I won't have anything to do with the plan, nor will I sanction it. The board of control, Warden Wolfer, and the state board of pardons should be consulted first. When they are ready to act, they will."[112]

In July, Elwin sold out and Jim was out of a job. He complained to Wolfer that his landlord had attempted to scare him into paying his rent a second time for his apartment at 222 South Eighth Street in Minneapolis. He was very concerned about money, especially since with no job, there was nothing coming in. And he was still worried about Cole: "Cole, I hear is sick, but I do not know where he lives, and I would not like going around inquiring."[113]

By August, Jim was thoroughly depressed over having no food to eat nor a job to make money. And, of course, the failed attempts at securing a pardon and the refusal of the state to permit his marriage to Alix weighed heavily on his mind. In his parole report for August when asked to state his surroundings and prospects, he answered with one word, "Gloomey [sic]."[114]

Jim wrote in a letter to Wolfer that same week that, with no money, he "had the hardest time to keep to an even notch." He said also his "board bill is higher than the average, because I have so much trouble getting food that I can eat."[115]

Just when his prospects began to improve—he had been promised a job with the Hartford Insurance Company—he was denied a license. Since the company could not advance him wages, and the union workers refused him—one man calling him "Wolfer's pet"—he could not work.[116]

On September 29, F.A. Whittier found work for Jim with the F.R. Yerxa Company selling office supplies. Whittier wrote Wolfer saying he had received a "very doleful" letter from Jim stating that "he had nothing to do and no way to make a living," so he decided to find Jim employment at once.[117] But, Jim could make no money. "Well, I walked about thirty miles per day," he said, "and talked myself hoarse, and got left, absolutely. And quit."[118]

Wolfer wrote back to Whittier the following day and

stated "[Jim] seems to be nearly as helpless as a baby. I cannot understand how he has been able to support himself during the long period he has been out of employment unless he receives help from some other source other than he has been able to provide for himself. I think it might be well to keep in pretty close touch with him from now on."[119]

Wolfer also wrote that he was not pleased with the Cole Younger situation and wondered if Chief O'Connor used him in anyway that violated his parole. He said he felt Cole should be doing "something more definite and regular."

Cole met with Jim on October 16, and the pair had a long talk. In no way did Jim share his destitution with his brother. Cole went away from the meeting thinking his brother had sufficient funds and was at least tolerating his position.[120]

But Jim had reached the end of his rope. He told a friend: "I am a mere nothing in the world's affairs from now on, old man. I'm a ghost, the ghost of Jim Younger, who was a man, not an extra good one, but I'm nothing." After telling his friend he was no longer the man who had ridden with Quantrill or the outlaw who entered Stillwater Prison, he added, "The fact is that I believe there is nothing left of me but the soul I started with."[121]

On October 19, at 4:30 in the afternoon, Jim Younger was found dead in his room in St. Paul's Reardon block, Seventh and Minnesota streets. Wearing only his suit of underwear, a .38 caliber revolver was found in Jim's right hand, and his left hand was covered with coagulated blood. Jim had been dead for hours from a bullet hole in his right temple.[122]

"A quarrel with his brother Cole, an infatuation for a young woman beyond his station, which resulted in a conflict between him and the friends that had been most instrumental in his liberation from the penitentiary, are assigned as the motives which prompted him to end his life," read a local newspaper.[123] Allegedly, the dispute with Cole was over money. Cole had received money from friends in the South, and, although very generous, his brother, Jim, thought he had not been as liberal as he could have been. Of course the quarrel may have been conjecture on the part of over-zealous journalists.

The newspaper account also attributed Jim's depression to persistent pain from the gunshot wound suffered in the 1876 capture near Madelia. Some of Jim's friends took the view that he shot himself to put an end to the pain.

Jim had only been living in the Reardon-block apartment a few weeks. Mr. O'Connell, manager of the building, said guests had informed him they had heard heavy groaning from Jim's room as early as eight o'clock in the morning. But no one investigated the sounds until a clerk tried to enter the room in the afternoon but found the door locked. The clerk reported the locked door, and, following an investigation, Jim's body was found in bed. His hand was clutching the revolver.

On a table next to a glass of water, a pen, and ink, was a large manila envelope that contained a stack of letters from Alix. On the face of the envelope, Jim had scrawled an affectionate note to Alix in big bold print: "To all that is good and true I love and bid farewell—Jim Younger." On the reverse side of the envelope, he penned, "Oh! Lassie! Good Bye. All relatives just stay away from me. No crocodile tears wanted. Reporters, be my friend. Burn me up."[124]

Next to the large envelope, Jim had placed a letter apparently written the night before, in which he addressed the public: "October 18—Last night on earth. So, good by, Lassie, for I still think of the A.U.G. Forgive me, for this is my only chance. I have done nothing wrong. But politics is all that Van Sant, Wolfer, and others of their stripe care for. Let the people judge. Treat me right and fair, reporters, for I am a square man. A socialist and decidedly in favor of woman's rights. Bryan is the brightest man these United States have ever produced. His one mistake is in not coming out for all the people and absolute socialism. Come out, Bryan. There is no such thing as a personal God. God is universal, and I know him well, and am not afraid. I have pity for the pardoning board. They do not stop to consider their wives, or to think of the man that knows how to love, and appreciate a friend in truth. Good bye, sweet lassie.—Jim Younger."[125]

Dr. J.M. Finnell, acting for Coroner A.W. Miller, had the body taken to the morgue, then to O'Halloran & Murphy Undertakers. Dr. Finnell believed Jim had shot himself in the head about eight o'clock in the morning and had been in a sitting position when he pulled the trigger. He said the coagulated blood on the left hand indicated Jim did not die instantly and that he had placed the hand to the wound before expiring.

Cole was shocked over the death of his brother and, at the time, was sick in bed in his room at 136 West Fourth Street. Cole said he had nothing to say to the press. Warden Wolfer also could not comprehend Jim's suicide. He knew Jim had been despondent because of his inability to hold jobs, owing to poor health, but he never realized how depressed he had really been.

"Jim carried a bullet in his head, and I believe that it caused him to become insane," related Wolfer. "He had acted strangely of late. I saw him coming down the street in St. Paul only a few days ago, and I expected that he would stop and speak to me, but he walked right by."[126]

Alix was in Boise, Idaho, where she had gone in August to avoid publicity over her relationship with Jim, when she received the news. Said Alix: "Jim wrote me under date of

October 16, stating he had given up all hope and was out of work. Saturday he telegraphed me, 'I won't write.' He was driven to this act by his persecutors. I am his wife, understand spiritually. No scandal has ever attached to my name. But before God he is mine and mine alone. My life work will be to place him right before the world. I have wired the authorities to cremate his body, it was his request."[127]

Many persons gathered outside the funeral parlor hoping to get a glimpse of the body of Jim Younger. However, Cole made a special request that the remains of his brother be excluded from public viewing, and the wish was carried out. Other morbid curiosity seekers tried to get a look at Jim's room at the Reardon, and Cole was so besieged with visitors, physicians had to call a halt to the visits.

The body of Jim Younger was not cremated to comply with his wishes or those of Alix Muller. C.B. Hull, Jim's nephew-in-law, who accompanied the body to Lee's Summit, Missouri, for burial, stated, "Jim never wanted to be cremated. The story probably grew out of a line written on an envelope before he died. He told the newspaper men in the note to treat him fair and not to burn him up. Out of that had grown the impression that he wanted to be cremated."[128]

When the coffin arrived in Missouri, it was discovered that many splinters had been cut from the pine box enclosing it; the grisly work of relic hunters who had met the funeral party along the way. According to a local newspaper: "The four corners had been whittled with knives and long slivers were cut off, while along the top of the lid wherever entrance could be obtained for the point of a knife the vandals had desecrated the coffin. Tucked under the undertaker's card was the waybill providing for the transportation of the body. Even this had been torn and the fragments carried off, until but little except the bare address was left."[129]

On February 4, 1903, a special meeting of the Board of Pardons met and voted unanimously to grant Cole Younger a conditional pardon, thus letting him return to Missouri. By "conditional," Cole had to sign that he could not place himself in exhibition in any way and that he would never return to Minnesota.

Shortly after returning to his former home in Lee's Summit, Cole went into partnership with Frank James and started their own Wild West show, although, technically, Cole did not exhibit himself. Anxious to get the conditions attached to his Minnesota pardon removed, especially that which forbade his return to Minnesota, Cole wrote Warden Wolfer to intercede with the state board of pardons and have the conditional pardon made unconditional. Cole hoped he could travel through Minnesota on tour with his Wild West show.[130]

Wolfer blasted Cole in a reply letter saying he once

thought Cole was a brave man and would prove it by living up to the conditions of his pardon. Wolfer termed Cole "a coward," and warned him that if he ever returned to Minnesota, he would place him behind bars.

Henry Wolfer was not the only person in the prison system perturbed with Cole's actions as evidenced by a letter the warden received from a prison official at the United States Penitentiary at Leavenworth, Kansas: "Please send me a copy of your reply to Cole Younger. He deserves a good warning since it is not possible now to give him the good hanging that he ought to have had years ago."[131]

After giving up the Wild West show, Cole sought to promote an electric railway between Kansas City and Lee's Summit. His later years were spent quietly with relatives in the Lee's Summit area. He died March 21, 1916, at the age of seventy-two, following a long illness. His last words were: "I have tried to make amends for the crimes of my younger days and hope, under God's mercy, for forgiveness."[132]

Notes

1 *The* (Stillwater Prison) *Mirror*, Vol. 103, No. 1, Anniversary Edition, August 11, 1989.

2 Brent T. Peterson & Dean R. Thilgen, *Stillwater, A Photographic History, 1843-1993*, Valley History Press, Stillwater, 1992, pp. 51-53.

3 Document signed by Warden John A. Reed for receipt of prisoners from A. Barton of Rice County. Author's collection.

4 *Faribault Democrat*, Friday, November 24, 1876, "In Prison."

5 Cole Younger, *Cole Younger By Himself.*

6 Brent T. Peterson & Dean R. Thilgen, *Stillwater, A Photographic History*, p. 51.

7 W.C. Heilbron, *Convict Life at the Minnesota State Prison*, W.C. Heilbron, St. Paul, 1909, pp. 13-16, 23-27.

8 Ibid., pp. 115-116.

9 Marley Brant, *The Outlaw Youngers*, p. 217.

10 Ibid.

11 W.C. Heilbron, *Convict Life at the Minnesota State Prison*, p. 97.

12 F.E. Stratton letter to daughter Alice, February 1904, published in *Historical Whisperings*, Washington County Historical Society, Vol. 9, No. 1, April 1982, pp. 1-2.

13 "Life in Minnesota in St. Paul's First Hundred Years," undated newspaper article, Northfield Public Library collection.

14 Ibid.

15 C.W. Deaton, "Plot to Free the Youngers Failed," published in *Northfield Independent*, Date Unknown, collection of Northfield Public Library.

16 *St. Paul & Minneapolis Pioneer Press*, Wednesday, January 9, 1884, "Fire Within Prison Walls;" *Stillwater Messenger*, Saturday, January 12, 1884, "Minnesota State Prison Fire."

17 Brent T. Peterson & Dean R. Thilgen, *Stillwater, A Photographic*

History, p. 57.

18 *Stillwater Gazette*, May 10, 1894.

19 *St. Paul & Minneapolis Pioneer Press*, Wednesday, January 9, 1884; *Stillwater Messenger*, Saturday, January 12, 1884.

20 *Stillwater Messenger*, Saturday, January 26, 1884, "Another Pion Conflagration."

21 *St. Paul & Minneapolis Pioneer Press*, Sunday, January 27, 1884, "Painting the Town Red."

22 Ibid.

23 *Stillwater Messenger*, Saturday, January 26, 1884.

24 *St. Paul & Minneapolis Pioneer Press*, Sunday, January 27, 1884.

25 *Stillwater Messenger*, Saturday, January 26, 1884.

26 *St. Paul & Minneapolis Pioneer Press*, Sunday, January 27, 1884.

27 *St. Paul & Minneapolis Pioneer Press*, Saturday, January 26, 1884, "The Prison Again Ablaze."

28 *St. Paul & Minneapolis Pioneer Press*, Sunday, January 27, 1884.

29 Marley Brant, *The Outlaw Youngers*, p. 227; Brent T. Peterson & Dean R. Thilgen, *Stillwater, A Photographic History*, pp. 59-60; *St. Paul & Minneapolis Pioneer Press*, Sunday, January 27, 1884.

30 *St. Paul Pioneer Press*, Thursday, July 11, 1901, "Prison Doors are Opened."

31 *St. Paul & Minneapolis Pioneer Press*, Sunday, January 27, 1884.

32 Ibid.

33 Brent T. Peterson & Dean R. Thilgen, *Stillwater, A Photographic History*, pp. 57-59.

34 W.C. Heilbron, *Convict Life at the Minnesota State Prison*, p. 97.

35 Marley Brant, *The Outlaw Youngers*, p. 229; Carl Hage, interview with author, Madelia, Minnesota, February 27, 1982.

36 Brent T. Peterson & Dean R. Thilgen, *Stillwater, A. Photographic History*, pp. 57-59.

37 Dr. William A. Settle (ed. Marley Brant), *Cole Younger Writes to Lizzie Daniel*, James-Younger Gang, Liberty, Missouri, 1994, p. 1.

38 Marley Brant, *The Outlaw Youngers*, pp. 231-236.

39 Carl Hage interview with author, February 27, 1982.

40 *The Mirror*, Anniversary Edition, Vol. 103, No. 1, August 11, 1989, "Mirror Turns 103."

41 *Stillwater Evening Gazette*, Friday, November 9, 1979, "Younger Brothers Play Role in First Prison Paper."

42 Ibid.

43 *The Mirror*, August 11, 1989.

44 *Butler Times*, Thursday, June 12, 1889.

45 Carl W. Breihan, *Younger Brothers*, pp. 183-184; *St. Paul Pioneer Press*, Tuesday, September 17, 1889, "Bob Younger Free."

46 *St. Paul Pioneer Press*, Tuesday, September 17, 1889.

47 *St. Paul Pioneer Press*, Thursday, September 19, 1889, "Stillwater Old Settlers of the St. Croix Valley Meet—Bob Younger's Funeral."

48 *The Prison Mirror*, Thursday, September 19, 1889, "Bob Younger."

49 Peter Brennan letter to Retta Younger dated September 23, 1891, Bronaugh-Younger Papers, Northfield (Minnesota) Bank Robbery of 1876: Selected Manuscripts Collections and Government Records,

Microfilm Edition, Minnesota Historical Society.

50 George T. Barr, "Account of Northfield Bank Robbery in 1876," Unpublished manuscript in archives of Blue Earth County Historical Society, Mankato, Minnesota.

51 A.E. Hedback, M.D., June 7, 1921, "Cole Younger's Story of the Northfield Raid in his own Handwriting," William Watts Folwell and Family Papers, Northfield (Minnesota) Bank Robbery of 1876: Selected Manuscripts Collections and Government Records, Microfilm Edition, Minnesota Historical Society.

52 Ibid.

53 The St. Paul Pioneer Press, Tuesday, July 13, 1897, "Arguments on the Younger Pardon."

54 Ibid.

55 Ibid.

56 Ibid.

57 The St. Paul Pioneer Press, Wednesday, July 14, 1897, "Held Fast in Prison."

58 The Minneapolis Journal, Friday, July 9, 1897, "Victim of Youngers Speaks Out."

59 Ibid.

60 The "defenseless Swede" is referred to in the article as Anderson, a misnomer. It should have read Nicholaus Gustavson.

61 The Minneapolis Journal, Friday, July 9, 1897.

62 Northfield News, Saturday, July 17, 1897, "Pardon Denied."

63 The St. Paul Pioneer Press, Wednesday, July 14, 1897, "Pardon is Denied."

64 Ibid.

65 Ibid.

66 Ibid.

67 Northfield News, Saturday, July 17, 1897.

68 Marley Brant, The Outlaw Youngers, p. 260.

69 St. Paul Pioneer Press, date unknown.

70 Madelia newspaper, title and date unknown.

71 Lee's Summit Journal, Friday, July 3, 1981, "Cole Younger Tells His Life Story."

72 St. Paul Pioneer Press, Wednesday, July 10, 1901, "Youngers to be Paroled."

73 St. Paul Pioneer Press, Thursday, July 11, 1901, "Prison Doors are Opened."

74 Ibid.

75 Ibid.

76 Stillwater Gazette, July 12, 1901.

77 St. Paul Pioneer Press, Thursday, July 11, 1901, "Will Make Good Citizens."

78 St. Paul Pioneer Press, Friday, July 12, 1901, "Youngers Will Drop From Sight."

79 St. Paul Pioneer Press, Sunday, July 14, 1901, "He Won't Hide the Youngers."

80 St. Paul Pioneer Press, Monday, July 15, 1901, "Youngers Are Out Of Prison."

81 *St. Paul Pioneer Press*, Tuesday, July 16, 1901, "Youngers Are Ready For Work."

82 Letter from W.C. Bronaugh to Henry Wolfer dated July 16, 1901. Stillwater State Prison Case File: Younger Bros.: Selected Manuscripts Collections and Government Records, Microfilm Edition, Minnesota Historical Society.

83 Letter from George M. Bennett to Henry Wolfer dated July 22, 1901. Stillwater State Prison Case File: Younger Bros. Selected Manuscripts Collections and Government Records, Microfilm Edition, Minnesota Historical Society.

84 Monthly Parole Report of Jim Younger dated July 20, 1901. Stillwater State Prison Case File: Younger Bros. Selected Manuscripts Collections and Government Records, Microfilm Edition, Minnesota Historical Society.

85 Letter from Jim Younger to Warden Henry Wolfer dated August 14, 1901. Stillwater State Prison Case File: Younger Bros. Selected Manuscripts Collections and Government Records, Microfilm Edition, Minnesota Historical Society.

86 Letter from Jim Younger to Warden Henry Wolfer, August (undated) 1901. Stillwater State Prison Case File: Younger Bros. Selected Manuscripts Collections and Government Records, Microfilm Edition, Minnesota Historical Society.

87 Letter from Jim Younger to Warden Henry Wolfer dated September 1, 1901. Stillwater State Prison Case File: Younger Bros. Selected Manuscript Collections and Government Records, Microfilm Edition, Minnesota Historical Society.

88 Letter from Cole Younger to Warden Henry Wolfer dated August 31, 1901. Stillwater State Prison Case File: Younger Bros. Selected Manuscripts Collections and Government Records, Microfilm Edition, Minnesota Historical Society.

89 Monthly Parole Report of Cole Younger dated August 31, 1901. Stillwater State Prison Case File: Younger Bros. Selected Manuscripts Collections and Government Records, Microfilm Edition, Minnesota Historical Society.

90 *Madelia Times*, October 18, 1901, "Jim Younger's New Job."

91 Marley Brant, *The Outlaw Youngers,* pp. 260-271.

92 Undated letter from Jim Younger to Warden Henry Wolfer. Stillwater State Prison Case File: Younger Bros. Selected Manuscripts Collections and Government Records, Microfilm Edition, Minnesota Historical Society.

93 Letter from Cole Younger to Warden Henry Wolfer dated September 20, 1901. Stillwater State Prison Case File: Younger Bros. Selected Manuscripts Collections and Government Records, Microfilm Edition, Minnesota Historical Society.

94 Monthly Parole Report of Cole Younger dated September 20, 1901. Stillwater State Prison Case File: Younger Bros. Selected Manuscripts Collections and Government Records. Microfilm Edition. Minnesota Historical Society.

95 *Madelia Times*, October 18, 1901.

96 Undated letter from Jim Younger to Warden Henry Wolfer.

Stillwater State Prison Case File: Younger Bros. Selected Manuscripts Collections and Government Records, Microfilm Edition, Minnesota Historical Society.

97 Letter from Jim Younger to Warden Henry Wolfer dated October 10, 1901. Stillwater State Prison Case File: Younger Bros. Selected Manuscripts Collections and Government Records, Microfilm Edition, Minnesota Historical Society.

98 Monthly Parole Report of Jim Younger dated October 20, 1901. Stillwater State Prison Case File: Younger Bros. Selected Manuscripts Collections and Government Records, Microfilm Edition, Minnesota Historical Society.

99 Letter from Warden Henry Wolfer to Jim Younger dated October 24, 1901. Stillwater State Prison Case File: Younger Bros. Selected Manuscript Collections and Government Records, Microfilm Edition, Minnesota Historical Society.

100 Undated letter from Jim Younger to Warden Henry Wolfer. Stillwater State Prison Case File: Younger Bros. Selected Manuscript Collections and Government Records, Microfilm Edition, Minnesota Historical Society.

101 Letter from Jim Younger to Warden Henry Wolfer dated November 5, 1901. Stillwater State Prison Case File: Younger Bros. Selected Manuscript Collections and Government Records, Microfilm Edition, Minnesota Historical Society.

102 Letter from Jim Younger to Warden Henry Wolfer dated November 15, 1901. Stillwater State Prison Case File: Younger Bros. Selected Manuscript Collections and Government Records, Microfil Edition, Minnesota Historical Society.

103 Monthly Parole Report of Jim Younger dated November 20, 1901. Stillwater State Prison Case File: Younger Bros. Selected Manuscript Collections and Government Records, Microfilm Edition, Minnesota Historical Society.

104 Letter from Cole Younger to Warden Henry Wolfer dated October 21, 1901. Stillwater State Prison Case File: Younger Bros. Selected Manuscript Collections and Government Records, Microfilm Edition, Minnsota Historical Society.

105 Monthly Parole Report of Cole Younger dated October 20, 1901. Stillwater State Prison Case File: Younger Bros. Selected Manuscript Collections and Government Records, Microfilm Edition, Minnesota Historical Society.

106 Monthly Parole Reports of Cole Younger dated November 20 and December 20, 1901. Stillwater State Prison Case File: Younger Bros. Selected Manuscript Collections and Government Records, Microfilm Edition, Minnesota Historical Society.

107 Marley Brant, *The Outlaw Youngers,* pp. 274-275; Monthly Parole Reports of Cole Younger dated January 20 and February 20, 1902. Stillwater State Prison Case Files: Younger Bros. Selected Manuscript Collections and Government Records, Microfilm Editions, Minnesota Historical Society.

108 Letter from James Elwin to Warden Henry Wolfer dated February 12, 1902; Employment Agreement Between James Elwin and Henry

Wolfer dated February 13, 1902; Monthly Parole Reports of Jim Younger dated January 20, February 20, and March 20, 1902. All documents in Stillwater State Prison Case Files: Younger Bros. Selected Manuscript Collections and Government Records, Microfilm Edition, Minnesota Historical Society.

109 Monthly Parole Reports of Cole Younger dated April 20, May 20, and June 20, 1902. Stillwater State Prison Case File: Younger Bros. Selected Manuscript Collections and Government Records, Microfilm Edition, Minnesota Historical Society.

110 Letter from Jim Younger to Warden Henry Wolfer dated June 26, 1902. Stillwater State Prison Case File: Younger Bros. Selected Manuscript Collections and Government Records, Microfilm Edition, Minnesota Historical Society.

111 Letter from Warden Henry Wolfer to James Younger dated June 27, 1902. Stillwater State Prison Case File: Younger Bros. Selected Manuscript Collections and Government Records, Microfilm Edition, Minnesota Historical Society.

112 *Minneapolis Times,* June 1902. Stillwater State Prison Case File: Younger Bros. Selected Manuscript Collections and Government Records, Microfilm Edition, Minnesota Historical Society.

113 Letter from Jim Younger to Warden Henry Wolfer undated (July 1902). Stillwater State Prison Case File: Younger Bros. Selected Manuscript Collections and Government Record, Microfilm Edition, Minnesota Historical Society.

114 Monthly Parole Report of Jim Younger dated August 20, 1902. Stillwater State Prison Case File: Younger Bros. Selected Manuscript Collections and Government Records, Microfilm Edition, Minnesota Historical Society.

115 Letter from Jim Younger to Warden Henry Wolfer dated August 24, 1902. Stillwater State Prison Case File: Younger Bros. Selected Manuscript Collections and Government Records, Microfilm Edition, Minnesota Historical Society.

116 Letters from Jim Younger to Warden Henry Wolfer dated September 8, September 19, another undated September, 1902; Monthly Parole Report of Jim Younger dated September 20, 1902. Stillwater State Prison Case File: Younger Bros. Selected Manuscript Collections and Government Records, Microfilm Edition, Minnesota Historical Society.

117 Letter from F.A. Whittier to Warden Henry Wolfer dated September 29, 1902. Stillwater State Prison Case File: Younger Brothers. Selected Manuscript Collections and Government Records, Microfilm Edition, Minnesota Historical Society.

118 Undated letter from Jim Younger to Warden Henry Wolfer. Stillwater State Prison Case File: Younger Bros. Selected Manuscript Collections and Government Records, Microfilm Edition, Minnesota Historical Society.

119 Letter from Warden Henry Wolfer to State Agent F.A. Whittier dated September 30, 1902. Stillwater State Prison Case File: Younger Bros. Selected Manuscript Collections and Government Records. Microfilm Edition. Minnesota Historical Society.

120 *Kansas City Star*, Monday, October 20, 1902.

121 *Kansas City Star*, Tuesday, October 21, 1902.

122 *St. Paul Pioneer Press*, Monday, October 20, 1902, "James Younger Commits Suicide."

123 Ibid.

124 Ibid.

125 Ibid.

126 *St. Paul Pioneer Press*, Tuesday, October 21, 1902. "His Romance Ends in Death."

127 Ibid.

128 *St. Paul Pioneer Press*, Thursday, October 23, 1902. "His Coffin is Hacked."

129 Ibid.

130 May 1908 Newspaper article. Stillwater State Prison Case File: Younger Bros. Selected Manuscript Collections and Government Records, Microfilm Edition, Minnesota Historical Society.

131 Letter from R.W.M. Daughery to Warden Henry Wolfer dated May 30, 1908. Stillwater State Prison Case File: Younger Bros. Selected Manuscript Collections and Government Records, Microfilm Edition, Minnesota Historical Society.

132 Newspaper clipping, Northfield Public Library, Newspaper unknown, dated March 22, 1916.

Chapter 7

The Dirty Little Coward

WAS IT YOU JESSE

In the streets of Northfield
With Frank at your side
And malice in your heart?

And was it you
Who parleyed deep in Monegaw
    With Bob and Stiles
      To ride many miles
To faraway Northfield?

And was it you, Frank
Who pulled the trigger
On brave Mr. Heywood
And any hope of salvation?

Pray tell was it you
Who defied Cole's orders
    And with Pitts and Bob
    Bungled the job
With the curse of drink?

Was it Zerelda's boys
Who galloped into Dakota
Leaving Youngers to their fate
And a widow to her grief?

Across the Big Muddy
    You rode home empty handed
      With your gang disbanded
Jesse . . . Frank . . .
Was it you?

WITH THE GANG ALL BUT DISBANDED, Jesse and Frank James had to seek new personnel. In 1877, lying low in Tennessee under the alias of John Davis Howard, Jesse attempted to go straight by living the life of a farmer and wheat speculator. His luck at the gam-

Bill Ryan. (Courtesy of Armand De Gregoris Collection)

Artist's interpretation of Jesse James. (Drawing by John Stevens)

bling table ran out in 1878, and he decided to recruit a new gang. Among the outlaws to join the gang was Bill Ryan. On October 8, 1879, Jesse, Ryan, and company robbed the Chicago and Alton line train of $6,000 at Glendale, Missouri.[1]

Frank, meanwhile, who was also living in the Nashville area, had managed to keep out of trouble and had gained the reputation as a hard-working, law abiding citizen under the name Ben J. Woodson. Frank was angry when Jesse brought outlaws Bill Ryan and Dick Liddil with him to Nashville during the summer of 1880.

But the outlaws went right to work. On September 3, 1880, Jesse James and Bill Ryan held up two stagecoaches near Mammoth Cave, Kentucky, and on March 11, 1881, the gang relieved a Federal Paymaster of $5,200 near Muscle Shoals, Alabama.[2] Two weeks later, Ryan was arrested after bragging, while under the influence of liquor, about being an outlaw. Jesse, Frank, as well as Dick Liddel, hurriedly left Nashville.[3]

Back in Missouri, Jesse gathered others into his little band of outlawry, and on July 15, 1881, they robbed a Chicago, Rock Island, and Pacific passenger train near Winston. The robbery was attributed to a band of five to seven men, among them Jesse and Frank James, Dick Liddil, Jim Cummins, and Ed Miller. Still, Jesse's outlaw career was coming to an end.[4] After robbing

a Chicago and Alton train at Blue Cut, Missouri, in September 1881, Jesse shook the conductor's hand and said, "You'll never hear from me again."[5] Jesse intended to give up his life of crime and move to a farm in Nebraska with his wife and two children.

But one more robbery, a bank in Platte City, had been in the planning stages for April 4, 1882. Robert and Charles Ford, newly recruited youthful members of the band, had been staying with Jesse and his family at their temporary residence on the corner of Thirteenth and Lafayette Streets in St. Joseph, Missouri. Charles had helped rob the Chicago and Alton train the past September, but Bob, only twenty years old, had never been involved in a robbery.[6]

Jesse James home in St. Joseph, Missouri. (Photo by author)

Unbeknownst to the gang, Bob had been meeting secretly over several weeks with Liberty, Clay County Sheriff James Timberlake, Kansas City Police Commissioner Henry Craig, and Governor Thomas Crittenden. The governor had related to Bob Ford that, "I want Jesse James brought in, and I will give you $10,000 for him, dead or alive." Commissioner Craig armed Ford with two revolvers belonging to the state. Ford then sent a dispatch to Timberlake stating, "I have gone after Jesse James, and in ten days I'll have killed him or he'll have killed me."[7]

Bob and Charley Ford watched Jesse every minute and waited for the right opportunity to kill him. Jesse, however, was always heavily armed and ever watchful. They discarded any plan of taking him alive, considering the attempt suicidal. But, following breakfast, on April 3, 1882, thirteen days after Bob Ford said he'd get Jesse, the opportunity presented itself.[8]

Charley Ford and Jesse had been out in the stable preparing the horses for that evening's intended Platte City robbery. Returning inside the house, Jesse said to Bob, who was seated in the room, "It's an awfully hot day." Jesse pulled off his coat and vest and placed them on his bed. Then he said, "I guess I'll take off my pistols, for fear somebody will see them if I walk in the yard," and unbuckled his gun belt. Placing his two .45s—a Smith & Wesson and a Colt, on the bed, he picked up a brush to dust some pictures on the wall.[9]

When Jesse turned his back to his friends, they stepped between him and his revolvers, and at a motion from Charley, both drew their pistols. Robert drew quicker than his brother and fired at the back of Jesse's head from a distance of only two to four feet. Jesse heard the slight motion and began to turn his head, but he fell to the floor with no outcry. The fatal bullet had entered his skull.

Charles Ford. (Frank Leslie's Illustrated Newspaper, Apreil 22, 1882)

The wall Jesse James was facing when shot. (Photo by Diana Pierce)

Jesse's wife had been in the kitchen during the shooting and, hearing the shot, raced into the front room to find her husband lying dead on his back and the Fords, each holding a revolver, making for the fence at the rear of the house. As Robert scaled the fence, Mrs. James shouted, "Robert, you have done this. Come back." Robert answered, "I swear to God, I didn't" and came back. Bending over her husband, Mrs. James tried to wipe the blood from his forehead, but it flowed so fast, wiping was impossible. He died, his head in her hands, as the Ford brothers rushed off to report their deed to the authorities.

Jesse's death started a souvenir stampede. Playwright Oscar Wilde passed through town shortly after Jesse's demise and noted, "They sold his dustbin and footscraper yesterday by public auction, his door knocker is to be offered for sale this afternoon. . . . The citizens of Kansas have telegraphed to an agent here to secure his coal scuttle at all hazards, and at any cost. . . ."[10]

Wilde knew what he was talking about. Jesse's widow auctioned off $177 worth of household goods. Jesse's dog brought in the highest bid at fifteen dollars. Other relic hunters carried off pieces of the James stable and sections of his fence.

Bob Ford. (Frank Leslie's Illustrated Newspaper, April 22, 1882)

Pinkerton guards at the Jesse James gravesite. July 18, 1995. The body was excavated and reburied in the cemetery in Kearney. (Photo by Mrs. Merri Vinton.)

Down to the rotted coffin. (Photo by Mrs. Merri Vinton.)

Confererate Honor Guard march at Jesse James' third funeral (1995). (Photo by Marvin James.)

Jesse's third funeral. (Photo by Marvin James.)

Despite her grief, several years after her son's death, Jesse's mother, in need of money, held court at the James Farm and charged curiosity seekers to hear her tell the story of Frank and Jesse James. In later years, visitors paid fifty cents to the ticket taker, Frank James, before entering the property. Zerelda sold rocks from Jesse's grave, and, when she ran out of stones from the grave, she carted them up from the river and sold them. She also sold horseshoes from Jesse's horses, and, since the supply could not last indefinitely, the shoes were not always "the originals."[11]

Within weeks of Jesse's demise, a mysterious pair of unexplained explosions rocked the Northfield area in Minnesota's Rice County. The first of these strange explosions was felt only two and a half weeks after Jesse's death, according to a local newspaper report: "At about 7:30 o'clock, yesterday morning, a violent explosion was heard in the direction of Willis Hall. Many thought it was caused by the blast of rock on Division Street, but investigation showed that some crank had filled a piece of gas pipe with powder and firecrackers and placed it in the southwest window of the gallery in Willis Hall. A string leading to the ground was tied to something arranged to fire the powder, which was done at the time of the explosion and evidently premature. Probably the plan was to have the explosion take place during morning devotions, when a panic would have unavoidably been the result, accompanied by loss of life and limb."[12]

The article went on to say that the blast could have been the work of a practical joker, but whoever had caused the mishap, needed to be punished. Nonetheless, the perpetrator of the blast was not apprehended.

Another explosion occurred in Northfield on May 12, not far from the bank robbery site: The same newspaper stated: "At about 9:30 o'clock Friday evening last, Northfield people were startled by the violent report of an explosion, which sounded as if it occurred in the vicinity of the bridge. Upon investigation it was found that an attempt had been made to blow up Dr. Greaves' office. It appears from what was found among the debris, that a short bag was filled with powder and after being wound with stout cord, and a fuse attached was placed under the building and touched off. The explosion was of sufficient power to blow off all the boards which enclosed the space under the building, and break several bottles which were in the room above, but aside from this did no particular damage."[13]

Whether the blasts were related in any way to the death of Jesse James or the 1876 downfall of the gang is not known. It is doubtful, however. There was no real motive for the crimes, and there simply weren't any James gang personnel left that would have been in the area at that time. The blasts must have had people wondering, however, and to many, they brought back unpleasant memories of a town disaster only six years earlier.

Rumors about Frank James were numerous following the death of Jesse. One report stated he may have attended his brother's funeral and was "seen" in the St. Joseph area. Others insisted he had been spotted in St. Louis, New York City, and Kansas City, or he was hiding out in Texas or Kansas. There was widespread belief that he would avenge his brother's death but those rumors faded within a few months.[14] (Robert Ford would be shot down in a silver mining camp in Creede, Colorado, by Ed O'Kelley on June 8, 1892.)[15]

Throughout the summer of 1882, negotiations were being made with Governor Crittenden, through writer John Newman Edwards, for the surrender of Frank James. On October 4, Frank accompanied his friend Edwards to Jefferson City. Crittenden invited several state officials, as well as newspapermen, to a meeting with James and Edwards. After Edwards introduced Frank to the governor, the former outlaw removed his pistol and cartridge belt, and handing them to the governor said, "Governor Crittenden, I want to hand over to you that which no living man except myself has been permitted to touch since 1861, and to say that I am your prisoner."[16]

As Frank awaited trial while in jail at Independence, rumors circulated that the governor of Minnesota would have him brought to that state on charges stemming from the Northfield robbery and murder of Heywood. In January 1883, the governor of Minnesota did send a requisition to Crittenden asking for Frank's removal to that state, but Crittenden refused to honor it. He did so on the grounds that he would honor no out-of-state requisitions until all Missouri charges had been settled.[17]

Following a series of delays, Frank James finally went to trial in Gallatin, Missouri, on August 21, 1883. Several days of testimony ensued, but Frank was found not guilty. The jury needed only three and one-half hours to reach its verdict. When Frank heard the verdict, he turned to his wife and embraced her amid a loud applause. Frank had other charges to face but was eventually found not guilty on those charges as well.

While awaiting trial in a Huntsville, Alabama, jail cell, Frank was visited by a cousin, William St. John. According to family papers, St. John rode a mule from Huntsville to Bibb County following the visit and told another relative of his visit to Frank: "He [cousin William] loaned him [Frank] $50. He said his cell in the jail was furnished like a palace."[18]

Minnesota officials showed up at the Frank James trial in Huntsville, planning to arrest the outlaw once another verdict of not guilty was announced. However, as soon as the trial ended in a not guilty verdict, Sheriff John F. Rogers of Cooper County, Missouri, arrested Frank for his participation in the 1876 Otterville robbery. The arrest was a hoax. Frank was brought back to Missouri to keep him away from the Minnesota officers, killing any chance of his being returned to Minnesota to face charges for his alleged involvement in the Northfield robbery. A local newspaper branded it the work of ruling Bourbons in Missouri.[19]

Frank, forty-two, was finally released in February 1885 and went to work as a race starter at county fairs and race tracks. He also worked "regular" jobs selling shoes in Nevada, Missouri, and he spent four years in Dallas, Texas, employed by the Mittenthal Clothing Company. During one two-year span, he lived in Texas, Louisiana, and New Jersey working as a livestock importer, race timer, and even as a doorman at a burlesque house.[20]

After playing roles with traveling stock companies, Frank joined Cole in 1903 to form the James-Younger Wild West Show. After 1901, he lived at the James farm near Kearney, Missouri, except for four years while he lived on a small farm near Fletcher, Oklahoma. He passed away at the Kearney homestead on

February 18, 1915, at the age of seventy-two. He widow, Annie, continued to live on the farm until her demise on July 6, 1944.

With Frank's death, and that of Cole Younger's the following year, the truth about what really happened at Northfield went to the grave with them. Many important questions remained unanswered: Who pulled the trigger on Joseph Lee Heywood? Was there a ninth, or even tenth, man in the outlaw band? And perhaps the most significant question of all, were Jesse and Frank James really at Northfield? Historians have argued these questions for nearly one and one-quarter centuries, and the truth is as clouded today as it was in the swirling dust of Northfield in1876.

When Cole Younger was captured in September, 1876, he denied that the two men who had escaped were Jesse and Frank James. According to an 1876 newspaper account, the two escapees did not resemble the Jameses: "They are larger, coarser and much heavier men. One of them wore full, heavy red whiskers, and he was one of the men who entered the bank and the one who shot Heywood; the other wore full and heavy black whiskers. Before the robbery, these men braided their whiskers and tucked them in under their vests, and after the robbery they took them out."[21]

According to this same account, Cole Younger allegedly stated he had not spoken to either of the James boys in six years, but if he ever did see them again, he would do so at the point of a revolver. Mrs. Twyman, the Youngers' aunt who came up to Minnesota following the capture, agreed with Cole's story and said if the Youngers were in Minnesota, the Jameses were not. She attributed her remarks to a deadly feud between the Youngers and Jameses.

No "deadly feud" existed between them, and Cole did not plan to shoot Jesse and Frank if he ever saw them again. When Cole was released and sent back to Missouri on a pardon in 1903, he wasted little time in looking up Frank James and teaming up for a wild west circus. The two were close friends. Obviously, the feud and would-be gun battle were contrived to protect his friends. Cole had already been sentenced to life; he could gain nothing by tattling on his accomplices. He simply referred to the two men who had escaped as "men which none of you know."

In 1903, Cole Younger published an autobiography stating the Jameses were not at Northfield. Although he again would not identify the pair, he wrote that one of the men had been killed in Arizona and the other died from fever. The deaths were very convenient. Since they were both gone and could not speak for themselves, there need be no mention of their names. Honor the dead.

And, of course, since to Cole the story had ended, the Jameses had to be left out of it.[22]

Cole did write that the two unidentified men who took part in the robbery were named Woods and Howard. Jesse had been living under the alias "J.D. Howard" when he was killed. When Frank surrendered, he was living near Nashville under the name "B.J. Woodson." It was not simply a coincidence that Cole gave the names of Woods and Howard. Judge William H. Wallace, who, as prosecuting attorney of Jackson County, prosecuted Frank James at Gallatin, stated he had received a full account of the Northfield robbery from Dick Liddil, who was given it by Jesse James. According to Wallace, the eight names were the same as those given by Cole Younger, including the names Howard and Woods.[23]

Some historians believe Frank James was at Northfield but Jesse was not. It is quite well documented that Jesse was in Nashville during August and September of 1876. Plus there were no indictments and no extradition of the James brothers by the State of Minnesota because of the lack of hard evidence that they participated in the robbery. Frank James and Cole Younger were good friends, but Cole and Jesse were anything but cordial by the summer of 1876. And it is doubtful that Jesse would have permitted such an undisciplined job as the Northfield robbery with men who had been drinking that day.[24]

While it is true that Jesse would not pull a job with men who had been drinking, it is doubtful that Frank or Cole would have either. Cole, more than any of the others, was visibly upset when he found that the men who had entered the bank had been drunk and had blamed the bungled bank attempt on the liquor.

Scholars point out that between the issue of hard drinking, the Pinkerton files that placed Jesse in Nashville at the time, the Younger brothers defense files, the Nashville files, Jesse's September 5 birthday (would he really have went away to rob a bank on his birthday?), his son's birthday, and the lack of warrants, indictments, or extradition, there is a case for Jesse's non-participation. But how strong a case? Jesse may have been away robbing a bank on his own birthday, but would he do so on his son's first? The birthday was not an issue. Jesse's son was born in Tennessee on December 31, 1875. Jesse was back in Tennessee well before December.

Todd M. George of Lee's Summit, Missouri, befriended Cole Younger following his return to Missouri in 1903. According to George, Cole talked openly about his career as an outlaw, although never pointing a finger at Jesse James. Said George: "So many of the writers of true and fiction have made the true history of these notorious characters here in Jackson

County almost impossible to know what to believe, but from the words of Cole Younger himself he always insisted to me that Jesse James was not present with the seven that made this raid. In the first place Cole did not like Jesse James, but his close relationship and friendship of Frank James always did exist and he tole [sic] me truthfully that Frank James is the only one that made a safe escape to get back to Missouri."[25]

George offered other information that implied that Frank James was at Northfield: "I have been asked so often if Cole Younger ever tole [sic] me who in the group committed the murder. On a number of occasions when I asked Cole if he could ever tell me who did this his answer was always, 'Frank James knew who did it.'"[26]

Jim Younger wrote to a sweetheart and stated that the James boys had been in Northfield and that it was Frank who killed Joseph Heywood.[27] Jim also indicated that "Jesse seemed to disappear part of the time during the Northfield episode."[28] A manuscript written by Cora McNeill, as related to her by Jim Younger, also establishes the fact that the James boys were there. And, of course, it states that Jesse talked Bob Younger into going and Bob's brothers went along in part to protect him.[29]

Both Cole Younger and Frank James were storytellers of the first magnitude. When cornered, they liked to confuse their interrogators and keep the public guessing . . . and second guessing.[30]

Cole was known to lie. He once said it was recorded in his family Bible that his ancestors came from Germany. That same Bible was lost in a fire. Most researchers have found that the Youngers were of Scotch-Irish stock. He had a poor memory for dates, not only days and months, but years as well. He once claimed the Northfield raid was the only robbery in which he had participated. History knows better.[31]

Author Robertus Love, who published a respected biography of Jesse in 1925, was convinced Jesse and Frank were both in Northfield. Love bases his conclusion on many factors, including the sighting of Jesse James by a Mankato man who, prior to the robbery, alerted the police. Love contended it was Frank and Jesse who rode double, with Frank wounded in the leg. And at Sioux City, "they visited a doctor who dressed Frank's wound." When questioned after their capture, the Youngers answered they would remain in true faith to their friends.[32]

Dallas Cantrell, in her book, *Younger's Fatal Blunder*, (1973), described an incident when Chief King of St. Paul showed photographs of Jesse and Frank James to Cole Younger after his capture. Cole readily admitted they were the Jameses but said they had changed so much a "stranger" would not recognize them. When shown a photo of himself taken at the same time, he merely said, "it was a good one."[33]

Homer Croy in *Last of the Great Outlaws* (1956) doesn't even debate whether the Jameses were a part of the robbery. He clearly states that they initially planned to rob the First National Bank in Mankato. Jesse rode in first to give the signal. He rode in at noon and was not happy with a crowd that had gathered to watch city repairs across the street from the bank. He rode in again at two o'clock to check the situation which was still ongoing. Disgusted they rode out of town and on to Northfield. Page 113 states that Frank James came out of the bank and that he had killed Cashier Heywood. Frank was shot in the thigh upon exiting the bank. Page 127 has Cole asking the posse (upon his capture) if Frank and Jesse got away.[34]

In Marley Brant's, *The Outlaw Youngers, A Confederate Brotherhood* (1992), Chapter 16 begins with Jesse and Frank accompanied by Charlie Pitts or Bill Chadwell beginning their trip to Minnesota.[35]

George Huntington, in *Robber and Hero* (1962), stated: "Of course they passed under assumed names, introducing themselves as J.C. King, Jack Ward, etc. It is now known that the band consisted of the following men: Jesse James and his brother Frank, Thomas C. Younger (commonly known as Cole Younger), and his brothers James and Robert, Clell Miller, William Stiles, alias Chadwell, and Charles Pitts, alias George Wells. Some persons maintain that there was a ninth man, but he has never been identified, and is commonly believed to be mythical."[36]

James Horan's *Desperate Men* (1949) again lists the same eight in Chapter 15.[37]

And the list goes ever on. Nearly all books written about Jesse and Frank James place them at Northfield. As Maria Younger said: "Cole Younger was a liar. He had to cover for his friends. Seeing a possibility of freedom by pleading guilty, Cole had hopes of leaving prison at some point in time. Looking toward this future would have meant lying was in order to reestablish himself upon his release. And without question, his friendships were important to him. In retrospection of the Youngers and James lives, their friendships were all they had—no one place they called home, families disgraced and disheveled by the war, loved ones killed by the war or the Pinkertons, staying 'on the run' to avoid capture."[38]

Because of these strong friendships, Jesse and Frank would have been there because Clell Miller was there. Clell followed them. Clell Miller would not have gone to Northfield by himself or with anyone else. He trusted Jesse James.[39]

In a letter to Maude Williamson James, Frank wrote that stories published in the newspapers about Jesse killing Heywood in Northfield were false. He said Jesse was not even in the bank, and it may have been Bill Chadwell who shot him. According to the Frank James letter, Jesse was outside the bank beside Frank's horse when they heard two shots ring out from inside the bank. Both Jesse and himself, he said, hadn't wanted to go to Minnesota because they expected trouble there, and the whole thing had been "Bill's" idea.[40]

Although the Frank James letter's authenticity could be challenged, since it was not discovered until several decades later, the missive does have some very good internal clues. In the letter, Frank referred to Jesse as "Dingus," which was his nickname. He also explained that Jesse never mistreated women and did not brag, both of which were true. Frank mentioned names of persons only a few members of the James circle might recognize such as "Doc" McCoy and also touched on the shooting of Frank Mott by Jesse.[41]

Adding to the evidence that Frank and Jesse James had been involved in the Northfield robbery was a June 25, 1941, visit by the daughter of Frank James to the Hospital Caves in St. Peter. Charles W. Meyer, who conducted the tours, related that Frank's daughter wanted to "see the place where her father and uncle stopped before they went to Northfield for the big bank robbery."[42]

According to Meyer: "An elderly lady about sixty-five came to me and asked all manner of questions. Then she said she was a daughter of Frank James. 'I always wanted to see the place but do not tell the crowd as I do not want to be looked at by everybody. We are also on the way to Northfield to see the bank.'" Mr. Meyer showed them through the cave, and when his visitor left, she thanked him and said it was indeed a wonderful place.[43]

The fact that Frank's daughter came all the way to Minnesota to see the places "her father and uncle" had visited is a pretty strong indication that the brothers were indeed in Minnesota in 1876. Undoubtedly, the daughter would not have made the trip otherwise.

The most convincing evidence of all was a deathbed confession by Cole Younger to Jesse's son, Jesse Edward James, and to a close friend, Harry Hoffman. After Jesse's death, the blame for Heywood's murder had been placed on him in an attempt to protect the real killer. Cole admitted to Jesse's son and Hoffman that Jesse had not committed the murder. For years he had not identified the real killer stating only that the killing had been done by "the one who rode the dun horse."[44]

Cole stated that Jesse and Frank had been at Northfield under the names of Howard and Woods. He had lied to protect Frank James. If the authorities had learned that Jesse had not done the killing, then "Yankee Bligh" and several detectives from St. Louis would have arrested Frank for the murder. He said

Jesse James circa time of death. Frank Leslie's *Illustrated Newspaper*, April 22, 1882.

Frank had killed Heywood and ridden the dun horse, which he had stolen from a man probably named Stewart in Kansas City. The dun horse had been known as a fast sprinter, which attracted Frank.

If Jesse Edward James and Harry Hoffman can be believed, there can be little doubt that Jesse and Frank James were at Northfield. They had been blamed for several robberies in which they had taken no part, but with the strong friendship ties that bound the outlaw band together, they have confused serious scholars even today.

"The James boys were blamed for many things they did not do—but, the James boys did do a lot of things the 'smart' fellows could never figure out," wrote one man in 1948. "Pinkerton detectives never caught any James gang members—but the James gang caught a lot of Pinkertons!"[45]

So confused were authorities, as well as the general public, that fact and fiction often became one, as evidenced by an 1882 newspaper account: "The rumor prevails in England that the late Jesse James was a member of Congress. For one we think this is too much. The late Mr. James was not what might be termed a proper citizen under all circumstances, neither was he altogether bad. He would rob anything from a palace car to a hen roost, and shoot an infant in arms if it barred the road to a nickel, but he never was a member of Congress. We believe the former rumor, that he was a member of the Chicago Republican Convention of 1880, has already been denied."[46]

Notes

1 Ted P. Yeatman, *Jesse James and Bill Ryan at Nashville*, Depot Press, Nashville, 1981, p. 7.

2 Ibid., pp. 7-8.

3 *The* (Nashville) *Tennessean*, August 7, 1983, Max York, "Jesse James: Nashville Citizen."

4 William A. Settle, Jr., *Jesse James Was His Name*, pp. 107-108.

5 *Minneapolis Tribune*, Sunday, April 4, 1982, Mark Peterson, "A Century After his Death, Jesse James Still Good Copy"; *Duluth News-Tribune*, Sunday, April 4, 1982.

6 *The* (St. Joseph) *Daily Gazette*, Wednesday, April 5, 1882-EXTRA, "Jesse, By Jehovah;" William A. Settle, Jr., *Jesse James Was His Name*, pp. 117-118.

7 *Frank Leslie's Illustrated Newspaper*, April 22, 1882, "The Jesse James Tragedy," p. 135.

8 *The* (St. Joseph) *Daily Gazette*, Wednesday, April 5, 1882-EXTRA.

9 Ibid.

10 *The Milwaukee Journal* (Green Sheet), Friday, April 2, 1982, John F. Bordsen, "Jesse James: He's Still Holding Up the Tourists."

11 Marie Gery Interview with author, Northfield, Minnesota, August 22, 1997.

12 *Faribault Democrat*, Friday, April 21, 1882.

13 *Faribault Democrat*, Friday, May 12, 1882, "Villainous Work."

14 William A. Settle, Jr., *Jesse James Was His Name*, pp. 130-131.

15 Judi Ries letter to author dated December 12, 1996.

16 *St. Louis Missouri Republican*, October 6, 1882.

17 William A. Settle, Jr., *Jesse James Was His Name*, pp. 136-144.

18 James family records and papers in the possession of Grace James White of Brent, Alabama.

19 *St. Joseph Herald*, April 27, 1884.

20 William A. Settle, Jr., *Jesse James Was His Name*, pp. 163-164.

21 *Faribault Democrat*, Friday, December 1, 1876, "A Few Particulars."

22 *The Northfield Saga*, pp. 13-14; *Minneapolis Sunday Tribune*, January 18, 1948; Joseph W. Zalusky, "Oh Where Were the James Boys When the Northfield Bank Was Robbed," *Hennepin County History*, Hennepin

County (Minnesota) Historical Society Bulletin, Spring 1963, pp. 20-22.

23 *Kansas City Star*, September 22, 1929.

24 B. Wayne Quist letter to author dated December 28, 1996.

25 Todd M. George letter to Owen Dickie dated February 22, 1968, Le Sueur County Historical Society, Waterville, Minnesota.

26 Ibid.

27 Carl W. Breihan letter to author dated January 15, 1982.

28 Wilbur Zink letter to author dated January 7, 1997.

29 Wilbur Zink letter to author dated March 25, 1982.

30 Marley Brant letter to author dated January 17, 1983.

31 Maria Younger letter to author dated February 1, 1997.

32 Robertus Love, *The Rise and Fall of Jesse James*, pp. 194, 213, 225, and 228.

33 Dallas Cantrell, *Younger's Fatal Blunder*, p. 72.

34 Homer Croy, *Last of the Great Outlaws*, Duell, Sloan and Pearce, New York, 1956, pp. 113, 127.

35 Marley Brant, *The Outlaw Youngers*, p. 169.

36 George Huntington, *Robber and Hero*, p. 3.

37 James D. Horan, *Desperate Men*, G.P. Putnam's Sons, New York, 1949, p. 107.

38 Maria Younger letter to author dated February 1, 1997.

39 Ruth Coder Fitzgerald letter to author dated January 15, 1997.

40 *Old West Magazine*, March, 1983, "Letter from Frank James, Former Outlaw Reveals his Thoughts in Unpublished Letter," pp. 48-49.

41 Milton F. Perry letter to author dated February 18, 1983.

42 *Northfield News*, July 10, 1941, "Daughter of Frank James of Bank Raid Fame a Visitor."

43 Ibid.

44 *The Northfield Magazine*, Vol. 6, No. 2, 1992, "Who Killed Joseph Lee Heywood?" p. 21.

45 Lee Hawk letter to Mr. Olsen dated September 13, 1948. Copy in author's collection.

46 *Faribault Democrat*, Friday, June 2, 1882.

Chapter 8

Dead Men Tell No Tales

POOR OLD CHARLIE PITTS IS DEAD

But his skull won't fit inside his head.
Never-the-less they think he's dead
'Cause they's the bullet hole—besides his head.

They dug him up from in the ground
And all these years he's been hauled around.
They think it's Charlie Pitts they found,
So they dug him up and hauled him 'round.

They run a wire right though his chest
Where a bullet hole come through his vest.
They laid Charlie's bones from east to west
But the hole don't 'zactly fit his chest.

Now who's to judge from where they sits
What might have happened to Charlie Pitts!
Is some skull duggery goin' on there
Beneath what used ter be Charlie's hair?

Let's pause a moment in our chores today
And think what Charlie Pitts might say-
Like the old woman of years gone by-
"If that be me, then who is I?"

—Harold W. Dickinson[1]

THE STREETS OF NORTHFIELD WERE QUIET THE NIGHT after the bank robbery attempt. Local citizen Will Ebell later recalled: "That night there wasn't a soul on the streets, and as far as I could find out only a single light was burning in town. This light was in a vacant building next to John Morton's store. The bodies of two of the dead robbers were lying in there on the floor with a lantern standing on the counter."[2]

Ebell may have been one of the last persons to see the bodies of Chadwell and Miller. The remains of the two outlaws were exhumed on September 9 by, ironically, Henry Wheeler and

213

two of his University of Michigan classmates, Clarence Persons and Charles Dampier.[3]

The mysterious disappearances of the two bodies of robbers killed at Northfield, and also that of Charlie Pitts who had been killed near Madelia, remain as sketchy as the escape of two very alive robbers who may have been Frank and Jesse James.

A diary kept by a Northfield area man, Newton Persons, for 1876 provided the first clues of "foul" play. Persons' entry for September 7, 1876, began: "O [Orville] & I take C [Clarence] pile a load of hay 16.80 lbs. And plows in A.M. & draws straw till 3:00 P.M. then goes to town. I cut corn and C. draws straw. Eight robbers ride into Northfield & attempt to rob the bank but Heywood not unlock it for them they kill him and I hear Bunker through the shoulder. Manning and H. Wheeler each kill a robber & wound another & kill one horse they then leave."[4]

The entry for the following day, September 8, starts off as innocent as the entry preceding it, but ends on a somewhat cryptic note: "I go to town to see the dead men this morning and I ran manure. O. helps Weeks thrash with his team and Nelly to draw straw in P.M. I finish cutting corn in P.M. C. does some work tonight."[5]

Newton did not reveal the nature of Clarence's nocturnal work in this entry, but the words "does some work tonight" by a man who usually works during the day imply more than a casual reference. Under his entry for Saturday, September 9, Newton explains: "A rainy day core and string apples is about all we do today. Clean up a load of wheat just. Night Clarence, Orville & Wife come home today & Albert comes at night. C. ships two barrels of mixed paint this morning to UV.????Ann Arbor."[6]

While a posse was forming to chase down the fleeing live bandits, Henry Wheeler, more than aware of the scarcity of cadavers at medical school, may or may not have pursued the outlaws for the handsome reward offered. Instead he thought of a different treasure. There were more corpses lying in Northfield than the University of Michigan's dissection laboratory would see in a semester, and he must have felt two of the corpses belonged to him.[7]

Wheeler, Persons, and Dampier volunteered for burial detail and the two dead outlaws were quickly buried in a Northfield cemetery. But Wheeler and his two cohorts returned to the graveyard that night and had no trouble finding the shallow and carefully marked graves. A nervous black wagon driver accompanied them, and the bodies of Chadwell and Miller were hastily dug up, nailed inside two barrels marked "paint" and driven out of town. The bodies were placed on a train in Minneapolis/St. Paul bound for Michigan.

Another account reported Wheeler did join the posse, but in leaving Northfield, yelled to his friend, Persons, "Clarence, see if you can get the bodies." Clarence Persons stayed up all night preparing the bodies for the curious barrel shipment.[8]

Still another report alleged that the future Dr. Dampier "retrieved" the outlaw corpses from the graveyard while Wheeler was out with the posse. Initially, Mayor Solomon Stewart of Northfield had said the medical students could have the bodies, but later his authority to give them up was questioned. But he did relate to the students that, while he had to bury the bandits, he did not think it necessary to bury them deeply. Of course, the young medical students took that as tacit permission to commit an act of good old-fashioned grave robbing.[9]

The three students soon returned to the University of Michigan campus with their two barrels of "paint." They were regarded as nothing short of heroes by their classmates because the cadavers were in the prime of life and in excellent condition. When Wheeler was asked by a friend where he got his cadaver, he answered proudly, "I shot him."[10]

Only a month following their return to school, the *Ann Arbor Courier* ran an account of their endeavors next to an advertisement for Ayers Sarsaparilla: "The students of the medical department will this winter have the pleasure of carving up two genuine robbers, being members of the Northfield, Minnesota, gang."[11]

How much dissection was carried out on the bodies is open to speculation. Another account reported the body of Clell Miller was exhibited around the state of Minnesota in the paint barrel filled with alcohol. Sensationalism may have been the rule of the day since the photographer at Northfield, who had captured the bloody remains of the town the day of the battle, had sold over 50,000 pictures only one month after the robbery.[12]

The story of the outlaw corpses gained wide circulation and indignant relatives of Clell Miller decided to rescue the corpse from the anatomy lab. Ed Miller, brother of Clell, was afraid to go to Minnesota, but former Liberty resident, Samuel Hardwicke, who had moved to Minnesota in 1875, assured him he would be safe.[13]

Ed Miller's task upon reaching Michigan was not an easy one since time had been at work on the corpses. Neither Wheeler, Persons, or even Ed Miller could be certain which of the corpses was Chadwell and which was Miller. But Wheeler and Persons surrendered one corpse to Ed Miller and turned their scholastic interests to the remaining body.[14]

Ed Miller quickly left Minnesota with what he believed to be his brother's body still in the barrel. It cost the Miller family about nine hundred dollars to bring Clell's body home, and the ride back to Missouri did more damage to the already decomposing corpse. The motion of the train rubbed the skin partially off Clell's head as it bounced against the side of the barrel.[15]

A funeral was held at the Miller home about three miles north of Kearney, Missouri, and the body believed to be that of Clell was laid to rest in Muddy Fork Cemetery alongside a brother, Francis. A Liberty newspaper ran the following: "We have sometimes been asked as to the family of Clell Miller who was killed in the Minnesota bank robbery. It is sufficient to say, that there are no better people than Moses W. Miller and his wife, the father and mother. If their son had been unfortunate, it was not from a want of proper parental training. Mr. M. and family have the sympathy of all who know them, in their great trouble."[16]

Since the body had been unrecognizable, the Millers may or may not have received Clell for burial. Henry Wheeler had killed Miller in the streets of Northfield and may not have wanted to part with the body, so the family could have been given the body of Chadwell instead. (Some accepted biographies even state Miller's body remained with Dr. Wheeler.) Or it may have been an inadvertent switch. There is even some speculation that Miller's unrecognizable body was switched with an unknown cadaver and given to the Miller family.[17] (The body believed to be Miller was stolen from the grave by an entrepreneur and placed in a glass case that toured Midwestern fairs.)[18]

When Wheeler graduated in June 1877, all that remained of the skeleton in his possession—Chadwell or Miller—was a sack of carefully picked bones. Wheeler and his cronies assembled the skeleton and shellacked it. Wheeler then left medical school, taking the shellacked skeleton with him, opening up a practice in Northfield where he could show-off his proud possession.[19] Wheeler received another proud possession from the First National Bank of Northfield—a gold watch for helping to repel the James-Younger Gang during the bank raid.[20]

In 1879, he went to New York City where he entered the College of Physicians for additional training. One year later, Doc Wheeler established his practice in Grand Forks, North Dakota; of course he took the skeleton with him. (The reconstructed skeleton stood across from the safe in his office until Wheeler's retirement in 1926.)[21]

Wheeler's arrival in Grand Forks with his skeletal prize caused quite a stir in the frontier community. It is alleged that the father of outlaw Bill Stiles, who lived in nearby Mallory, came in to Dr. Wheeler's office to see the skeleton. Mr. Stiles said he had lived in St. Cloud, Minnesota, from where his son also came, and told Wheeler young Bill had disappeared from there about the time of the Northfield robbery. Of course, the skeleton, res-urrected from a bag of picked bones, was impossible to identify.[22]

In Grand Forks, Dr. Wheeler immediately combined with a Dr. Collins, who was already practicing in Grand Forks, forming Wheeler and Collins, and later, Wheeler and Logan. In 1887, Dr. Wheeler was admitted to membership of the Dakota Medical Society in Huron, South Dakota, and, that same year, he co-founded the Valley Medical Associates in Grand Forks. He served as president of the North Dakota Medical Association in 1895 and 1896 and secretary of the Board of Medical Examiners from 1894 to 1911.[23] Dr. Wheeler served one term, 1913-1914, as city alderman. In 1917, at the age of sixty-four, he was elected mayor of Grand Forks and served two terms.[24] He was also presi-dent of the Grand Forks Gun Club.[25]

Dr. Wheeler retired in 1926 and left the skeleton behind in his office. What became of the "unknown" outlaw skeleton is, like that of Miller, open to speculation. In 1927, Doctor Wheeler's former office was destroyed by fire, and the skeleton that had been left behind may have burned with it.

Yet, other accounts indicated that the skeleton had not been destroyed in the fire. One such report alleged that Dr. Wheeler donated the skeleton to the Masons, of which he was a member, for use during initiation rites. The skeleton was then given to a local fraternity.[26]

A collector in North Dakota stated that Dr. Henry Wheeler, Jr., after receiving threatening letters, sold the rifle which had killed Chadwell. Dr. Wheeler's pocket watch, pistol, and the skeletal remains of a Northfield outlaw were dealt to another collector.

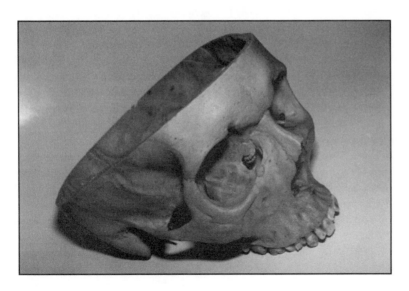

Skeleton of robber brought to Grand Forks by Dr. Wheeler. (Photo by Dr. Keith W. Millette, M.D.)

Skeleton of robber brought to Grand Forks by Dr. Wheeler. (Photo by Keith W. Millette, M.D.)

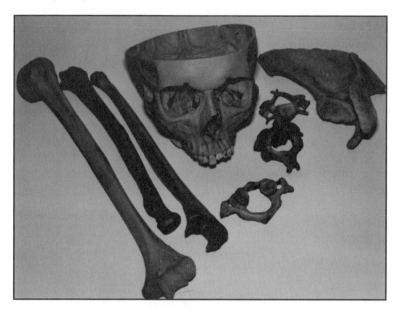

Perhaps the most credible account alleged that the bones remained the property of the medical profession. Upon Wheeler's retirement, he reportedly gave the bones of the gang member to a Dr. Campbell at Valley Medical. When Dr. Campbell retired, he in turn gave the bones to another Grand Forks physician, Dr. Walter C. Daily. That physician was certain the skeleton had come from Dr. Wheeler, but he could not be sure if it had been that of a gang member who had been shot. The doctor, upon his own retirement, gave the skeleton to another doctor, Bill Powers, living in LaPorte, Minnesota, who in turn, passed it on to a physician back in Grand Forks, Dr. Keith W. Millette.[27]

As to whether the skeleton is that of Clell Miller or Bill Chadwell, or . . . even that of Charlie Pitts, may never be known. It is possible also that the skeletal remains could be parts of two robbers since Wheeler and Persons had little more than a collection of bones at the time of their graduation. And since the body of Nicholaus Gustavson, the innocent Swede killed in the streets of Northfield, "seemed to disappear," some persons believed Wheeler's bones even may have belonged to him.[28] Rumors circulated over the years that Gustavson's skeleton found its way to Dr. Wheeler's office in Grand Forks while others alleged the Swede had been buried in an unmarked pauper's grave in Northfield.[29] An unmarked grave in a Northfield cemetery, believed to be that of Gustavson, was located in May 1994, and a stone monument was dedicated during a ceremony on September 7 of that same year.[30]

A forensic specialist examined the bones but was only able to determine that the bones "were of recent origin and probably male." He did find, however, that the skeletal parts possessed the typical markings of bones used by medical students in their studies on cadavers.[31]

One doctor and recipient of the skeleton declared, "After examination of the bones, I am not certain that they all belong to the same individual. The dentition on the skull is in excellent shape. . . . If the skull is from Charlie Pitts he apparently did take care of his teeth."[32]

So how did Charlie Pitts, killed near Madelia, two weeks after the other robbers, become a skeletal candidate believed to be either Bill Chadwell or Clell Miller?

Following Pitts' demise, crowds poured into the Madelia jail to stare at his body. Since Minnesota law determined that unclaimed bodies could be used for science, Pitts' body was packed in ice, shipped to St. Paul, and embalmed by Surgeon General Dr. Frank W. Murphy. The body was then displayed in a wing of the State Capitol, located at Tenth and Wabasha, for two days. Over 2,000 visitors showed up, paying ten cents each "to stare at the unpleasant and disgusting spectacle."[33]

One woman, who was growing up in Minnesota during the time of the Northfield raid, recalled the excitement that erupted when Charlie Pitts' body was delivered to St. Paul. After meeting another woman her own age, she reflected: "Just a few years ago, I met a woman who was a little school girl at the time of the Raid; she lived in St. Paul and attended a school near Rice Street. She told me, 'All us school children were ordered to go and look at that dead man. We had to walk by where he lay stript [sic] to the waist, and that awful bullet hole in his breast.' [Perhaps that was the way in those days of curbing juvenile delinquency.]"[34]

In March 1877, Dr. Murphy handed over Pitt's skeleton to his nephew, Henry F. Hoyt, a young medical student, who had just returned home to St. Paul from Rush Medical College in Chicago. Hoyt found the bones in excellent shape and decided to mount the skeleton for use in his office following graduation. After dissecting the skeleton, he bleached the bones under water for more than a year. With the help of a brother, he carefully packed the bones in a shoe box, adding a few large rocks as sinkers. The two brothers drove out to the south side of St. Paul's Lake Como, rowed the box out in a boat, and sank it in the middle of the lake.[35]

During the Christmas holidays 1878, a year-and-a-half after the Lake Como sinking, Dr. Hoyt was in Las Vegas when he received some interesting letters and newspapers from home.

Lake Como had, of course, frozen over for the winter, and a life-long friend as well as neighbor, August Robertson, had gone after muskrats with spear and hammer. As he walked across the ice of Como, he discovered the corner of a box sticking out of the frozen lake. Smashing open the box with his hatchet, he discovered the bones of a human being![36]

But initially, Robertson failed to deduce the bones belonged to a man. He had recently lost his dog and decided the bones belonged to his favorite animal. When he reached home, he told his father about the strange box containing the dog bones. His father grew suspicious and decided to investigate. He strode out onto the ice and knocked off the entire end of the box. Out rolled a human skull!

Lillie LeVesconte recalled the incident many years later: "The body was put into a box and with weights, it was lowered into Lake Como. This happened at a part of the lake usually covered with water lilies and rushes. Joshua Robertson's farm bordered that part of the lake, too, and during the winter, his boys chopped holes in the ice; the cows drank there. Now it happened the ice was clear—boys and men could 'see a box down there.' The mysterious box was brought up and ours was a horrified community."[37]

After the sheriff and coroner were notified, newspaper headlines told of a horrible murder. The unidentified bones were full of bullet holes in five different sections of the body. The Associated Press quickly picked up the story, and St. Paul police and detectives were criticized for their inability to capture the killer. When Dr. Murphy learned of the box of bones, he immediately squelched the murder theory and took charge of the bones. When Dr. Hoyt did not return home when expected, Dr. Murphy gave the bones to a physician in Chicago. Of course, the name of that physician remains a mystery to this day.

Although Dr. Hoyt no longer had a skeleton, its memory continued to haunt him. His father forwarded him a letter from an unknown source that condemned him for his inhumane treatment of "pore charley pitts." The unsigned missive ended with "I'll git yu yit."

The Northfield bank robbery lingered on in Dr. Hoyt's life. Not far from Las Vegas, just over the New Mexico line, Hoyt claimed he shared a table with three men at a restaurant. He recognized one of the men as Billy the Kid, allegedly, and insisted that Billy pointed to a friend and said, "Hoyt, meet my friend Mr. Howard from Tennessee." According to Hoyt, Jesse, and Bill were together, and Jesse was missing the tip of a finger on his left hand.[38]

During the summer of 1928, after Hoyt had written about his meeting with "Jesse James," Harrison Leussler, Western representative of Hoyt's publisher, Houghton Mifflin, informed him about a recent interview with a reformed outlaw living in Los Angles. The man, named Bill Stiles, said Jesse James had never been in New Mexico and had never lost a part of any fingers.

After publication of Dr. Hoyt's book, *A Frontier Doctor*, in which he wrote about Pitt's skeleton and his alleged meeting with Jesse James and Bill the Kid, the physician no longer connected himself with the 1876 Northfield bank robbery. The skeleton of Charlie Pitts, via its unknown benefactor, simply disappeared. Decades later a skeleton said to be that of Charlie Pitts was given to the Stagecoach Restaurant and Museum near Shakopee as a trade-in on an antique gun. A retired Minnesota sheriff had owned the skeleton and stated he had purchased it from Dr. Henry Wheeler.[39]

According to the story of the sheriff who had owned the skeleton, Pitts' body had been sent to the dissecting tables at a medical school in Wisconsin following his death. There, it was alleged, the students wired the skeleton together and sent it back to Dr. Wheeler for a souvenir. However, it was explained, Wheeler had not sent the body intact to the students, having cut off an ear and part of "Pitts'" scalp. The ear later turned up at the privately owned Schilling Museum in Northfield and was displayed in recent years as Charlie Pitts' ear. The brown shriveled ear was attached to a scrap of leathery skin.

But Charlie Pitts' had been killed near Madelia, fully two weeks after the Northfield disaster, and his body had never been taken by Dr. Henry Wheeler. Chadwell and Miller, yes, but certainly not Pitts. So whose skeleton turned up in Shakopee, Minnesota? Who had lopped off the ear as a grisly souvenir and how did it end up at a museum in Northfield? And, of course, who was the mysterious Chicago doctor who had received Pitts' bones after their discovery in St. Paul's Lake Como?

Another account stated that Charlie Pitts' bones had been given to a Twin Cities doctor after leaving the physician in Chicago, and it was this doctor who donated the skeleton to the Stagecoach Museum.[40] But how the ear from the skeleton came to Schilling's museum has never been explained. When the Schilling Museum closed, the ear was given to the Northfield Historical Society, which received it with skepticism and displayed it with "the curious notation that it is not Charlie Pitts' ear."[41]

The owners of the Stagecoach Museum sought to buy the "Pitts" ear at the Schilling Museum auction, to combine it with the skeleton they owned and had for sale. When they discovered that Alice and Louis Schilling had given the ear to the Northfield Historical Society, they decided the body and ear should be reunited and donated their skeleton to the Northfield museum.[42] The remains, believed at that time to be those of Pitts, were placed on display in the museum office over the Fourth of July weekend and even appeared in the Saturday forenoon parade.[43]

According to one source, the doctor who had worked over Pitts' skeleton in 1876, had offered to amputate the trigger finger and mount if for Alonzo Bunker who had been wounded by the bandit in escaping out the back door of the bank. Bunker, however, had declined the offer. The saving of ears and skeletons was quite commonplace in the nineteenth century, and grave robbing for medical purposes took place fairly often.[44]

The Northfield Historical Society went to work immediately to determine whether their newly acquired bones were really those of Pitts. On August 3, 1982, the bones were carefully placed in a replica of a Jesse James coffin and taken to the Hennepin County Medical Examiner's office in Minneapolis for study by a team headed by Dr. Garry Peterson. The team's task was to reassemble the skeleton to determine sex, age, and height. Most important, bullet damage of the bones needed to be checked to see whether it corresponded with the known wounds suffered by Pitts.[45]

Then there was the question of the ear which, presumably, had belonged to Pitts. There were contradictory reports that when Dr. Wheeler "appropriated" the bodies of Chadwell and Miller, he cut off an ear from one of the cadavers, wrote a message on it, and mailed it to a friend. It was also the medical examiner's job to find out to who the ear belonged. Like a fingerprint, no two ears are alike.

Through modern medical detective work, Dr. Peterson determined, with a ninety percent accuracy, that the bones were not those of Charlie Pitts. The skull did not match photos taken of Pitts after his death. Although the examiner located a notch in a chest bone exactly where Pitts had received a bullet hole, the notch was either artificial or had been altered. This notch, which was too rounded, had been punched or filed, but had not come from a bullet. The "bullet" notch appeared to have been manufactured and x-rays detected no evidence of lead fragments.[46]

Photographs of the skull were superimposed on 1876 photos of the deceased outlaw's head. When the eyes and nose were lined up, the skull proved to be deeper than Pitts' chin, and when the top and bottom of his head were lined up, the eyes did not fit within the eye sockets.

Charlie Pitts had also been shot in the arm and leg. No evidence of bullets hitting leg or arm bones was found, although it is possible the gunshot wounds could have missed the bones.

The skull profile, jaw, and teeth, however, did match up pretty closely to photos taken of the dead Clell Miller. But that finding, too, showed discrepancies. Clell Miller stood six feet tall; the length of the skeletal thigh bone revealed a man no taller than five feet seven or eight. Clell's death photograph also revealed shotgun pellets in the forehead but no trace was found on the skeletal forehead. Miller died from a bullet which severed an artery in his left shoulder but the skeleton's shoulder was bullet-free. Again, there is a slight chance the bullet could have passed through the body without hitting a bone.[47]

The skull did not match the face of Bill Chadwell. During the autopsy, the names Chadwell, Chadwick, or Stiles did not appear in the newspapers, the only reference being to "the third robber."

It was impossible to draw any conclusions from the ear which had been purported to be that of Charlie Pitts. Although the age of the ear fit into the proper period, the ear was too dry to yield any explanations. Case ME-82-1618 of the Hennepin County Medical Examiner's office was put to bed in the "unsolved" file. As the *Minneapolis Tribune* of August 25, 1982, put it: "Although the bones may not be Old Charlie's [or Old Clell's], they certainly belong to Old Somebody."

Notes

1 Ballad in collection at Northfield Historical Society.

2 Will Ebell's account of the night after the Northfield Bank Raid from *Inland The Magazine of the Middle West* reprinted in *The Northfield Magazine*, Vol. 6, No. 2, 1992, Inside cover.

3 Clell Miller and William Stiles Files, Northfield Historical Society.

4 Transcription of Newton Persons' Diary for September 7, 1876, Northfield Historical Society.

5 Transcription of Newton Persons' Diary for September 8, 1876, Northfield Historical Society.

6 Transcription of Newton Persons' Diary for Saturday, September 9, 1876, Northfield Historical Society.

7 Sue Garwood DeLong, Executive Director Northfield Historical Society interview with author, January 27, 1997, Northfield, Minnesota; Charles N. Barnard, Editor, *A Treasury of True, The Best From Twenty Years of the Man's Magazine,* A.S. Barnes and Company, New York, 1956, "You Shot Him—He's Yours," by William Bender, Jr., p. 239; Francis F. McKinney, "The Northfield Raid, and Its Ann Arbor Sequel," *Michigan Alumnus Quarterly Review 61,* December 4, 1954, pp. 38-45; William Holtz, "Bankrobbers, Burkers, and Bodysnatchers, *Michigan Quarterly Review,* 6, Spring 1967, pp. 90-98; *St. Paul Pioneer Press,* September 5, 1981 under "Others Reap Northfield Raid Riches" by Roger Barr; Clell Miller and William Stiles Files, Northfield Historical Society.

8 *Rochester Post Bulletin,* Saturday, May 8, 1982, Ken McCracken, "Medical Research Got Help From James Gang."

9 *Grand Forks Herald,* Date Unknown, Jack Hagerty, "Skeleton Had a Life of its Own," in collection of Keith W. Millette, M.D.

10 *Rochester Post Bulletin,* Saturday, May 8, 1982, Ken McCracken, "Medical Research Got Help From James Gang."

11 William Bender, Jr., "You Shot Him—He's Yours," p. 239.

12 Ruth Coder Fitzgerald, "Clell and Ed Miller—Members of the James Gang, *NOLA Quarterly*, 1991, pp. 29-34; *The Liberty Tribune*, October 20, 1876.

13 *The Liberty Tribune*, October 27, 1876.

14 William Bender, Jr., "You Shot Him—He's Yours," p. 239.

15 Ruth Coder Fitzgerald, "Clell and Ed Miller—Members of the James Gang," pp. 33-34.

16 *The Liberty Tribune*, October 27, 1876.

17 Clell Miller and William Stiles Files, Northfield Historical Society.

18 *Northfield News*, September 2, 1982, "Skeleton Remains Mystery" by Mary Elster and Maggie Lee.

19 Sue Garwood De Long interview with author, January 27, 1997; William Bender, Jr., "You Shot Him—He's Yours," p. 239; Clell Miller and William Stiles Files, Northfield, Minnesota; Dr. Bill Powers, "History of Valley Medical Associates, Ltd."

20 *Compendium of History and Biography* under Dr. Henry Wheeler, p. 190.

21 Sue Garwood De Long interview with author, January 27, 1997; William Bender, Jr., "You Shot Him—He's Yours," p. 239; Clell Miller and William Stiles Files, Northfield, Minnesota; Dr. Bill Powers, "History of Valley Medical Associates, Ltd."

22 *Grand Forks Herald*, Date Unknown, Jack Hagerty, "Skeleton had a Life of its Own," in collection of Keith W. Millette, M.D.

23 Dr. Bill Powers, "History of Valley Medical Associates, Ltd."

24 National Register of Historic Places Inventory—Nomination Form, United States Department of the Interior National Park Service, Item no. 8, p. 2.

25 *Grand Forks Illustrated*, April 1891.

26 Sue Garwood De Long interview with author, January 27, 1997; William Stiles File, Northfield Historical Society.

27 Keith W. Millette, M.D. letter to author dated November 7, 1997.

28 *Grand Forks Herald*, Date Unknown, Jack Hagerty, "Did GF Physician Have Skeleton of Northfield Bank Robber?" in collection of Keith W. Millette, M.D.

29 *Minneapolis Star Tribune*, Saturday, September 11, 1993, Richard Meryhew, "Death of a Swede, Northfield Buffs Dig Up Old Story of James Gang and a Lost Body."

30 B. Wayne Quist, *The History of the Christdala Evangelical Swedish Lutheran Church of Millersburg, Minnesota*, p. 23.

31 Keith W. Millette, M.D., letter to author dated November 7, 1997.

32 Keith W. Millette, M.D., letter to Sue Garwood, Northfield Historical Society dated September 23, 1993.

33 *St. Paul Dispatch*, September 5, 1981, "Others Reap Northfield Raid Riches" by Roger Barr; Charlie Pitts File, Northfield Historical Society.

34 Lillie LeVesconte, from a letter to Mr. Hodnefield of St. Paul, sent from Prior Lake, Minnesota, February 19, 1945, roll 1, 67-68. Northfield, Minnesota Bank Robbery of 1876; Selected Manuscripts Collections and Government Records, Microfilm Edition, Minnesota Historical Society.

35 Henry F. Hoyt, *A Frontier Doctor*, Houghton Mifflin Company, Boston & New York, 1929, pp. 17-19.

36 Ibid., pp. 109-110.

37 Lillie LeVesconte, from a letter to Mr. Hodnefield of St. Paul, sent from Prior Lake, Minnesota, February 19, 1945, roll 1, 67-68. Northfield, Minnesota Bank Robbery of 1876; Selected Manuscripts Collections and Government Records, Microfilm Edition, Minnesota Historical Society.

38 Henry F. Hoyt, A *Frontier Doctor*, pp. 111-112.

39 Action Line, *St. Paul Dispatch and Pioneer Press,* in collection of Northfield Historical Society.

40 Charlie Pitts File, Northfield Historical Society.

41 *St. Paul Dispatch*, September 5, 1981, "Others Reap Northfield Raid Riches" by Roger Barr.

42 Article in Northfield Historical Society Collection, "Long Division," Tuesday, June 30, 1981.

43 *Northfield News,* July 9, 1981, "Pitts' Skeleton Given to Society" by Rosemary Cashman.

44 Ibid., Maggie Lee, then secretary.

45 *St. Paul Pioneer Press,* August 3, 1982, "Bone Exam Could Rattle Legend, Is Skeleton Charlie Pitts?" by Bill Gardner.

46 *Minneapolis Star and Tribune*, Wednesday, August 25, 1982, "Autopsy Proves Northfield Skeleton is Old—But Not That it's Charlie Pitts" by Lewis Cope.

47 *Minneapolis Star and Tribune*, Tuesday, August 31, 1982, "That Old Skeleton May Be Another of Jesse's Gang" by Lewis Cope; *Duluth News-Tribune Herald*, Sunday, August 29, 1982, "Autopsy May Show if Skeleton is That of James Gang Member;" *Duluth News-Tribune Herald*, Wednesday, September 1, 1982, "Identification Not Certain of James Gang Skeleton."

Chapter 9

Too Many Bandits

SLOUCHING FROM NORTHFIELD
(In My Wheel Chair–Can't Mount a Horse)
by Emmett Hoctor

(*My interpretation of W. B. Yeats' poem, "The Second Coming," to
be read with the musical score composition heard on Joni Mitchell's album,*
Night Ride Home, *"Slouching to Bethlehem," and with a tardy note it is
dedicated to my great uncle James Hoctor and any and all James Gang members who have not been credited with their role in the Northfield, Minnesota,
Bank Robbery of September 7, Eighteen Hundred and seventy-six. . . .*)

Ten years with posted names
Trying to recapture an unCivil War
Our memorable trace
With murmurs of our Southern persecution
Taunting us into many other places out of Missouri State
Our secret visits to California, Chicago, New York
And jobs we pulled in between. . . .
With would-be gangsters
Trekking across the plains
Civilized kin and friends nodded knowingly
The nations herd heard only a few real names
Forlorn names like Berry, Judson, Martin,
    Stiles, and Jimmy Hoctor, too . . .
And in a saloon it was decided Minnesota
Under the sign of Virgo and blue-moon
Time and tide choose Northfield
But center could not hold
As our men in the street were cut-down with bullet holes
Driven in widening circles of desperation
From field to forest lost in space
Our plan to pillage Yankees-blew up in our bloodied faces
The papers told of the bank teller and predicted our fates
Like beasts driven to madness
Two groups wondered into ways of escape
Brothers and friends parted with curses spoken in haste

227

The Youngers found unexpected mercy
Jesse and Frank escaped yet another time
Others hid in Minnesota; Fort Dodge, Iowa,
Others to Omaha, Brownville, and Nebraska City,
    Nebraska, until it was past time
To leave their "safe retreats" Jesse wrote about on time
Later I mused about Jesse's underlined Bible
And Frank quoting Ingersoll both believing in bullets
    to save their kind
Now my last breaths of polluted air
As I slouch over this electric pen
Wishing not to be the last left for dead
Slouching to Northfield in my head
My memories to the cemetery boxed in lead
Slouching to my appointment in Samarea-just ahead . . .
Slouching to the last job-unadorned
Slouching into the history books too late and so forlorn.

ON JANUARY 3, 1877, J.C. NUTTING, president of the First
National Bank of Northfield issued the following proclamation:
"TO WHOM IT MAY CONCERN, Pursuant to resolution of
the Board of Directors of the First National Bank of Northfield,
adopted January 2d, 1877, the reward offered for the capture of
the men engaged in the bank raid of September 7th, is hereby
withdrawn, so far as it affects the two who are still at large."[1]

But had only two members of the gang escaped when as
many as nine or ten had been seen? Had the old man in Los Angeles,
professing to be Bill Stiles, told the truth after his conversion to
Christianity, or was he just another quack looking for publicity? And
what about the others? Bill Stiles was not the only outlaw who at one
time or another had claimed to have been at Northfield.

Yet would Jesse James, undoubtedly a very smart outlaw,
employ a large gang of nine or ten men to rob a bank in a small
town, knowing all the while that so many men would draw suspicion on themselves? Jesse did not anticipate trouble inside the
bank; any problems would occur outside.[2]

Russell Yates, whose two uncles had been in on the capture of the Youngers, made a life-long study of the event and col-
lected many documents in connection with the capture.
According to James historian Carl S. Hage, Yates told him he had
"a letter written to his grandfather by George Bradford from
Oregon not long after the capture here at Madelia. In the letter
he tells of a man named Cummins who was supposed [sic] have
been a ninth member of the gang and made his escape alone. I
have heard of this, but never gave it much credence, but according to this letter there may be something to it."[3]

The Cummins referred to was James Robert Cummins (also known as Jim Cummings) who, born January 31, 1847, near Kearney, Missouri, had enlisted with Jesse James in guerrilla service during the Civil War and fought under Bloody Bill Anderson. Cummins had spent nearly twenty years "just roaming," and had once been a cobbler, a breaker of horses, a government scout in Texas during the Indian Wars, and later a deputy United States marshal. Cummins' career was not easy to follow since he used several other names, although he always kept "Jim," and many other persons masqueraded under his name. Although he was accused of many crimes by "fiction" writers, he was exonerated of any crimes committed after the death of Jesse James through confessions of Dick Liddel and Clarence Hite. About 1899, he settled on a farm in Lafayette County, Missouri, before spending his last days in a home for Confederate veterans in the same state. Many of Cummins' own statements contradicted one another, but in his last letter to author Robertus Love, in whom he had revealed some truths, he stated, "Don't forget to protect my confidence."[4] The "confidence" reference to Love undoubtedly involved

Jim Cummins (standing) with friend or relative. (Courtesy Armand DeGregoris Collection.)

Cummins in the Northfield episode. Soon after the robbery, Cummins had told others he had been involved in the robbery. Afraid of persecution, he then modified his statement, insisting he had been the ninth man, but only as far as Mankato, where he alleged he turned back. (Another account states a ninth man accompanied the outlaws only as far as Omaha where he turned back.)[5] Finally, he denied any participation in the ordeal at all. Cummins was considered a liar by many persons, so obtaining the truth was not an easy task.

In George A. Bradford's letter to Isaac B. Yates, Bradford referred to Cummins' "lies," but put stock in the outlaw being a ninth man at Northfield; at least, as far as Mankato: "Before I close, I must speak of the posthumous letter of Jim Cummins. His letter shows very plainly that he was not at Northfield. If he lied any stronger in his letter written while alive, he has certainly equaled it in this. I suppose you will remember that it was reported that while the robbers were in Mankato there were nine, and that one of them met a man that knew him and he left the gang. Not long after I went to Grant's Pass, an old Confederate asked to meet me in a real estate office and I met him there. He told me that he left college in St. Louis and joined Quantrell's [sic] company and served there with the James and Youngers, but when he was discharged he went to his old home in Missouri and went to farming and married there. He did not remain there long, however, as it was hard to make people believe that he was not one of the gang of robbers."[6]

Bradford was told by the "old Confederate" that he had moved to Grant's Pass, raised eleven children, and all had passed through the school system. Bradford continued: "In talking with him I asked him if he knew anything about the report of nine men being in Mankato. He said, 'Yes, that man lives right up here on Cow Creek Canyon.' I think that was Jim Cummins . . . had I time and space to explain. Trains were robbed up in that canyon afterward and the old Confederate soldier was accused of taking part and he left there."[7]

Following Cummins' death, a posthumous paper was left by him stating he had been with the gang in Minnesota. This contradicted what he had written in a book, *Jim Cummins' Book: Being a True But Terrible Tale of Outlawry*, published in 1905, where he wrote: "I was not in Minnesota when the bank at Northfield was robbed, and do not know who were there."[8]

According to the *Kansas City Star* on September 22, 1929, Cummins died leaving a false statement to be published after his death. The statement ends with: "I have written these things that justice may be done the public; that the world may know the truth about these men. I am leaving this to be printed when I am gone. I hope to go out with my boots on. It has been a hard life, uncertain; sometimes I think the future will be welcome, bring what it may. I have played it fair as I knew how: I am at peace with the world today. Good-bye."[9]

If Cummins was not at Mankato with the gang, who was the ninth man spotted in town? And if it was Cummins, would he have turned back to Missouri instead of remaining with the gang where there was strength in numbers? If Cummins had been the ninth man at Mankato, was there a tenth man guarding the escape at the bridge on the outskirts of Northfield? Or even an eleventh holding the horses during the shoot-out in the streets of Northfield?

According to some James family members, there was a man holding the horses during the shoot-out. This information is based on material from Jesse Edwards James (Jesse James, Jr.), an unpublished manuscript written by Jo James Ross in the 1930s who had interviewed friends and relatives from the late nineteenth century period, and rough handwritten notes scrawled by

Billy Judson who was said to have ridden with Jesse for eight years.[10]

According to this material published by James R. Ross, great-grandson of Jesse James, in his book, *I, Jesse James*, Cole, Bob, and John Younger, Jim White, and Jesse James rode into the Ozarks not long after robbing the Kansas City Fair in September 1872. Stopping at a store, they encountered a man beating a boy of about twelve years of age with a whip. When White objected, the man split White's skull with the whip, killing him instantly. Jesse then shot the man through the heart. The grateful boy rode off with Jesse and, thereafter, participated in robberies with the gang.[11]

During the Northfield robbery, Billy Judson was said to have held the horses while the three outlaws entered the bank, after he had ridden into town with Jesse James and Jim Younger. Leaning against a hitching post in front of the bank, Judson kept his hand near his gun, which was concealed by his long duster. During the shoot-out, Judson was hit in the side, a bullet he carried with him until he died fifty-eight years later. With two useless arms, Bob Younger rode out of town with Judson holding onto him on the same horse. The raid lasted but seven minutes. It would have been difficult during the chaos and confusion to count the number of robbers.[12]

Were Cummins and Judson involved in the Northfield robbery? And what about Jim Martin?

James Aron Martin was born in New York in 1858. Although too young to have fought in the Civil War, he had an older brother who had gone to Missouri and ridden with Quantrill. It is quite conceivable the older Martin met Frank James while riding with the guerrillas. During the early 1870s, Jim, in his early teens, went to Missouri in search of his brother.

Jim Martin died in 1923 at the age of sixty-five—killed by an angry stepson. Some time before his death, Martin had told his son—Frank James Martin—that "when he was eighteen, he was with the gang in Northfield." Although Jim Martin did not specify the name of the gang, he did reveal that the year was 1876.

According to Jim Martin, as the outlaws rode out of town following the raid, they did not take flight down the Dundas Road for several miles. Instead, they rode but three miles south of Northfield and hid in the woods, shielded by a bluff along the Cannon River.[13]

Billy Judson in 1885. (Courtesy of Hon. James R. Ross [Ret])

James Aaron Martin and wife, Caroline, with their son, Frank James Martin. (Courtesy Nicholis Martin)

The gang members spent the first night on the edge of the Big Woods. While present-day Northfield is a bit removed from the Big Woods, Martin's grandson is quick to point out that the area along the Cannon River outside town was on the perimeter a century ago. "My grandfather said they camped the first night on the edge of the Big Wood, not 'Woods' but 'Wood,'" explained Nicholis Martin. "Where it starts is where the discrepancy comes."[14]

With a posse in hot pursuit, a posse that expected the boys to make tracks as fast as they could away from Minnesota, the outlaws rested over night at a bend in the river, in hopes of stopping the bleeding from some of their wounds. The men had stayed there, not only to mend their wounds, but, as Jim Martin said, to rest. Some of the men had ridden from Millersburg, about fifteen miles distant, the morning before the raid, and their horses were too tired to make many miles after the raid.

"One of the men took a plow horse just outside of town," Nicholis Martin stated. "A plow horse could not make it as far as a good horse."[15]

Jim Martin told his son that half the group—those who had not ridden in from Millersburg—had spent the night before the robbery at this very same campsite. The secluded spot had probably been at one time an Indian campsite since many arrowheads were found there in later years. Following the raid, the men beat it back to this same secluded hideout. During the night, the posse came so close to the robbers that the fugitives had to hold their hands over the noses of the horses to keep them quiet.

Martin said the men buried some gold near a big rock and a large tree near the river. If they were captured in the woods, it would not go well for them to be carrying loot. Martin, however, did not specify whether the gold was picked up in Northfield or from an earlier robbery in Iowa.[16] In the morning when the coast was clear, the men left their hiding place and slowly groped their way through "enemy" territory.

Grandson Nicholis Martin said that, during the search for the fugitives, a print found in the mud at one of the gang's campsites, revealed that its bearer wore a size-six boot. That size of boot meant that the man may have worn a size-five shoe. "Grandfather never wore more than a size-five shoe," he insisted.[17]

Nicholis Martin always wondered about his grandmother's fascination with Frank and Jesse James. "When she came to visit us, she would always pay our way to go see any Frank and Jesse James movie being shown for some unknown reason," he said, insisting she did not attend other movies. "Perhaps she was trying to tell us something about our ancestry."

James and Caroline Martin, 1909. (Courtesy Nicholis Martin.)

Martin also insists that a photograph of the James-Younger gang members includes an unidentified man who closely resembled his grandfather. The unknown man in the photograph had very curly hair as did Jim Martin when he was young. After Jim suffered a somewhat prolonged high fever, his hair went straight. Cole Younger said that one of the men in the raid suffered from a high fever. Since any of the outlaws could have been stricken with such a fever due to the severity of their wounds, it is impossible to ascertain with any degree of certainty, who the wounded man to whom he was referring may have been.

The wounded man could have been Omaha outlaw, Jim Hoctor, who is believed by some to be a possible ninth or even tenth member of the gang that struck at Northfield. Hoctor was living in the Omaha area in 1875, only a year before the Northfield raid. Frank James had married in Omaha that same year, and Jesse James was seen in town about this same time. Bill Stiles was in Omaha that year also and even got into a gunfight there. Bad Jim Berry, rumored to be a sometime-member of the gang, operated a store in nearby Plattsmouth. The James-Younger boys had used Omaha as a favorite hiding place for years, even stopping there in 1873 on their way to rob a train near Adair, Iowa. And when Frank James came to Omaha, he would head to St. Elmo's dance hall, which just happened to be where Jim Hoctor had set up his headquarters.[18]

Hoctor had relatives in Minnesota, and, like Bill Stiles, he probably was familiar with the territory. Hoctor's uncle, Dennis Kennedy, had lived with the Minnesota branch of the family since the 1850s and had survived the Sioux Uprising of 1862 and the smaller Santee Sioux massacre of 1867. Kennedy had a long criminal record in both Minneapolis and St. Paul, which was probably responsible for his taking a quick leave of the city in 1875 and turning up in Omaha.

Kennedy was arrested several times in Omaha for burglary. He once tunneled out of the local jail but lingered in Omaha and was recaptured. A second attempt at freedom was unsuccessful. Nonetheless, an uncle like Kennedy may have made quite an impression on the much younger Hoctor.

The outlaw career of Jim Hoctor ended with his death on May 31, 1883, in Fremont, Nebraska. A local newspaper reported the incident: "Two men arrived at Fremont from Bell Creek about 11:15 A.M., yesterday. They were suspicious looking characters and were followed to that place by some Bell Creek citizens. They were suspected of being train robbers from Lyons, Iowa. The citizens telegraphed Sheriff Gregg in Fremont to be at the depot when the train arrived and to take charge of them, and he deputized some of the citizens to assist him. They met the robbers at the train and told them that they were their prisoners, upon which, one of the strangers drew a revolver and fired, the ball taking effect, striking Mr. Morse in the mouth, and coming out at the right side of the lower part of the neck, inflicting what is feared to be a fatal wound. The sheriff, with a posse of men, attempted to arrest them when they leaped from the train and started for the Platte River, the Sheriff and his men shooting at them as they ran from the train. The strangers returned the fire and one shot took effect. The sheriff shot and killed one man instantly and the other one was captured and brought back to the city."[19]

The surviving outlaw was identified as twenty-seven-year-old George Swain. Swain claimed that he did not know his dead companion, having only met him the day before in Council Bluffs, Iowa. Swain insisted that his companion, Jim Hoctor, had shot the dying Mr. Morse although several eye witnesses claimed it was Swain, and not Hoctor, who had pulled the trigger.

The *Sioux City Journal* published a story the same day linking the two men to a bank robbery in Lyons, Iowa: "After entering the Lyons bank one outlaw gave some kindly advice to young Everette, the teller, saying 'say nothing about this.' No one would miss the $500.00 taken if the bank would just raise the level of interest! They skipped out, leaving him still gagged, stole two horses and started in the direction of Decatur [sic, Nebraska]." The article also linked them to a Bancroft, Nebraska, post office heist two weeks earlier.[20]

The Lincoln, Nebraska, newspaper linked the pair to other robberies in an exclusive interview with Sheriff Gregg: "The two desperadoes who arrived at Fremont on the train from the north are without doubt the same two men who robbed the

Patrick and Julia Hoctor home, 2701 Harrison Street, Omaha. Their former home had been burned to the ground under mysterious circumstances following the death of their son, James, and the exposure of his outlaw career. (Photo courtesy Emmett C. Hoctor.)

post office at Fort Calhoun and cracked a safe in another town. Upon the person of the man shot and killed by Gregg, was found a map of the State of Nebraska, with names of the towns marked, and the names of banks located therein, written on the margin of the map. Upon the other man, now a prisoner in the jail in Dodge County, was found a long piece of putty covered with bladder, used in covering glass, before cutting, and a particular formal pair of pincers, that may be used in twisting keys that are inside the door locks!"[21]

That Jim Hoctor knew Bill Stiles as well as Frank and Jesse James is more than just a possibility. A wedding picture of Jim with his wife Annie Hoctor bares an uncanny resemblance to an unidentified young man pictured with James gang member Bill "Whiskey Head" Ryan in the Frank James photograph collection.

In 1995, the photo of Jim Hoctor was sent to a highly respected photo identification expert in outlaw/lawmen circles who compared it to the man pictured with Ryan. His answer: "No doubt about it, as far as I'm concerned. . . . The man seated next to the illustrious Bill Ryan is none other than Jim Hoctor. . . . Too many factors indicate that the man seated is Jim Hoctor: Features are more than just similar . . . they are identical. If it isn't Jim Hoctor, he is his twin. The anatomy of the hands and fingers [is] identical. The anatomy of the neck, trapezius, and shoulder structure, is the same. Knee, calf, and thigh structure [are] the same. There couldn't be more than five years in age difference between the pictures of Jim Hoctor seated, and more than five pounds in difference in body weight. The odds are just too much in favor of it being Hoctor. The picture of Hoctor and Ryan would have been taken anytime between 1878 and 1883."[22]

On June 6, 1884, Annie Hoctor gave birth to a daughter, Mary Ella Hoctor, but the baby died a month and one-half later. Her husband, Jim Hoctor had been dead for thirteen months, thus making it impossible for him to have been the father. This death was followed by three other deceased children in March 1891, December 2, 1891, and July 1892; their ages two and one-half years, six months, and five days respectively. But why were the children named Annie Ryan, Rose Ryan, and William Ryan?

BIll Ryan(standing) and Jim Hoctor. (Courtesy Armand DeGregoris Collection.)

235

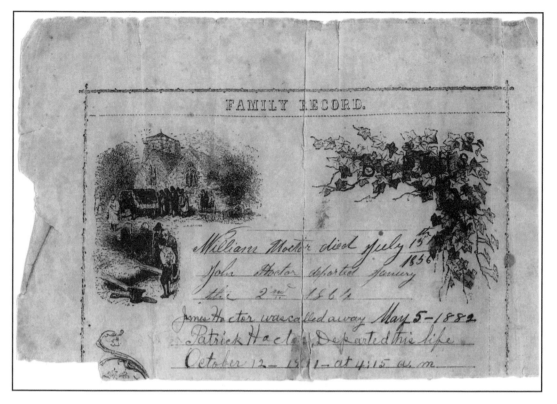

FAMILY RECORD.

William Hoctor died July 15th 1856
John Hoctor departed January the 2nd 1864
James Hoctor was called away May 5—1882
Patrick Hoctor Departed this life October 12—1911—at 4:15 a. m.

Hoctor family Bible with entry of Jim Hoctor's death. (Courtesy Emmett C. Hoctor.)

The evidence that Jim Hoctor and possibly Annie had at least known Bill Ryan, and probably the Jameses and Bill Stiles, is more than circumstantial. With the Jameses and Stiles in Omaha at the same time as Hoctor, only one year before the Northfield affair, the plans for a robbery in Minnesota could quite well have been considered. Although Hoctor probably remained in Omaha for the remainder of the year, the Jameses and Bill Stiles did not.

Following his Omaha gunfight in 1875, Bill Stiles showed up in Texas in December of that same year, vowing to return to Cannon Falls, Minnesota, soon—with plenty of money. While it has been rumored that Stiles had been in the mining camps around Joplin, Missouri, and probably met members of the James gang there, Stiles' trips to Texas (circa 1874 to 1876) are of interest. The James and Younger brothers had friends in Texas dating back to the Quantrill days and sometimes stayed with them when they were wanted men.[23]

At least one 1876 newspaper stated that the Northfield bandits left Sherman, Texas, on August 23, traveling by train. If there is any truth to this, it is possible Stiles met the Jameses in Texas, and not in Missouri, which most writers claim.[24]

Stiles' background is quite sketchy. He is attributed to be of both Minnesota as well as New York background, and it is more than possible, that one of these men was, in reality, Bill Chadwell. A St. Paul newspaper from 1861 describes a William Stiles as quite a character, if he was, in fact, the Stiles (or one of them) in question. Stiles, stated the newspaper, was "the man who fought the bull dog on Third Street a short time ago" and was said to have dived from the steamer *Alhambra* to a depth of thirty feet to hitch a hawser to the shaft lying on the bottom of the river. Stiles was described as the most noted diver on the river and a person who lately offered to jump into the river from the St. Paul bridge for a consideration.[25]

A separate article referred to the arrest of W. Stiles by Officer Morton of the St. Paul Police Department on August 23 for disorderly conduct.

Los Angeles Bill Stiles told writer Ed Earl Repp in a 1931 interview that the confusion between him and that other Stiles—Chadwell—had always presented historians with a problem. According to Stiles, in Northfield "they killed Clell Miller, Bill Chadwell, and almost got me, but I'm still kickin'!" Stiles said Chadwell's body was mistaken for his because the other man had often posed around Northfield as Bill Stiles. "I had a reputation which he liked to usurp occasionally," insisted Stiles.[26]

Bill Stiles was believed to be not only Bill Chadwell, but Jack Ladd and Jay Ward as well. Rumors floated that he was born in Nova Scotia, and, according to the 1870 Census, a William Stiles was living in Minneapolis that year. This Bill Stiles, who may not have been *the* Bill Stiles, was a half-breed Cherokee living in Ponca City, Oklahoma, when the Northfield raid occurred. Because he was suspected of being at Northfield, he went to Oregon City, Oregon, following the raid to be left alone.[27]

But Los Angeles Bill Stiles revealed to Repp that he was born October 27, 1850, near New York City, of well-to-do, respectable parents while Chadwell was born in Minnesota. Initially, he was afraid to talk with Repp for fear that he might be taken back to Minnesota to stand trial for his part in the Northfield raid. Repp brought in a lawyer who explained to Stiles that he was safe as long as he did not leave California. Only then did Stiles speak with considerable freedom.[28]

At the age of fourteen, Stiles said he began to steal. His first victim was a sleeping man in a foundry yard near his home. Stiles lifted the man's wallet. Young Bill was apprehended by a police officer, and, after hearing the officer discuss with his father a plan to put him aboard the prison ship, *St. Mary,* he stowed away on a Hudson River steamer and went to New York City.

In the city, the boy attempted to pick the purse of a well-dressed lady who caught him in the act. Instead of turning him over to the police, she entered him in her crime school where she served as teacher. He quickly learned that she was the mistress and matron of a "Fagin School," which produced young criminals.

In school, he was given "pick-pocket" lessons. Stiles was ushered into a dark room where there were dummies with small sums of money stashed in their pockets. The problem was these same dummies had tiny bells sewed into their clothing. Bill was told he could keep what money he lifted if no bells rang, but he said he rang many bells before developing his touch.

Sent out to try his craft on the street, he lifted a watch and wallet from his first "customer." In Stewart's Big Store, he even lifted the matron's purse. The matron, convinced he had graduated, gave him a letter of introduction to a man named McGirk, who ran a crime school in Chicago. Bill stayed for several months, then oddly enough, a Chicago policeman taught him to shoot with two guns. But the young man had to leave town in a hurry after being discovered for a crime he committed. He hid out in the woods of northern Wisconsin with the Chippewa Indians and became familiar with the country in Minnesota, northern Wisconsin, and a bit of Canada.

Stiles remained with the Chippewa nearly a year before heading west. In Omaha, he stole a horse from a man who turned out to be a Pinkerton detective. Stiles said he then fled to Minnesota where he met Bill Chadwell, son of a rich merchant and member of the James gang. Stiles, dodging the law from Nebraska to Missouri, with bounties totaling $10,000 on his head, encountered Chadwell, who was being hunted for a Minneapolis killing, among other crimes, in the town of Stillwater. Chadwell saved Stiles from arrest at the hands of two Pinkerton agents in a small saloon, in the shadow of Stillwater Prison. The two men got along well and Chadwell introduced him to Frank and Jesse James, who took him in on a trial basis.[29]

Chadwell told Stiles his real name was Alvin Stevens and that he only used the name "Chadwell" so as not to disgrace his family. He also used the name Alvin Stubler. Chadwell said his father owned timberland, stores, and lumber mills in St. Paul and in other parts of Minnesota and was one of the richest men in the state. He claimed Stevens County was named after his father. He said he did not rob for money but did so for kicks—he liked taking it from behind a gun. Stiles said he had never been sure if Chadwell had told him the truth or had been pulling his leg.

After joining the James gang, Stiles ran into some "Pinkerton agents" and tried to shoot it out. During the shoot-out, he was not able to hit any of the lawmen, who quickly strung him up and demanded he tell where the James gang was hiding. After refusing to give any information, the men cut him down and explained that Jesse had set him up as part of a test of his loyalty. His shots had not hit anyone because the boys had substituted blanks for the cartridges in his guns the night before.[30]

Stiles said he rode with the gang for five years and participated in several holdups including the Otterville Missouri-Pacific train robbery, the Glendale assault on the Chicago and Alton Railroad, and the East Winston raid on the Rock Island Line.[31] At the 1879 Glendale Train job, he said his fellow robbers were Frank and Jesse James, Ed Miller, Red Bill (no one knew his last name), Bill Williamson alias "The Parson," Bill Ryan, Tucker Bassham, Big Nick Nicholson, Cock-Eye Shepherd, and Jim Anderson.[32] Belle Starr, he said, had helped the boys plan the Northfield robbery but she did not take part in the raid. She did, however, according to Stiles, play a part in the Ste. Genevieve Savings Bank robbery in Missouri.[33]

He claimed there were ten men in the Northfield raid but he did not know the identity of the tenth man. Stiles had ridden a black stallion he had stolen in Omaha for the Northfield job and he said someone (he believed it to be Manning) had shot him in the back with buckshot. The Los Angeles Stiles then showed Repp his back, which was covered with small, purple welts.[34]

During the flight from Northfield, Stiles said he drew upon his knowledge of the Wisconsin timberlands and led the gang into the Big Woods. After splitting with the Youngers and Pitts, Repp said Stiles told him that he had guided Jesse and Frank to Grantsburg, Wisconsin, on to Clam Lake, and then to a band of Chippewas at Yellow River. Stiles allegedly referred to the Indians as a "bad lot" because many renegade whites from Minnesota, Missouri, Wisconsin, and Illinois lived with them. (Stiles later said the Wisconsin story was partially incorrect and overly embellished.)

But, said Stiles, he and the James brothers made their way to Shell Lake and Chief Chinaway's village. Stiles had once saved the chief's life from scalp hunters so the grateful Indian had some women tend to the trio's wounds. As their condition slowly improved, Jesse and Frank laid plans to rebuild the gang with new personnel and conduct raids in Texas. Chippewa runners informed the bandits that Pinkerton agents were searching relentlessly for them throughout Minnesota and Missouri. Jesse had sprouted a black beard, Frank sandy-colored whiskers, but Stiles, despite being twenty-six years old, could not grow facial hair except for a mustache.[35]

When they reached Chinaway's camp, Stiles was in the worst shape, although all three suffered multiple wounds. The cantle of his saddle was soggy with blood, which caused the seat of his pants to stick to the saddle. Squaws removed the buckshot from his back, first heating their knives before using the sharp points to cut into the skin. His infection was treated with kinnickinnic (wild tobacco), which was chewed, made into poultices, and rubbed into the wounds. Frank and Jesse were treated in the same way.[36]

Stiles learned later that during the operation he had passed out and remained unconscious for three days. The tribal medicine man used magic on him, and when he awoke, a pretty Chippewa girl named White Fawn was mopping sweat from his face. Said Stiles, "I never saw anything more beautiful in my life!"[37]

Jesse's wounds had healed more quickly than Frank's or Bill's and he paced back and forth through the camp like a caged animal. As cruel as Jesse could be, Stiles called him "a home-loving man" and it was obvious to Stiles that Jesse wanted to go home to Missouri. Frank's leg, meanwhile, had healed somewhat, although he walked with a limp.

Stiles' back was scabbed but there was no sign of infection. White Fawn carefully padded the buckskin with a soft moss so his shirt would not rub against his shoulders. The wounds hurt Stiles most when he lifted his arms, and he refrained from the act whenever possible.

In October, after a month at Chinaway's camp, Jesse crawled out of his blankets on a cold, windy morning and announced he was going home. Frank and Bill attempted to talk him out of it, but Jesse was adamant. The squaws filled their saddlebags with jerky and parched corn. After thanking the Indians, the boys rode out of camp with only Jesse in high spirits. Upon reaching Missouri (Stiles did not elaborate upon the route they had taken), Stiles said he spent a few hours with the brothers in St. Joseph, then left to stay with friends in Independence, promising to meet them in the spring. The friends to whom he referred included Bill Ryan and Bill (not Jim) Cummings. But Stiles stayed too long and missed the gang when they rode out of St. Joseph.

Stiles rode first to Oklahoma in search of the James gang, and then traveled on to Texas, New Mexico, and Arizona. He rejoined the gang in Missouri after Jesse and Frank had returned from Mexico. Among the new members of the gang were Jim Cummins, Ed Miller, Wood Hite, Bill Ryan, Tucker Bassham, Dick Liddel, and one other man he did not identify. Stiles remained with the gang until Jesse's death at the hands of Bob Ford.

Throughout this period, Stiles realized he was fairly safe from the hands of lawmen because of the confusion with Chadwell. Since Chadwell had used Stiles' name in canvassing Northfield the day before the robbery, the body in Northfield was identified as that of Bill Stiles. He hoped to keep Bill Stiles dead as long as he could and picked out an alias, which he used from then on. During Repp's eight-year friendship with Stiles, the former outlaw refused to reveal his new name. Said Stiles, "There are things in the lives of a lot of men that's best kept secret. Things he might be very much ashamed of. This is one of those times."[38]

Ten years after Jesse's death, Stiles contended he rode to Creede, Colorado, to kill Bob Ford but found Ed O'Kelly had beaten him to it. As the gang slowly disintegrated, Stiles returned to the Big Woods of Wisconsin where he lived with the Indians, once again, for several weeks. The Chippewa bestowed upon Stiles the name "The Wolf," likening him to the timber wolves that travel alone except in mating season.[39]

At Chinaway's village, Stiles married White Fawn, the girl who had nursed his wounds in 1876, under Indian rites, and they spent the winter together. In the spring, White Fawn, pregnant with Stiles' child was killed by a jealous Indian. The angry Chippewa had meant to shoot the outlaw but hit White Fawn in the breast instead. Stiles pulled both his hip guns and shot the brave in the face, killing him instantly. Berserk with rage, Stiles raced into the forest and shot the Indians who had accompanied his wife's killer on his mission of death. Stiles then returned to the white man's world.

According to a 1935 interview writer Ed Earl Repp conducted with outlaw Emmett Dalton, Stiles showed up at the Dalton farm near Coffeyville, Kansas, in 1887. The Dalton Gang had planned several robberies including a raid on the Condon Bank of Coffeyville, and Stiles was ushered into the gang "on probation" because of his experience. Emmett Dalton, however, never trusted Stiles and felt he had gotten too friendly with people in Northfield before the 1876 robbery and may have sold out the gang to the "bankers and townsmen."[40]

Despite's Emmett Dalton's hatred of Stiles, he did explain that Bill had a better eye for details than had any of the Daltons, and he had been blessed with a photographic mind. When Bob Dalton conceived the idea of robbing both the Condon and Coffeyville banks simultaneously, Stiles was asked for his input. Grat Dalton sent Stiles into Coffeyville, according to Emmett, to study entrances and exits, the times the banks opened and closed, and whatever else he could find out. Emmett protested, saying the same thing had happened before the James-Younger raid on Northfield and that Stiles had sold out for "thirty pieces of silver."[41]

Emmett Dalton conveyed to Repp that Bill Stiles accompanied the three Dalton brothers (Bob, Grat, and Emmett), Dick Broadwell, and Bill Powers on their October 5, 1892, ride to

Coffeyville for the raid that would be their last. Just outside town, Stiles halted and complained of bad pains in his lower abdomen and gasped with every step of his mount. Stiles told Grat he could not go on because he was suffering from a double rupture but that he would catch up with them later. The rest of the Coffeyville story is history.

Stiles, after hearing Emmett's accusations, told Repp in an interview that same year that he'd put a hole through Emmett "you could use for a trolley car tunnel." He admitted he had started out for Coffeyville with the gang but had ruptured his privates on the saddle swells and nubbin after a horse had been shot out from under him on a previous raid. Without embarrassment,

Jesse James grave. Kearney, Missouri. (Photo by Diana Pierce.)

he dropped his drawers in front of his interviewer and showed him his testicles, which were enlarged to the size of "toy footballs." He also revealed his buckshot-scarred back and insisted he would not sell out for a load of buckshot.[42]

If Stiles had made the whole thing up, it is interesting to note that Emmett Dalton, a bitter rival, had corroborated his enemy's insistence that he had been in on the Northfield raid. It must be taken into account also, that Stiles' own father had publicly stated that Chadwell's body, not his son's, lay in a Northfield mortuary following the raid. And sworn affidavits from the staff at the Union Gospel Mission in Los Angeles declared that Stiles was a sincere Christian convert and certainly anything but a liar. He was to them, Bill Stiles, "our faithful night watchman, alert and watching while his fellows sleep, much as he used to, only for a different purpose."[43]

Eight men? Nine? Ten? Even more? With the passing of Cole Younger in 1916, the truth may never be known. Or did the truth survive another two decades, its flame snuffed out on August 16, 1939, with the passing of an old man in a gospel mission in Los Angeles, after "a wonderful change had been worked in the heart of Bill Stiles?"[44]

Notes

1 *The Northfield Magazine,* Vol. 6, No. 2, 1992, p. 12.

2 N. Dave Smith telephone interview with author November 28, 1997.

3 Carl S. Hage letter to author dated March 26, 1982.

4 Ruth Yates letter to author dated January 8, 1997.

5 Gregg Higginbotham telephone interview with author November 28, 1997.

6 George A. Bradford letter to Isaac B. Yates dated December 9, 1929, reprinted in *Madelia Times-Messenger,* Friday, January 3, 1930, "Interesting Letter by Geo. A. Bradford to His Late Friend, Mr. Isaac B. Yates."

7 Ibid.

8 *Kansas City Star,* September 22, 1929, Section C.

9 Ibid.

10 James R. Ross, *I, Jesse James,* Dragon Publishing Corp., 1989, p. i.

11 Ibid. pp. 128-129.

12 Ibid., pp. 201-214; Hon. James R. Ross (Ret.) letters to author dated December 17, 1996, and May 14, 1997; Sue Garwood DeLong, Executive Director, Northfield Historical Society, interview with author January 27, 1997, Northfield, Minnesota.

13 Nicholis Martin interviews with author December 9, 1996, and December 16, 1996, Lakeville, Minnesota.

14 Nicholis Martin interview with author November 6, 1997, Lakeville, Minnesota.

15 Ibid.

16 Grandson Nicholis Martin currently has three surveyors looking for the campsite and the gold.

17 Nicholis Martin interviews with author December 9, 1996, and December 16, 1996.

18 Emmett C. Hoctor letter to author dated December 5, 1996; "Just Like Jesse James," unpublished manuscript by Emmett C. Hoctor; Ed F. Morearty, *Omaha Memories; Recollections of Events, Men and Affairs in Omaha, Nebraska, from 1879 to 1917*, Swartz Printing Co., Omaha, 1917, p. 8.

19 *Omaha Daily Bee*, June 1, 1883.

20 *Sioux City Journal*, June 1, 1883.

21 *Lincoln Daily State Journal*, June 5, 1883.

22 "Just Like Jesse James," unpublished manuscript by Emmett C. Hoctor.; Emmett C. Hoctor letters to author dated December 4, 1996, and December 5, 1996.

23 Emmett C. Hoctor, "Bill Stiles Fan Club" article.

24 *The Liberty* (Missouri) *Tribune*, October 6, 1876.

25 Emmett C. Hoctor, "Bill Stiles Fan Club" article.

26 Bill Stiles, as told to Ed Earl Repp, "Bill Stiles' Story," *Frontier Times Magazine*, Vol. 43, No.1, December-January 1969.

27 Gregg Higginbotham telephone interview with author November 28, 1997; Richard Ensminger letter to Gregg Higginbotham dated March 22, 1996.

28 Bill Stiles, as told to Ed Earl Repp, "Bill Stiles' Story."

29 Bill Stiles, as told to Ed Earl Repp, "Who Was Bill Chadwell?" *Golden West Magazine*, Vol. 9, No. 12, November 1973.

30 Bill Stiles, as told to Ed Earl Repp, "I Was Hanged by Jesse James," *The West*, Vol. 17, No. 4, November, 1973.

31 Bill Stiles, as told to Ed Earl Repp, "Bill Stiles' Story."

32 Bill Stiles, as told to Ed Earl Repp, "The James Gang and the Bounty Hunters," *Real Frontier Magazine*, Vol. 1, No. 4, August 1970.

33 Ed Earl Repp, "Belle Starr Saved My Life," *Real West Magazine*, Vol. XIII, No. 79, February 1970.

34 Bill Stiles, as told to Ed Earl Repp, "Bill Stiles' Story."

35 Bill Stiles, as told to Ed Earl Repp, "I Was the Last of the James Gang," *True Frontier Magazine*, No. 27, June 1972.

36 Bill Stiles, as told to Ed Earl Repp, "The Chippewa Saved Our Lives," *The West Magazine*, Vol. 16, No. 9, April 1973.

37 Ibid.

38 Ibid.

39 Bill Stiles, as told to Ed Earl Repp, "My Chippewa Bride," *True Frontier Magazine*, Vol. 1, No. 11, December 1971.

40 Ed Earl Repp, "Last of the Old Time Outlaws," *True Frontier Magazine*, No. 36, January 1974.

41 Ibid.

42 Ibid.

43 Forty-First Annual Report of the Union Gospel Mission, Los Angeles, California.

44 Ibid.

Acknowledgments

For sixteen years, on, and frequently, off, I have researched the Northfield bank raid. True, that no man is an island, but true also, that no historian puts together a volume of this nature all by himself. This book is the work of many persons, both living and dead, and without their precious assistance, there would be no book at all.

A special thanks to Diana Pierce, who kept the flame burning and who spent hours upon hours in proofreading—thus saving me from numerous errors. I also wish to thank Ed Wilks, who also burned the midnight candle, red-penciling my gibberish and offering innumerable insights. Thanks as well to Emmett C. Hoctor for sharing a "suitcase" of his research with me; material he could have used to produce a similar, if not better, volume. A special word of gratitude is extended to my "computer doctor," Zach Pierce, who answered my call day or night to nurse an ailing electronic patient.

I cannot thank enough of you who shared your time, research, photographs, opinions, and family heritage: Arnold D. Alberts, Mayor Gail Anderson of Jordan, Jörg Bashir, Erich Baumann, Marley Brant, Carl W. Breihan, Eldon J. Bryant, Eric Carlson, Tracy Christensen, Marilynn Cierzan, Robert Cole, Julius A. Collier II Attorney at Law, Mary Elizabeth Counselman, Andy Decker, Armand DeGregoris, Olive C. Dickie, George Diezel II, Darlene Egolf, Steve Eng, Walker Fischer, Ruth Coder Fitzgerald, Irene Fosdick, Louis Garcia, Marie Vogl Gery, Mrs. B. A. Gilmore, Carl S. Hage, Donald R. Hale, Christopher W. Hawes, Thomas P. Healy, Gregg Higginbotham, Mouraine R. Hubler, Margarette B. Hutchins, Len James, Marvin James, Merrill E. Jarchow, Ray G. Juergens, Cathy Keller, Ralph Keller, Arthur Knight, Kit Knight, John S. Koblas, Sarah Koblas, Dr. Arthur Larson, Paul Lunden, Rex Macbeth, Elmo Martin, Nicholis Martin, Millie Miller, Grace Sumner Northrop, Garlyn Johannsen-Leary, Dave Page, Chuck Parsons, Keith Pierce, B.

Wayne Quist, Stacy Radcliff, Judie Ries, Judge James R. Ross, Stephanie Rugg, Tom Ryther, Marty Schnatz, Robert L. Shelburne, Lucius A. Smith Attorney at Law, N. Dave Smith, Lee Stangler, John Stevens, Jim Stoesz, Matt Stoesz, Chip Stroebel, Mrs. Herbert E. Summers, Merri Vinton, Mrs. Ed Weinzeirl, Patrick Wells, Mrs. Fred Wingert, Ruth Yates, Ted Yeatman, Maria Younger, and Wilbur A. Zink.

Additionally, I am indebted to the following individuals and organizations in various states for sharing valuable information with me: CALIFORNIA: Thomas R. Ankrom and Art Purner, Union Rescue Mission, Los Angeles; IOWA: Mrs. Jackie Wilson, Jesse James Museum, Adair; W. E. Littler, Jr., The Adair News, Adair; Hugh Doty, The *Times-Republican*, Corydon; Lowell R. Wilbur, Iowa Historical Library, Des Moines; David Parker, Fort Dodge Historical Foundation, Fort Dodge; Kelly Green, The *Messenger*, Fort Dodge; Librarians, Fort Dodge Public Library, Fort Dodge; Karen Laughlin, Iowa State Historical Society, Iowa City; Jim Driscoll, Plymouth County Historical Society, LeMars; Scott Sorensen, Sioux City Public Museum, Sioux City; KENTUCKY: Louise W. Hampton, Scholl Family Research Association of America, Winchester; MICHIGAN: D. Wayne Stiles, Fort St. Joseph Museum & City of Niles Historical Commission, Niles; MINNESOTA: Reference Librarians, Faribault County Historical Society, Blue Earth; Marion Jamieson, Wright County Historical Society, Buffalo; Jane George, Burnhaven Library, Burnsville; Tracy DuToit Swanson, Chaska City Hall, Chaska; Shirley Brewers, Chaska Historical Society, Chaska; Catherine Harber, Martin County Historical Society, Fairmont; Janet N. McCorkell, Deputy Clerk of District Court of Rice County, Faribault; LeAnn Dean, Buckham Memorial Library, Faribault; Emily Mae Buth, Rice County Historical Society, Faribault; Lester E. Swanberg, *Faribault Daily News*, Faribault; Judy A. Nelson, Jackson County Historical Society, Lakefield; Sr. Mariella Hinkly, Rock County Historical Society, Luverne; Mrs. Alton Anderson, Watonwan County Historical Society, Madelia; John Whalen, Madelia Times-Messenger, Madelia; Marcia T. Schuster and Audrey Hicks, Blue Earth County Historical Society, Mankato; Paul Klammer, Brown County Historical Society, New Ulm; Sue Garwood DeLong, James Beving, Ron Morris, Northfield Historical Society, Northfield; Marston Headley, Northfield Public Library, Northfield; Margaret Lee, Northfield News, Northfield; Shirley Lohmann, Steele County Historical Society, Owatonna; Orville Olson, Goodhue County Historical Society, Red Wing; Alice Befort, *Republican Eagle*, Red Wing; Dallas R. Lindgren, and Bonnie Wilson, Minnesota Historical Society, St. Paul; Kim

Berg, Nicollet County Historical Society, St. Peter; Louise Johnson, Washington County Historical Society, Stillwater; Donna Fostveit, Waseca Secretarial & Research Service, Waseca; Peg Korsmo-Kennon, Waseca County Historical Society, Waseca; James E. Hruska, LeSueur County Historical Society, Waterville; Ed Teater, North Ridge Farms, Wayzata; Christine Taylor Thompson, Cottonwood County Historical Society, Windom; Lucretia F. Moran, Winona County Historical Society, Winona; Helen Towne, Nobles County Historical Society, Worthington; MISSOURI: Milton F. Perry, Friends of the James Farm, Kearney; Janice L. Fox, Missouri Historical Society, St. Louis; Reference Department, St. Louis Post Dispatch, St. Louis; NEW YORK: George F. Neill, Pinkerton Inc., New York City; NEBRASKA: Ann E. Billesbach and Chad Wall, Nebraska State Historical Society, Lincoln; NORTH DAKOTA: Keith W. Millette, M. D., Altru Clinic, Family Medical Center, Grand Forks; Douglas W. Ellison, Book Corral, Medora; SOUTH DAKOTA: Jan Jones, Palisade State Park, South Dakota Department of Game, Fish & Parks, Garretson; Robert Kolbe, Minnehaha County Historical Society, Sioux Falls; and Joanita Kant Monteith, Codington County Historical Society, Watertown.

Index

About the Author

John J. Koblas is the author and/or editor of six books on the lives of F. Scott Fitzgerald and Sinclair Lewis. His book, *F. Scott Fitzgerald in Minnesota: Toward the Summit*, was a 1996 Minnesota Book Award nominee. Other works include: *F. Scott Fitzgerald in Minnesota: His Homes and Haunts* (Minnesota Historical Society Press, 1978), *Sinclair Lewis: Home at Last* (Voyageur Press, 1981), *Selected Letters of Sinclair Lewis, Sinclair Lewis & Mantrap: The Saskatchewan Trip*, and *Sinclair Lewis: Final Voyage* (1985).

Five years ago, Mr. Koblas' work was featured on a national television segment of *Good Morning America*. In 1985, he was a guest of Charles Kuralt on *CBS Sunday Morning* in New York for the Sinclair Lewis Centenary. That same year, Koblas was chosen by the Postmaster General in Washington to present the Sinclair Lewis Stamp at its First Day of Issue Ceremony. The following year, he received an award from the governor of Minnesota for his Fitzgerald work at the Minnesota Walk of Fame dedication.

In addition to biographical endeavors, Koblas has been a visiting instructor of writing at Brevard College in North Carolina, feature writer for the *Daytona Beach* (Florida) *News-Journal*, and author of a syndicated column that was carried in 105 newspapers nationwide. He is the author of more than 500 short stories, articles, and verse published worldwide.

Recently, Mr. Koblas taught courses on Fitzgerald and Lewis at the Elder Learning Center of the University of Minnesota and Elder Hostel sessions.

Another book by Koblas, *H.V. Jones, An Adventure*, will be published this year.